The Craft of
Modular Post & Beam

*Building Log & Timber
Homes Affordably*

The Craft of Modular Post & Beam

Building Log & Timber Homes Affordably

J A M E S   M I T C H E L L

Hartley & Marks
PUBLISHERS

In dedication to Saxe and Haley, Meghan and Eric, Pippa and Zoë

Published by
HARTLEY & MARKS PUBLISHERS INC.
P. O. Box 147   3661 West Broadway
Point Roberts, WA Vancouver, BC
98281   V6R 2B8

Printed in the U.S.A.

Mitchell, James, 1952–
     The craft of modular post and beam : building log and timber homes affordably
  / James Mitchell.
          p.   cm.
     Includes bibliographical references and index.
     ISBN 0-88179-131-8
     1. Wooden-frame houses—Design and construction.   2. Log cabins—
Design and construction.   I. Title.
TH4818.W6M58   1997   690'.837—dc21   96-52327

The designs, methods, and details shown in this book are not intended to be appropriate in all situations. The authors and their agents assume no responsibility for the use of the information in this book by anyone. Each design, method and detail should be assessed and verified by a qualified professional, ensuring its safety, durability and appropriateness for the individual situation, and its compliance with all applicable codes and regulations.

Contents

Introduction/Author's Preface

This is a how-to building book. But, more importantly perhaps, it is also about the potential that post and beam, a form of wood joinery with roots reaching deep into our past, holds for the solitary owner/builder and the environment. It is a book about how you can build the house of your dreams without debt and without even owning the land first.

I was born and raised where big trees, rocky mountains, and the sea were my playground. Building has always been a passion for me. When I was a kid I loved to build forts—on the ground, underground, in the trees, on the water, out of sand, snow, straw, wood, or whatever I could find. Later, as a young man in the 1970s I subscribed wholeheartedly to the philosophy of going back to nature, living debtless and uncontrolled. I then became interested in domestic architecture in general, and log and timber in particular. I taught high school industrial arts, and adult log and timber house construction.

My interest led me to build numerous log and timber homes for others and eventually stimulated my desire to travel and learn about building in other parts of the world. My travels opened my eyes to a world of possibilities. I had been conditioned to believe that real building materials came from building stores. Apart from my interest in building with logs and timbers, I had never imagined the variety of natural materials available and the ways they could be used for building. Imagine my astonishment to see the same type of seaweed that I had kicked around on the beach used as thatch on a roof! The resourcefulness of other cultures amazed me, and I became fascinated by the concept of using natural and recycled materials and one's own sweat equity to create a home without debt. I learned a great deal in parts of the Third World where housing debt is virtually unknown.

On my return home I picked up where I had left off, building log and timber houses for people who could afford them. But I soon became disillusioned with society's pursuit of the almighty dollar. I realized that underlying our work-frenzied attitude was a deep-seated fear of unemployment and potential homelessness, with debt as the common denominator. Debt, primarily for one's home, often forces people to lead lives of constant financial stress and worry, and prevents them from considering environmental factors in their home-buying decisions. When even the cheapest mass-produced house is beyond the reach of most, concerns about quality and the environment are often forgotten. My disillusion turned to despair when I realized that I too would not be able to afford to build the home I had always envisioned, living and thinking the way I did.

When it was time to settle down and have a family, the pieces came together like a big jigsaw puzzle. My knowledge of building techniques, my realization that in parts of the world it was possible to build debt-free, and my familiarity with the prefabrication and modularity methods used in the Arctic allowed me to formulate my building strategy.

I decided I would build my house my own way, as I could afford it, even though I had no land to put it on. And it would not be some cheap box, but rather the home of my dreams. Based on the same "knock-down" principles of cabinetry, dividing the building into structural and passive elements, I would construct it in modular pieces, prefabricating and storing the components of the building shell until the time was ripe to assemble it on the site foundation. The trick was to reduce the number of pieces and simplify the process, so that the builder could accomplish the individual tasks in his or her spare time with minimal assistance and money.

I considered and quickly discarded several building types. Conventional stud frame has too many pieces that can twist and distort over time. A notched-corner log house (blockwork) wouldn't work for me because the size and weight of the logs meant that construction would be difficult and storing the pieces would be impossible. Braced timber framework would require long members that would be susceptible to twisting during storage. Also, the sandwiched exterior panels (called stress skin) used in braced timber framework are expensive and wasteful, especially after the window and door openings are cut out. Assembly would require a crane and ultimately, the finished building would look like any other standard stud frame house.

Post and beam was the logical answer for my home. Its design aesthetics, modularity, and ease of construction lent themselves to my project. Post and beam has the flexibility of interchangeable parts within the structural and passive components of the building shell. It would give me the option of salvaging shorter-length wood members from the beach nearby and building the house in round or square form. As an alternative to a solid wood infill, I developed a modular panel system which, when compared with the commercial stress skin panels, creates much less waste and is a fraction of the weight and price. Storing the components meant simply banding the wood beams and posts together in a stickered pile to prevent warping, with the walls stacked upright like a deck of cards. Everything fit nicely in the corner of my barn (for those without a barn I have shown in the book how to build an inexpensive storage hut). With the building form identified, I was free to gather and store recycled elements such as doors, windows, wood flooring, and fixtures, which I got at a fraction of the price they would have cost new.

In a perfect world all housing would be recyclable—it would be possible to take it apart and move it if necessary. Such housing would be less likely to end up as landfill in our throw-away society. Standard stapled-together particle board enclosures are not easily recycled, which is good for housing industry profits, but bad for the environment.

It is estimated that every dollar you save to spend on your house and mortgage requires earning fifteen dollars before taxes and the cost of living are deducted. This 15:1 ratio emphasizes the need for the average person to replace debt with sweat equity and smart recycling.

I want to make building a house possible for anyone who has passion and motivation. With this method I believe a home is within the reach of most people. I suggest building step by step, taking your future into your own hands. That is how I built my 4000 square foot dream home, debt-free.

My goal is to provide a new direction for owner/builders, and I have set about it in two ways: by learning and by doing. My house is now my workshop where I teach the material in this book.

Notes on Motivation

"Take delight in every step."
—SAYINGS OF A ZEN
MASTER

Twenty years ago I trekked into the forbidden kingdom of Sikkim. Deep in the Himalayan mountains I entered the Kar-Guypa monastery of Red Hat Sect Buddhists. There I gained an audience with the old lama. "What is the essence of happiness?" I asked him. He replied, "Happiness is creation . . ." I didn't realize it then, but today as I watch my three-year-old son absorbed in his play, I understand that from the moment we are able to manipulate objects we seek to create. As my son takes delight in his crayon creations, I remember how happy I was building my funky forts as a kid. It really didn't matter what I created then; rather it was the process of learning-by-doing which sparked my interest and motivated me to go further. Essential to creation are curiosity and interest, but these alone do not provide enough motivation to complete a large project such as a home. Breaking a large project down into smaller, simpler tasks, as is done with modular building, increases your chances of completing the job.

It has been said that the secret to success in building is the passion you bring to the project, because passion sustains motivation. Passion, however, if not reinforced with the drive to action and creation, will wither like fruit left on a vine. Find the passion and excitement of your undertaking and embrace it and let it lead you to creation. In this way you will surely take delight in every step.

CHAPTER ONE

Evolution of Post and Beam

Snow fell on me,
Rain beat down on me,
Dew fell on me,
Long I seemed dead.

—A STANZA FROM THE VIKING EDDA

The structure and style of mankind's dwellings have historically been closely linked to regional climate and the availability of suitable building materials and tools. It is not a coincidence then, that cultures living in similar regions around the world have come to similar solutions with respect to their housing needs: adobe in arid regions, sod and strawbale in the grasslands, thatch in the tropics, ice igloos in the Arctic, and of course, logs and timbers in temperate forest and mountain regions. During the Middle Ages vast forest regions stretched from Europe and Scandinavia to Asia and the Orient, forming a wooden girdle around the Northern Hemisphere. These regions excelled in the three wooden building methods: log blockwork, log and timber post and beam, and timber braced framework. The development of one method over another was directly related to each area's forest reserves and the tools of the day.

Figure 1-1 shows a map of northern Europe and the Orient during the Middle Ages where the different methods of wooden architecture became prominent. In eastern Europe and Russia, forest reserves were plentiful, while the available tools were rudimentary. Saws and drills were inaccessible for most people up to the nineteenth century and the common axe had to be relied upon for all manner of construction. As a

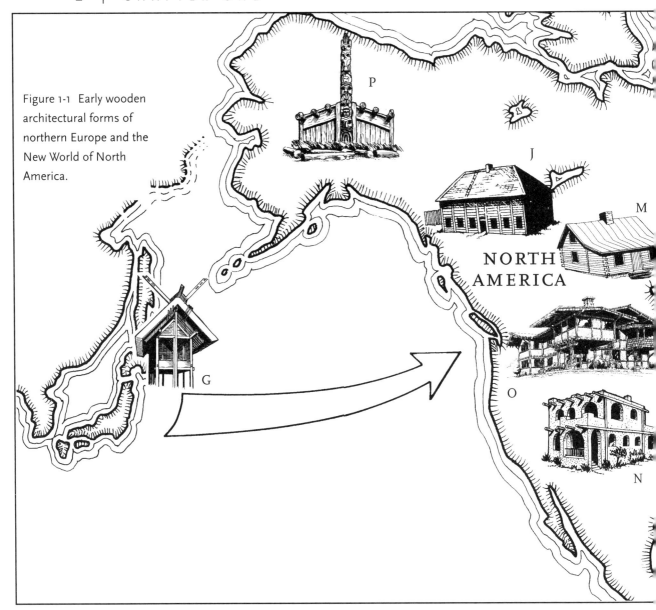

Figure 1-1 Early wooden architectural forms of northern Europe and the New World of North America.

MAP KEY

Europe

A Blockwork church, northwestern Russia (1400 A.D.), using notched corner log construction called "laft" in Norway.
B Framework building, western Europe (1500 A.D.), using braced timber frame construction.
C Stave church, Norway (1000 A.D.), using post and beam construction with plank infill between the posts.
D *Stav og laft* farmhouse of Norway and Sweden (1400 A.D.), combining stave and laft construction forms.
E *Stav og laft* church, western Russia (1400 A.D.), merging stave and laft construction to form true post and beam.
F Log posts and walls of earliest known post and beam structure, Poland (700 B.C.).

Orient

G Ise Shrine, Japan (6th century A.D.).

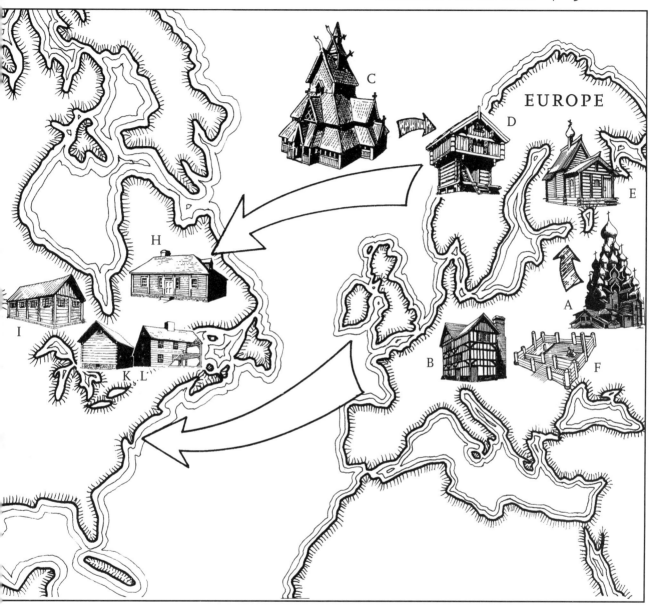

North America

H French (1600 A.D.) *pièce-sur-pièce* house.
I English (1700 A.D.) Red River frame house.
J Hudson's Bay (1800 A.D.) trading fort.
K Standard dovetail long log (blockwork) building.
L Timber (framework house), New England (1800 A.D.).
M Round notch long log (blockwork) building, western United States (1800 A.D.).
N Spanish Mission-style adobe post and beam building, southwestern United States, Mexico (1800 A.D.).
O Craftsman-style post and beam showing Spanish and Asian influence (1900 A.D.).
P Northwest Native Indian "Haida" post and beam long house.

result, the blockwork method was developed above others since trees could be felled and stacked in horizontal tiers with the ends notched together using a simple woodsman's axe. Russian mastery of the blockwork method is exemplified in the monastic Church of the Transfiguration in Figure 1-2 (building A).

In contrast to eastern Europe, the forest reserves of western Europe

Figure 1-2
Russian blockwork church
(Church of the Transfiguration)
1400 A.D.

were rapidly diminishing with increased population, and regulations were created to conserve wood supplies. In these more populous regions there were, however, numerous craftsmen's guilds and access to specialized woodworking tools which led to the development of timber framework architecture (building B). The braced frame required less wood and allowed infills such as stick wattle and clay surface daubing or simply rock rubble between the open frames (Figure 1-3). By the sixteenth century the scarcity of forest reserves in England and France forced buildings to be constructed almost entirely of stone.

The Scandinavian cultures between western Europe and Russia were

Figure 1-3
English Tudor
framework

Figure 1-4
Norwegian *reisverk*
stave church,
1000 A.D.

Figure 1-5
Reisverk Viking
stronghold in
the Netherlands
(Zeeland) ca.
1000 A.D.

fortunate in that they had the forest reserves, tools, and the geographic position to benefit from their neighbors' architectural influences. The result was a unique blend of both log blockwork and timber framework encompassed within the methodology of post and beam. Log post and beam construction did not demand the lengthy procedure of squaring the timbers, nor the intricate joinery of the braced framework bents, while the wood infill was substantially warmer than rock or clay. In addition, this method did away with restrictions to a building's size and the difficulty of handling the heavy, large logs used in blockwork construction.

Consider the famous stave churches of Norway, over 700 of which were built between 1000 A.D. and 1300 A.D. (Figure 1-4). "Stave" refers to the vertical stave or post used in this construction method, which they called *reisverk, reise* meaning "to place something upright" (i.e. the post) (Figure 1-5). The use of natural log posts and the absence of individually braced frame bents sets it apart from the framework methods of western Europe, though undeniably these are Christian churches which reflect the Gothic architectural influence of Christian Europe (building C). The Vikings had an advanced understanding of shipbuilding and frame and skin structure. On their expeditions of conquest they learned of new cultures and architectures, and were able to apply their shipbuilding skills to create new variations of post and beam construction. A merging of the two methods is seen in the typical Norwegian farmhouse in Figure 1-6. The Norwegian word for the horizontal notched-corner blockwork con-

struction method is *laft*, while the name of this combination of the two forms is *stav og laft* (a vertical post and horizontal beam) (buildings D and E). Another example integrating *stav og laft*, or post and beam construction, is shown in the Russian Church of St. Lazarus in Figure 1-7. In Denmark it was called *bulhuse* construction, *bul* or *bole* referring to the trunk wood of a tree, and *huse* meaning "house." In his book *Architecture in Wood*, Hans Jürgen Hansen refers to more than a hundred dwellings in Biskupin, Poland dating back to 700 B.C., constructed of vertical posts with horizontal log infill joined in tongue and slot fashion (building F).

Looking eastward beyond the great deserts of Persia and Afghanistan to the temporal regions of India, one finds examples of log and timber post and beam construction but no braced timberframe or log blockwork. Similarly in China, Korea, and Japan there is prolific log and timber post and beam architecture with some blockwork but no evidence of braced timberframe. In the sixth century, Buddhism spread religion and architecture from China to Japan. Temple scriptures and treasures were kept secure in fine storehouses called *kura*. These *kura* became the archetypes of two building types: log blockwork which was abandoned as a building method nearly a thousand years ago, and the post and beam type with heavy board walls as shown in the Ise Shrine in Figure 1-1 (building G).

Figure 1-6
Norwegian
farmhouse,
1400 A.D.,
showing the
stav og laft
method.

Examples of this style of post and beam can be found throughout the Orient. Today the more traditional forms of post and beam are reserved for ceremonial tea houses in Japan.

Wooden post and beam construction became the premier method of building in Japan because of its economical use of materials and its inherent ability to withstand the typhoons and earthquakes common to the Japanese archipelago. A wood frame merely shrugs in the presence of such stresses whereas stone and concrete crack. It must be mentioned that occasional failure of these structures under seismic stress has been attributed largely to the traditional, excessively heavy tiled roof supported by the structural whale-back beams which are unstable and lack bracing. (Sometimes tradition and religion outweigh practicality.) Moreover, earlier foundations lacked proper reinforcing and secure attachment to the posts, the result of a lack of technological understanding. In Japan today wooden post and beam construction is influenced by various sects (schools), and regional differences and differences in style technique such as *Karaya* (Chinese), *Tenjikuyo* (Indian), and *Wayo* (Japanese). The resulting array of hidden, complex joinery demonstrates the way competition, a keen blade, and a reverence for wood can hone the abilities of dedicated artisans.

Security, rather than tradition and religion, was the prime motivator dictating the development of construction methods during the colonization of eastern North America in the sixteenth century. Conflicts between the French, English, Dutch, and native Indians necessitated the building of strong fortifications. Post and beam was the preferred choice for building forts. The French initially used the method of *colombage*—a timber post and beam frame filled with rock and masonry rubble in between—which was common in France at that time. But the cold eastern and maritime winters made it wiser to exclude rock in favor of solid wood, which was a better insulator. The post and beam framing technique was called *poteaux sur sole,* meaning "post on sill." The method of wood infill between the posts was called *pièces de bois sur pièces de bois,* meaning "wood pieces on wood pieces" (building H). Soon, the common name became shortened to *pièce-sur-pièce,* a name by which it is still known today throughout Canada. Conventional *pièce-sur-pièce* houses in Upper Canada had wall timbers fully squared with a tenon or tongue at

each ending fitting into a vertical groove in the upright post of the frame.[1]

Enticed by news of a rich fur trade, the British were drawn to early Canada and into competition with the French. As established historical rivals, the only thing they did not disagree on was the use of the all-wood post and beam construction method for their houses and forts. Instead of using the French name, the English preferred to call the method "Red River frame" after the river of the same name in Manitoba (Figure 1-8a), or

Figure 1-7 Russian Church of St. Lazarus (ca. 1300 A.D.) which combines true post and beam with notched corner building methods.

1. Shurtleff, Harold R., *The Log Cabin Myth* (Gloucester, Mass.: Harvard University Press, 1939).

Figure 1-8a
An 1854 "Red
River frame"
house in
Manitoba.

Figure 1-8b
Fort Langley,
British
Columbia,
1800.

"Hudson Bay Corner," presumably after the Hudson's Bay Company,
which built most of its fortifications with this method. Post and beam forts
were built across Canada from the Atlantic to the Pacific, in a concerted
effort to exert dominance over the New World and to collect valuable furs
from the natives. In all, over two hundred forts were built by the North-
West and Hudson's Bay trading companies between the seventeenth and
nineteenth centuries, making log and timber post and beam colonial
Canada's first building method. Indeed, the plaque commemorating the
post and beam building of Fort Langley in 1827 records it as "the first Trad-

ing Post on the Pacific Coast of Canada" and the "Birthplace of the Colony of British Columbia."[2] (Figure 1-8b) (building J).

The flood of immigrants to eastern Canada and the U.S. that followed the fur trade included many northern and eastern Europeans. Homesteaders used axes to clear a spot within the forest and used the logs to build a house. Hastily erected log cabins with axe-notched corners and moss "chinking" between the layered logs sufficed (building K), but the winter winds of New England soon convinced these early settlers to try other methods. In his book *The Log Cabin Myth*, H.R. Shurtleff describes the type of construction that followed:

> *Their walls, instead of presenting the horizontally corrugated surface and projecting ends at the corners by which the true log cabin is universally recognized, were squared off smoothly by broadax; and the corners were either formed by posts in which the wall timbers were mortised, or else the timbers were evenly and neatly joined by some form of dovetailing.*"[3] Figure 1-8a.

As virgin forests gradually surrendered to agricultural use, settlements grew into townships, wood reserves diminished, sawmills cut square timbers from round logs, and braced timberframe emerged, covered by clapboard siding (building L). Blockwork, post and beam, and braced timberframe appeared again in a virtual reenactment in the New World of what had already happened architecturally in the Old World centuries earlier. By mid-nineteenth century, consumer demand and commerce resulted in the building medium of stud frame. Smaller dimension wood framing pieces were nailed together with clapboard and cedar shingles as an exterior covering. Ornate posts, fretwork, and brackets embellished these "Victorian" homes, mass-produced by newly invented woodworking machinery.

The Industrial Age had begun and cities were mushrooming in the east, influenced by the Victorian motif. The West Coast by contrast was still a hinterland and it was here that log blockwork and log and timber

2. Cullen, Mary K., *History of Fort Langley, 1827-1896* (Ottawa: Natural Historic Parks and Sites Branch, 1979).
3. Moogk, Peter N., *Building a House in New France* (Toronto: McClelland and Stewart, 1977).

post and beam once again emerged. Braced timberframe remained largely an eastern vernacular, presumably because the communal groups employing this method did not exist in the same numbers out west. Sawmills were few and far between, especially those capable of handling the large trees of the Pacific Northwest. Immigrant Swedes and Norwegians in particular took to the lumberjack trade flourishing in this region (building M). It is from these homesteaders that we find examples of scribe-fitted log blockwork and post and beam.

Further south the Spanish had, for many years, extended their influence from Mexico up to northern California. Spanish "mission" style architecture using a combination of wooden post and beam and plastered adobe dominated these more arid regions (building N). Adding to this architectural melting pot, a new tide of immigrants from Asia came to the western shores of North America. Lured primarily by the gold rush and the building of the transcontinental railroad, their influence upon western architecture would eventually play a significant role.

Early in the twentieth century an architectural rebellion began in England and spread to America. The Arts and Crafts Movement, as it was called, began as a reaction against the machine-made goods of the Industrial Revolution and the architecturally claustrophobic and grossly embellished Victorian housing style then common in eastern America and in most cities. It was a move towards a simpler, purer architecture both in form and function. In 1912 Gustav Stickley, a designer and publisher of *American Craftsman Homes*, wrote:

> *"People are also awakening to the fact that beauty in a building is not merely a matter of decoration, something to be added at will, but is inherent in the lines and masses of the structure itself."*

Prominent architects of the day who embraced this philosophy included Frank Lloyd Wright, Gustav Stickley, and the brothers Henry and Charles Greene. All dramatically changed interiors from Victorian cubistic to open and free flowing. In particular, the Greene brothers on the West Coast combined the regional influences of Spanish mission style and American shingle with an Asian expression of exposed timbers, wide, low pitched roofs, and projecting porches (Figure 1-9, building O).

The Arts and Crafts Movement produced some beautiful houses but

Figure 1-9
Timber post
and beam:
Craftsman
style.

they were affordable only for the wealthy. Soon efficient sawmills were mass producing smaller-dimension lumber inexpensively for the market. It became possible to buy an entire house precut and delivered, including windows, doors, and furnishings, through the Sears and Roebuck mail order catalogue. The housing industry was born and there was now little incentive to build with heavy logs and timbers. Log and timber building would remain dormant for the next half century.

By the mid-1960s, escalating building costs for materials and labor, government regulations, and bank mortgages caused disenchantment among homeowners. This disenchantment was mirrored by discontent with the established order in everything from housing and debt, to sex and politics, and caused a rethinking of the norms, similar in many respects to the Arts and Crafts Movement earlier but much greater in scope. This counterculture movement was the catalyst behind the resurgence of "alternative" building methods which emphasized freedom, individuality, and environmental responsibility. Old methods long forgotten were resurrected; building with logs, adobe, strawbale, rammed earth, and other natural materials became a link back to nature (Figure 1-10). Soon industry responded with a whole new generation of power tools which were portable and affordable. By the 1980s the log and timber housing industry was well established and was even touted as architecture nouveau. A log or timber home became financially out of reach for most people.

As we sit on the edge of the year 2000, all housing, whether log, timber, or standard type, is still too expensive for most people. However, there exists a counterculture of people today with similar attitudes to those found in the Arts and Crafts Movement of the 1900s and in the 1960s' Back to the Land Movement, who believe that a home should not be synonymous with long-term debt. These individuals, who set out to change the status quo by building their homes with their own sweat equity, are called owner/builders. The evolution continues and this book is one of the stepping stones.

Figure 1-10 Short log post and beam house, 1985.

CHAPTER TWO

Design

*"The more I design, the more
sure I am that elimination is
the secret of beauty in
architecture."*

—GUSTAV STICKLEY
(1858–1942)

The basic principles of design during the American Arts and Crafts
Movement were that buildings had to be suited to the way people actually
lived; they had to have the best structural outline and the simplest form;
and they should be made from indigenous materials and act in harmony
with the landscape. A home based on simplicity, utility, and organic harmony will never be out of date.

The design of your home affects the way you eat, sleep, work, and
play. It can make you comfortable or miserable. Many people relinquish
the design of their homes to specialists. In doing so, however, they di-
minish the extent to which their homes are expressions of themselves.

As with any building method, modular design requires a blueprint
and a plan for construction. Each component is broken down into a series of tasks, each requiring specific tools, materials, and procedures.

THE MODULAR APPROACH

Reducing a building into modular component pieces to enable quick assembly is not a new concept. Most highrise construction today consists of
a steel or reinforced concrete post and beam frame with a panelized skin

or infill. Modular sizing of conventional building components is apparent throughout the housing industry in such things as dimensional lumber sizing (2"× 4" studs), 4' × 8' plywood, concrete blocks, 16" joist and stud spacings, and so on.

The ability to assemble the modular components of a log or timber house shell can mean the difference between success or failure for the owner/builder. Ideally, the lock-up stage (the building shell sealed to weather) should be completed within one building season, which is the optimum time period to complete the shell before the detrimental effects of bad weather increase. Unless the builder is able to prefabricate and store the component pieces for assembly during the building season, the house may not be completed on time. A rushed schedule compromises quality and takes away from the enjoyment of building your own home.

Familiarize yourself with the phases of building: (I) land acquisition, (II) excavation and foundation, (III) lock-up, and (IV) utilities and finish. Each of these phases requires varying amounts of money to complete. The lock-up phase is the most critical because the entire house shell, from subfloor to roof covering, must be completed at one time to prevent deterioration caused by inclement weather. Most people cannot afford to complete all the building phases at once, however. By focusing one's resources solely on the house lock-up phase, building it modularly, success is possible on a limited budget.

Module

The module has been developed to simplify and standardize building practice and components. Represented in plan as a simple grid (Figure

Figure 2-1
Grid module.

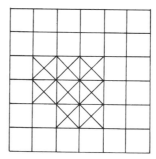

2-1), the modules, when grouped, form coherent shapes. The variety of possible shapes belies their simplicity. The Japanese base their building module on the 3' tatami mat. The North American building system is based on 4", resulting in combinations of 12", 16", 24", 48". From architectural scale on blueprints, to purchasing a 4' × 8' sheet of plywood to be nailed to joists 16" apart—it's all modules. To minimize waste, try to keep within industry parameters.Expanding the module three-dimensionally produces a cube shape which has volume (Figure 2-2). The module is made up of vertical and horizontal lines which, in a log and timber post and beam house, represent the center lines of posts and beams. The space in between represents the infill. All of these "modules" which together make the "modular whole" can be measured, reproduced, interchanged, or recombined to produce an entirely different shape. This is

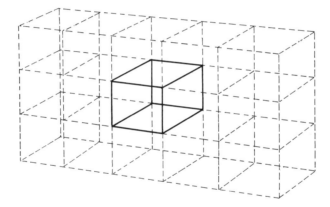

Figure 2-2
Cube module.

the essential concept of the modular post and beam system—plus the ability to store these modular components.

When building a post and beam house I prefer a module that is 10'–12' square with a 7'–8' height (Figure 2-3). The horizontal dimension relates to the post spacings and the beam span, whereas the vertical dimension relates to post height. Remember, these are center-to-center measurements. Variations of these dimensions depend upon the allowable beam span (refer to Structural Span Tables, Appendix III) and the economical use of available log or timber lengths. The module system allows for a consistency of heights and spans within the building's elevations and floor plans.

Figure 2-3
Post and
beam module.

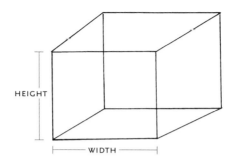

Golden Section

The mathematicians of antiquity determined a proportion which would form a harmonious relation of parts; this harmonious proportion is called the golden section. The pyramids of ancient Egypt, classical Greek architecture, and modern furniture design all employ the golden section, which is basically a rectangle whose short and long sides are expressed roughly in the ratio of 3 to 5. To be more precise, the ratio is 1:1.618 where the smaller length is to the larger as the larger is to the whole.

According to the golden section, to find the ideal proportion of a post and beam frame, multiply the post height by 1.618 to find the spacing (beam length).

For example, a 7' post (as measured centerline-to-centerline):

7' × 1.618' = 11'4", making the golden rectangle a 7' height with an 11'4" base (center-to-center).

Remember, the golden section relates to proportion only. The ultimate decision as to the span between the posts is regulated by the carrying capacity of the structural beam. For further information refer to Structural Beam Loading and Sizing in Appendix III.

Figure 2-4
How to find the
golden section.

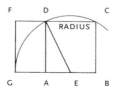

The long side of each rectangle, divided by the short side, equals 1.618.

1) Start with any size of square (A, B, C, D).
2) Bisect the base (A, B) and use point (E) to draw radius (E, D).
3) Extend the baseline of the square to the point where it intersects with the radius (G).
4) The new rectangle (B, C, G, F) is now in golden proportion.

Forces at Play

A frame can be strong but lack rigidity, meaning an unbraced structure can be distorted by the forces of gravity, weather, or seismic instability (Figure 2-5).

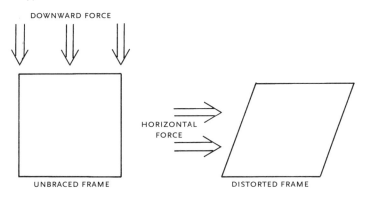

Figure 2-5
Frame distortion without bracing.

Bracing

In order to prevent a distortion of the frame, various methods of bracing are incorporated. These include triangular, diaphragm, and tensioning (Figure 2-6).

An example of triangular bracing in a post and beam frame are knee-braces. These are short-length timbers which bisect the corner of a post

Figure 2-6
Frame
bracing
methods.

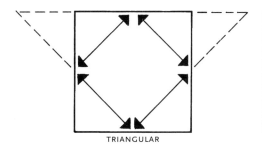
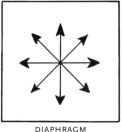
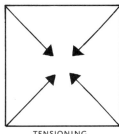

and beam frame at a 45° angle and give it rigidity. Kneebraces can be placed at any intersecting post and beam, but they are usually located at the outside corners (with an extended plate beam) to allow for the modular infill (Figure 2-7).

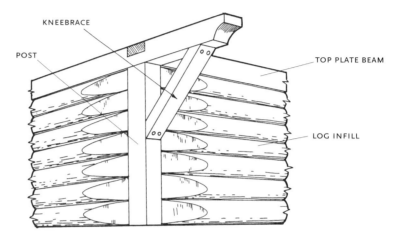

Figure 2-7
Triangle
bracing.

Diaphragm bracing enhances the ability of the infill material to withstand distortion which in turn makes the frame more rigid. For example, a conventional stud frame house relies on the diaphragm bracing of the plywood sheathing to impart rigidity to the structure. One of the post and beam methods shown in this book utilizes a rigid foam panel infill, and

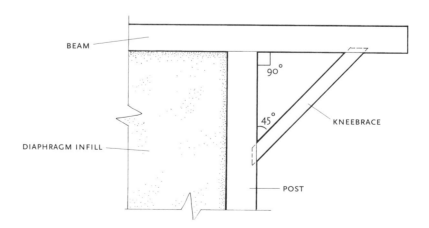

Figure 2-8
Triangle
kneebracing
with log infill.

relies on the combined components of the panel to provide diaphragm bracing, as well as kneebraces which provide triangular bracing (Figure 2-8). Solid log and timber infills, when properly pinned together, create both a diaphragm and a monolithic mass to resist distortion.

Tension is a pulling force that draws the opposite corners toward each other, and the resulting stress on the panel causes rigidity. When tensioning is applied to a rigid foam infill panel, the combined effect with its diaphragm potential is significantly stronger.

Tensioning involves taut wire or metal "T" spanning opposite corners to provide resistance and prevent distortion. Often a conventional stud frame infill (if plywood is not used as sheathing) employs "T" tensioning. In this case the tail of the "T" is fit into a shallow kerf cut in the studs and the flange is nailed to each individual stud. Tensioning would be applied to the interior studs prior to drywall.

THE HUMAN PERSPECTIVE

The intended purpose of a home is to be a nurturing environment, promoting the health and psychological well-being of the occupants. Obviously, the more the designer knows about the occupants, the better he or she can translate this knowledge into the structural design. A home is very much an expression of ourselves, so who better to design it than ourselves?

We therefore must begin by examining ourselves and our spatial requirements. We humans lead both active (extroverted) and passive (introverted) lives. Our extroverted, active self seeks freedom and movement in open, bright spaces. Our introverted, passive self seeks privacy and protection in enclosed, darker spaces. The architectural terminology for these dual human needs is ECTO (active, extroverted, open space) and

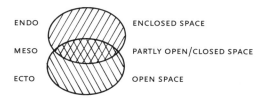

Figure 2-9
Active/passive
space.

ENDO (passive, introverted, enclosed space). The transitional space in between is called MESO (partly open/partly closed) (Figure 2-9). Both of these basic needs should be met in the design of our house.

When we allot functional space requirements to our basic human nature the picture takes on a clearer meaning (Figure 2-10).

Figure 2-10
Functional space.

ENDO — PRIVATE (SLEEP, STUDY)
SEMI-PRIVATE (BATH, DRESS)
MESO — OPERATIONAL (COOKING, LAUNDRY, UTILITIES)
SEMI-PUBLIC (RECREATIONAL, SOCIAL)
ECTO — PUBLIC (MAIN ENTRY)

Human actions relating to active and passive existence happen over time and are subject to the influence of the seasons and solar orientation. For example, experience the discomfort of trying to sleep at noon on a hot summer day in a bedroom facing south to appreciate this fact. Figure 2-11 shows the time/orientation relationship to active/passive space usage.

Once understood, these basic physiological and psychological requirements can now be applied to basic house form. As we can see in Figure 2-12 the private, enclosed space is separated from the public, open space by the operational space which is used both as a buffer and a link between the two zones. Operational space includes the kitchen, bathroom, and utility room.

This orientation of spaces locates bedrooms towards the cool, nighttime north; the kitchen towards the early morning east; the recreation

Figure 2-11
Space orientation.

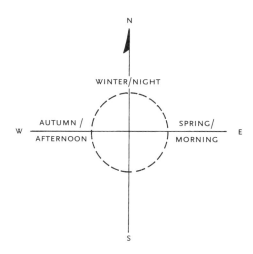

N

WINTER/NIGHT

AUTUMN /
AFTERNOON   SPRING/
W   E   MORNING

S

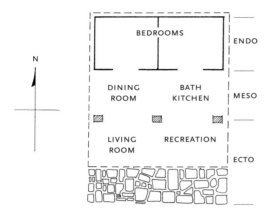

Figure 2-12
Functional space orientation.

and living rooms share a transitional role between indoor and outdoor space, positioned towards the warm noon south; and finally the dining room faces the late afternoon west. An arrangement of this sort allows for different activities to be carried on with maximum comfort and little disturbance between them.

Space Requirements

There are three stages to family life—early, crowded, and late—and these stages each have different space requirements. The early stage usually consists of a single person or couple who need only a basic unit for living, sleeping, cooking, and bathing. The crowded family stage requires more

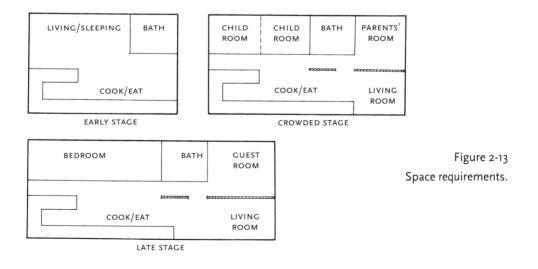

Figure 2-13
Space requirements.

space to afford more privacy for the occupants. During the late stage less space is needed as the children move out on their own (refer to Figure 2-13). When planning your house you will need to keep in mind which family life stage you are in or plan to be in.

Aesthetics: Art of Simplicity

Aesthetics refers to an appreciation for beauty. The degree to which you relate to your home aesthetically depends on how keenly responsive to beauty in art and nature you are. Since everyone has different tastes and interests in this regard, aesthetics are purely subjective. Keep in mind however, that if the ultimate purpose of a home is to be a nurturing environment, then our psychological well-being is as important as our physical health and the aesthetics of our home can have an impact on our psychological well-being.

Psychological well-being is increasingly more difficult to achieve when our lives are subjected to complex issues every day. Simplicity of form and function in the design of our home is necessary to create a balanced, restful state. The Greene brothers, architects of post and beam homes during the American Arts and Crafts Movement, said about simplicity in design: *"To simplify is never a simple attainment; it takes breadth of experience, confidence and cultivation."*

A post and beam structural frame with passive infill is a harmonious relationship—the former positive, the latter negative. Using solid and void, color and light, and surface contrast gives visual relief, achieving richness without unnecessary complication.

Massive vertical posts jointed to horizontal beams with diagonal kneebraces form the structural building frame. Nothing is hidden; the identity of each contributing part is visible, both externally and internally. The strength and simplicity of form implies a sense of security and coziness seldom equaled in other building types.

DESIGNING WITH LOGS AND TIMBERS

Building with logs and timbers allows for projections and cantilevers, which blur the division between nature and house. Figure 2-14 shows two simple rectangular house designs, one a conventional stud frame (including modern braced timberframe with stress skin panels) and the

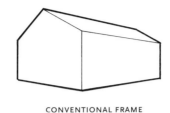

CONVENTIONAL FRAME

Figure 2-14
Designing with
logs and timbers.

LOG AND TIMBER
POST AND BEAM

other a log and timber post and beam design. The first example has a stagnant, box-like feeling. The second example gives the impression that the building has potential for growth, the opposite of stagnation. Projecting beams, cantilevering roofs, and decks give the feeling like branches of a tree reaching out.

Designing with logs and timbers is an interrelationship between Nature and Man. Nature provides the tree whose trunk (log) is round. Man transforms the round log into a square to make building easier. Each form has its own design potential and what's more, a new design potential is created in the transition of round to square. The following diagrams illustrate the design potential of post and beam: the round forms of log work, the square forms of timberwork, and the transitional forms of the two combined.

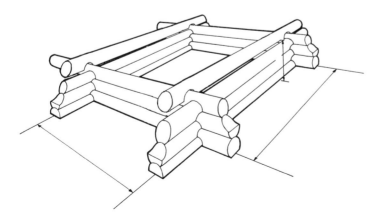

Figure 2-15
Round log blockwork.

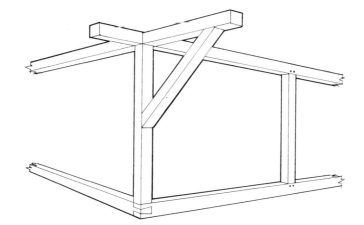

Figure 2-16
Square timber post
and beam.

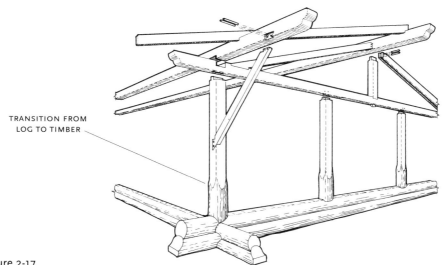

TRANSITION FROM
LOG TO TIMBER

Figure 2-17
Transitional log/timber
post and beam.

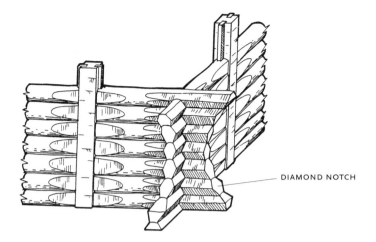

Figure 2-18
Shaping logs back from
the joinery intersection.

DIAMOND NOTCH

STRUCTURE

All structures in nature must stand up to the elements of gravity, seismic disturbances, weather, and human usage. We need to keep these forces in mind when designing our homes. The size and spacing of posts and beams, the method of anchoring the frame to the foundation, the roof slope and overhang, the choice of materials, and the arrangement and co-ordination of all the parts and details must be taken into consideration. Neglect or ignorance at this stage could result in structural failure.

In the post and beam construction method, a series of vertical posts unite with horizontal beams to form a structural framework. This frame defines the total building. Posts will be located at each corner of the building and spaced evenly between the corner posts to support the roof

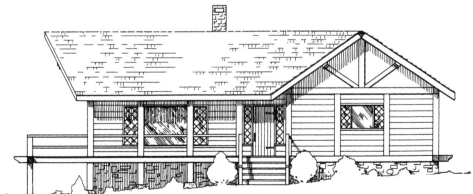

Figure 2-19
House designed with equal
post spacings.

Figure 2-20 Simplicity and harmony with the natural environment are the key to a successful rural or vacation home. In such areas tools, frame materials, and labor are scarce commodities. This log post and beam *pièce-sur-pièce* country cottage can be constructed by an owner/builder with materials gathered primarily from the land.

weight (Figure 2-19). Since the weight of the roof will be transmitted through the posts to the foundation, load bearing roof trusses and tie-beams should be placed directly over vertical posts. The distance between vertical posts should not exceed 12 feet for two reasons. First, a top plate (supporting the roof weight) could overtax its strength if made to span too long a distance (refer to Span Tables, Appendix III). Second, it is harder to construct solid wood infill panels if the distance between vertical posts is more than 12 feet. Equal post thickness and spacing will per-

Figure 2-21 *Stav og laft* revival. Round notched corner blockwork tapering to squared timber framework imparts a transition from natural to manmade. Infill types include glass, *pièce-sur-pièce*, and frame panel.

mit prefabrication of infill panels and the interchangeability of components from one house design to another.

The infill between the posts as described in this book can be as varied as high tech rigid foam panel, stud frame, log, or half timber, and can also include notched corners. An additional advantage of this method is that the structural framework can incorporate large glass areas without shrinkage or settling problems, as well as other infill types which afford adequate thermal and weather protection. The house's strength is achieved with solid beams and posts, leaving partition walls to act more as room dividers than as structural units.

The exterior finish of a wooden house should seek to reflect nature. In the forest the tree's roots grow from soil and rock; in the same way, a rock foundation gives the feeling a log or timber house is an integral part of nature. Try to reference the house to the building site—emphasizing the horizontal line gives one a grounded feeling, and a vertical line feels unstable, whereas ascending horizontal levels reflect the transition from

Figure 2-22 Timber post and beam with E.P.S. infill panel and acrylic stucco exterior finish.

anchored ground to free flight. Inside the house, highlighting the wood with contrasting materials works well. Drywall (gyprock) plastered and painted white is inexpensive, yet serves to enhance the wood's natural tones while at the same time providing the necessary reflective light. The colors red, orange, blue, and green look well with the golden hues of wood, and especially brighten the kitchen and bathroom areas.

CHAPTER THREE

Wood

And God said to Noah . . .
"Make an ark of wood."
——BOOK OF GENESIS

. . . and ever since, humans have exploited this most versatile of nature's materials. Log and timber homes raise the question of how environmentally sound building with wood really is. Uncontrolled, unsustainable logging created deserts where the great cedars of Lebanon once stood, and by the sixteenth century England's forests were devastated. Country after country has seen a similar scenario of deforestation. Our attraction to wood is both practical and psychological, an affirmation of the bond between nature and mankind. The question remains whether we can slow down the rapid extraction of this precious resource to a point of true sustainability in our natural forests rather than in tree farm mono-cultures. The natural forest is a diverse ecosystem of plants, birds, and animals, and clearcutting, no matter how controlled, devastates this fragile ecosystem. To replant with mono-culture trees invites species-specific predators which can wipe out an entire "farm."

Replacing clearcuts with sustainable, selective harvesting methods minimizes the impact and damage to the environment. Selective harvesting promotes faster growth of the surrounding trees by providing additional room and allowing sunlight to penetrate through the forest canopy.

When it comes to wood I believe in a philosophy of reduce, recycle, and replant. We have managed to reduce the life expectancy of houses from 100 years for those built prior to World War II, to 25 years for a house built today using composite materials, glues, and staples. By contrast, a log or timbered house has a life span of a thousand or more years.

Logs and timbers, unlike studs and particle-board sheathing, have a high recycle factor. A log or timber house can be dismantled and recycled rather than demolished. The result is housing for generations to come. Recycling logs, timbers, and other building materials is an effective, ecological way to reduce our demands on our forests. Wood is the primary material for the post and beam building methods described in this book. I urge you to educate yourself about the basic properties of wood and to nurture an appreciation for this most alive of our building materials.

STRUCTURE OF WOOD

Woods are classified into two broad groups: softwoods and hardwoods. This classification is somewhat misleading, for some so-called softwoods are harder than some species of hardwoods. A more accurate and simpler classification groups together as softwoods those trees which bear needles and, for the most part, retain them throughout the winter, and as hardwoods those which bear broad leaves and lose them over the winter months. Another feature which distinguishes the two groups is their overall size and shape. The needle-bearing softwoods generally grow tall and straight, with little tapering of the trunk, while the broad-leafed hardwoods tend to be shorter, with a more pronounced tapering of the trunk. For these reasons (size and taper), softwoods are frequently used in solid wood construction. Amongst the various species of softwoods some are stronger while others are more susceptible to rot and decay. Such characteristics help to determine where the various woods would best be placed in a building (see Appendix II).

Figure 3-1 shows the cross-section of a softwood tree. The outer bark protects the tree from injury and loss of vital fluids (sap). Just under the bark is the thin cambium sheath of active growth cells which creates the new growth. This "sapwood" transports water and nutrients from the roots to the leaves. (In conifers water moves upward almost entirely through the sapwood.)

The next layer is the heartwood, made up of matured sapwood cells which store resins and gums. This portion of the tree is sealed off from the growth process and serves primarily as the structural backbone. In comparison to the living sapwood, the heartwood is less subject to decay and shrinkage. The medullary rays which run at right angles to the axis

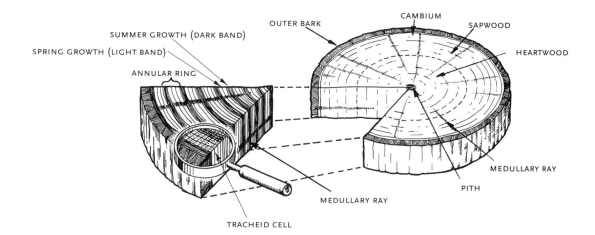

OUTER BARK
CAMBIUM
SAPWOOD
SUMMER GROWTH (DARK BAND)
HEARTWOOD
SPRING GROWTH (LIGHT BAND)
ANNULAR RING
MEDULLARY RAY
PITH
MEDULLARY RAY
TRACHEID CELL

are an alignment of additional storage cells which provide nutrition for the sapwood during winter dormancy. The pith is the first-year growth of the seedling tree which lies at the very center of the heartwood.

Figure 3-1 Cross-section of a softwood tree trunk.

The enlarged section of a tree trunk shows the annual growth pattern of the tree. During the winter the tree stores most of its watery sap in the roots, which keeps it from freezing and then splitting the wood. At this time no growth occurs. The warmth of spring stimulates a hormone which causes the sap to run and brings about the rapid growth indicated by the wide band of lighter, thin-walled cells. The heat of summer slows down the growth rate, producing a narrow band of darker, thick-walled cells. These two bands of light and dark wood make up an annular ring or one year's tree growth. The magnifying lens in the same diagram shows how the wood cells are arranged in a side-by-side vertical alignment down the length of the tree. Called tracheid cells, they comprise 90 to 95 percent of the tree's volume of wood. The length of their column-like bodies is approximately 100 times greater than the diameter. These facts explain why wood is stronger when it is vertical (in a post) rather than horizontal (in a beam).

Strength

When compared by weight, wood is stronger than steel. But as a natural material, wood is not homogeneous in consistency, and its strength is relative to its species, grain direction, the presence of defects, and moisture content. For example, the softwood species yellow cedar does not have the fiber strength of Douglas fir for reasons of fiber length and density. Thus the fir would be better suited for structural loading applications, such as floor joists or roof rafters. Wood is stronger by far where loading is applied parallel to the grain (as with vertical posts) than it is at right angles to the grain (as with horizontal beams). For this reason, additional care must be exercised when selecting wood structural beams. Defects such as loose knots, or cracks, splits, and shakes break the grain continuity and weaken the beam, most dangerously at its midpoint where stress is greatest. Furthermore, moisture-saturated wood will bend and become permanently deformed more readily than dry wood. Such deformities could, over time, cause sagging of load-bearing beams.

Thermal Value

Thermal value is a collective term for the two factors considered in determining the insulative worth of a material—specifically heat conductivity and thermal mass potential. Heat conductivity refers to the material's ability to conduct heat. The less well it conducts heat, the better its resistivity (R factor). Dry wood's R factor is between 1.8 and 2.0 per inch, compared with common fiberglass insulation which has an R factor of 3.3. This R factor rating indicates that the fiberglass has better heat resistivity than wood.

Thermal mass potential refers to the material's ability to trap and store heat energy within its physical mass. The larger the heat storage value, the slower the temperature change that is propagated through the material. This delay is called "time lag" and it gives an opportunity to store peak heat loads and release them at low-temperature periods. Solar heated houses rely heavily on the heat storage potential which only materials of large mass can provide. For comparison purposes consider a house which is insulated with typical fiberglass insulation, having a high R factor but low thermal mass. While the internal heat source is functioning the house is warm, but should the fires go out on a cold, wintry night, the short time lag due to a small thermal mass storage causes the house to cool quickly. Solid wood has millions of air cells and the physical mass of the wood traps and stores heat, allowing the house to stay warm throughout the night. According to the Timber Construction Manual of the American Institute of Timber Constructions, "Thermal conductivity is approximately the same in radial and tangential directions but is generally about 2 times greater along the grain." When examining a log wall, some building inspectors assess the thermal value of the wall based on its average thickness. For example, wall logs with a beam diameter of 12" (300 mm) and lateral groove width of 4" (100 mm) would be assessed on an average wall thickness of 8" (200 mm). This is a false assessment, since the heat flows into and through the wood twice as fast along the cellular alignment, which comprises the grain. As described above, the tracheid cell alignment is arranged in such a way that the heat path is down the length of the log, in toward its heart, and along the annular rings. In each case the path is not the shortest distance through the log, but rather a considerably longer distance into, around, and down the length of the log. This roundabout heat flow increases the wood's thermal mass potential. Hence, a correct thermal assessment should, at the very least, be based on the 12" (300 mm) wall thickness.

Note: A house's overall thermal effectiveness depends primarily on the amount of air exchange. Excessive drafts rob the average house of approximately 40 percent of the heat. Proper weather sealing and a heating system which creates a positive pressure inside the house by drawing its air source from outside will do much to rectify a cold house. In a hierarchy of heat-loss situations the roof is next in importance, since as heat rises it tends to concentrate near the ceiling. As well, large windows, not placed to take advantage of solar radiation benefits, amount to a large heat loss, as do lightweight doors. Unheated crawl spaces below the floor will absorb the damp cold like a sponge and displace the lighter warm air upward.

LOG SELECTION AND FELLING

Selection

Common methods of obtaining log materials include salvaging from concluded logging operations, harvesting trees privately, with a timber sales permit from the local Forestry Department, or by direct purchase from a logging contractor or mill. Although historically hardwoods have been used extensively for solid wood construction the majority of buildings today are built with softwoods. This, however, will depend entirely on the material's abundance in the area.

Generally, fir, spruce, larch, pine, and cedar are the softwoods most often used in log and timber construction (see Appendix II). Intermixing various softwood species in solid wood wall infill construction poses no problems, but strive to divide the mix equally amongst all the walls to avoid possible settling discrepancies. Logs ideally should have tops no smaller than 10" (250 mm). Square timbers used as posts or sill and top plate beams will be a larger size to offset wastage and minimize wane (rounded corners).

When scouting for trees it is best to avoid trees growing on river banks or near lake- and seashores. These trees serve to protect the area from wind and water erosion, and their removal can bring about adverse effects. Moreover, such trees have been exposed to high winds and, over a period of time, take on twisted growth patterns. This spiral wood growth goes unnoticed until the tree has been stripped of bark and dried. Building with such wood can cause beams and posts to twist out of shape after drying.

Seek out a thick growth stand on a north-facing hill or gently sloping mountainside. In such a location, due to the competition for sunlight, the trees grow straighter with least taper and fewer branches. On a south slope, sparsely populated stands will tend to have greater taper and more

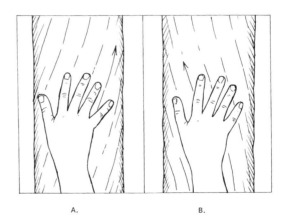

A.   B.

Figure 3-2 The traditional Bavarian technique for determining spiral grain. If the spiral follows the direction of the little finger (left), it is called right-handed; if it follows the thumb (right), it is left-handed. Right-handed wood is suitable for building, but left-handed wood is not.

branches. The tree stand should have road access for a skidder or horse team, and an area or landing to accommodate the stock-piled logs and a truck.

Once an area has been found with a suitable tree stand and accessible landing, individual tree selection can begin. To identify the trees for later harvesting you will need a tape measure and orange spray paint or surveyor's ribbon. As you scout through the forest, assess the individual trees of your preferred species: their girth, height, and their lack or abundance of limbs. Next "plumb" each tree for its straightness and direction of lean. Do this by sighting the tree from a distance of about 50' (15 m) or so. Take note of the following:

- The presence of excessive bows or dog-legs (S-curves).
- The direction and amount of lean, and how these will affect its later removal.
- Any possible snags or problems resulting from its direction of fall.

If the tree passes the test, mark it for later felling and move on to the next.

Girding

A traditional Bavarian method involved climbing the standing tree and removing a strip of bark from around the trunk, just below the crown. With photosynthesis cut off from the rest of the tree, the roots cease absorbing nutrients from the crown while the leaves continue to draw the vital fluids from the roots. Slowly the portion of the tree below the girdle dries out, in effect seasoning the tree while it is still standing. The problem with this method is the labor involved in climbing and girdling each tree. A slight adaptation of this process is to cut a deep girdle at the base of the tree, well into the sapwood, so as to "choke" it.

Felling

Warning: Tree felling is dangerous, and I do not recommend that you do it yourself. If you choose to learn to fall trees, guidance from an experienced faller is required.

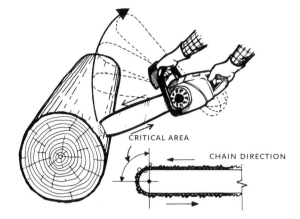

Figure 3-3
Kickback due to operating
the chainsaw too close to
the bar tip.

CRITICAL AREA

CHAIN DIRECTION

Chainsaw Safety Considerations

- Using the tip of the chainsaw bar can lead to severe kickback.
- Most accidents are caused by unstable footing, so before you begin, make sure you are in a stable position and that there is no debris to trip on.
- Let the saw cool off before refueling.
- Never let the chain become too loose on the bar.
- Always wear the appropriate safety gear when operating a chainsaw.

Safety Considerations for Felling

- Ensure all workers are clear of the hazardous area before felling a tree.
- Remove brush and debris from around the base of the tree, and establish a clear path to safety (to one side and behind the stump in relation to the direction of fall).
- Fell the tree in the general direction of its prevailing lean. Felling against the lean can be done to facilitate easier bucking or removal, providing the degree of lean is not considerable. Too much lean exists for this purpose when the weight of the tree forces it to fall in a particular direction.
- Ensure the undercut is complete and cleaned out (Figures 3-4a, b, c).
- Start a wedge in the backcut as soon as room allows.
- Observe the tree as it falls to the ground and guard against flying limbs and debris.

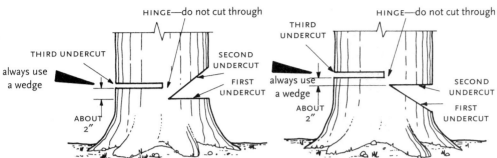

Figure 3-4a
Cutting procedures
for felling trees.

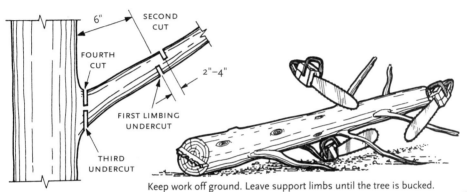

Keep work off ground. Leave support limbs until the tree is bucked.

Figure 3-4b
Procedure for
limbing.

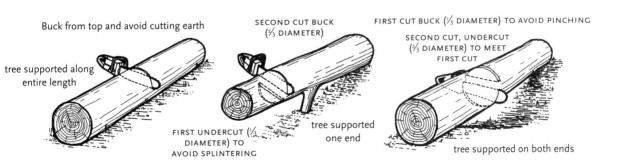

Figure 3-4c
Procedure for
bucking.

SEASONING WOOD

A tree standing in the forest is said to be in the "green" state, meaning that the wood is saturated with water. The amount of water it contains varies with the seasons, the least being in the winter and the greatest in the spring. Consequently, the best time to fell a tree is during the winter. Once the tree is felled it will begin to lose its trapped water until its moisture content equals that of its environment. During this time the wood cells will undergo their greatest amount of shrinkage. Figure 3-5 shows an individual wood tracheid cell before and after water loss. The dry cell has collapsed, shrinking in width but with no significant reduction in its length. Multiply this effect by the millions of tracheid wood cells in a tree, and the result is that the log shrinks in diameter while the length remains the same (Figure 3-6). When a number of horizontally placed green logs or timbers are fitted between vertical posts, their cumulative shrinkage, called settling, will lead to a reduced wall height, while the posts will stay the same height (Figure 3-7). The posts will shrink very little in width even if the wood is green, because the removal of the water-saturated sapwood in cutting flat surfaces for joinery has removed the cells most prone to shrinkage.

The too-rapid drying of green wood will cause excessive checking or cracking. Peeling a green log and leaving it in the hot sun will quickly dry the outer surface of the wood while the inner wood remains wet. The resulting cellular shrinkage around the outside will set up internal stresses leading to cracks (Figure 3-8). Such checks, especially the large ones, will look unsightly, collect dirt, and tend to widen over time due to the wedging action of freezing water. Extreme checking can cause structural weakening in loading carrying beams.

Figure 3-5
Tracheid cellular
shrinkage.

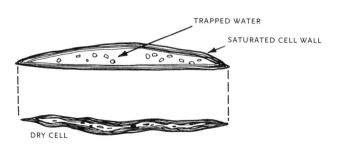

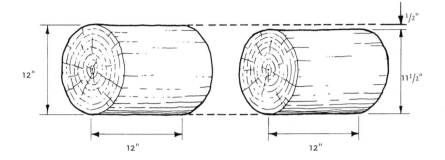

Figure 3-6
Log shrinkage.
Estimated at ½"
per 12" of log
thickness.

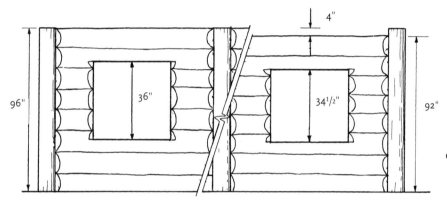

Figure 3-7
Shrinkage of
a log wall—
estimated at ½"
per vertical 12".

Checking can be reduced and practically eliminated by retarding the loss of surface moisture from the wood. To do this some people go to the extent of seasoning the wood for a year or two prior to construction. A practical alternative to this lengthy procedure would be to use fire-killed trees which have been naturally seasoned. Many builders prefer to work with green or slightly seasoned wood, both for the convenience and the ease of working with wood in this softer state.

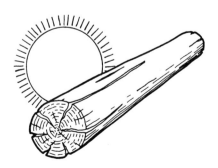

Figure 3-8
Cracks caused by
rapid shrinkage.

When building with green wood you run the risk of excessive checking unless some means of protection is applied to the log's surface right after peeling. This surface application can be thought of as an invisible bark. There are commercial sealers available to do the job, but a salt brine works just as well. The brine is made by dissolving as much salt as possible in water. (Heating the water increases saturation levels.) Salt retains water, and once the solution is brushed onto the surface, evaporation is inhibited.

An interesting, as yet experimental, alternative is the application of antifreeze to the surface of the wood. The sealing ingredient is ethylene glycol, which is the same as the P.E.G. (polyethylene glycol) solution that wood carvers use to prevent checking of their materials. It appears that this waxy, water soluble liquid penetrates into the wood, replacing the cell wall's moisture and preventing its collapse and shrinkage. How well various finishes will work with this surface application has not yet been thoroughly examined. In all cases a wax or paint should be applied to the end-grain surfaces of the wood, including log ends and any end-grain joinery locations as well.

Movement in wood is attributable to the stresses set up inside its fibers as a result of moisture fluctuations. For example, the heat of summer dries wood fibers, causing a contraction in tension while moisture from the fall rains expands the wood fibers, relieving this tension. We view the result as seasonal shrinkage and expansion. Depending upon the log's grain pattern, tension can become severe enough to cause distortions such as warping or twisting. This is especially true for a spiral grained wood. The potential for distortion is greatest as the wood changes from its green (i.e. water saturated) to its dry state. After this, the movement becomes less intensive and then minimal in relation to the yearly seasonal humidity conditions. Keep in mind that wood is alive, and even after a tree is cut the wood will respond to climatic changes.

Winter Cutting

Cutting trees in the late fall or winter when the sap is stored in the roots is essential, whether the intention is to build with green wood or to season it first. A method for determining if the sap has stopped running is to peel a small patch of bark off the trunk and wait a while. If no sap oozes from the wound it is time to cut. Cutting, then skidding after the first snowfall has the advantage of not scarring the logs too badly. Logs should be decked on pole skids spaced a few feet apart to keep the logs off the ground. When stored, the logs should be spaced to provide ventilation, and turned every few days to prevent bowing.

Seasoning Logs

Essentially the process of seasoning logs involves leaving on the protective bark at least over the hot summer, and waxing or painting the log ends. The sealed ends force the moisture to leave via the trunk's surface, thereby maintaining a stress equilibrium between the outer and inner wood. Sealing the end grain of all joinery after it has been completed but before assembly is recommended for this reason as well. Also during the hot summer, decked logs should be either shaded or sprayed with water each morning and evening to prevent rapid evaporation.

A note on air-drying versus kiln-drying. It is unfeasible to expect to kiln-dry a log or large timber due to the length of time required and the cost of kiln time. In addition, kiln-dried wood does not last as long as air-dried when exposed to dry-rot conditions or predators.

Figure 3-9
Seasoning logs.

Seasoning Timbers

Seasoning squared logs (timbers) is similar to seasoning logs with the advantage that timbers can be stacked to conserve space. Moisture loss is more rapid with the protective bark cut off, so ensure the timber ends are sealed and the stickered (spaced) pile is out of direct sunlight with good ventilation. The stack should be well supported above the ground to avoid contact with dirt or moisture. Figure 3-10 shows a stickered timber pile.

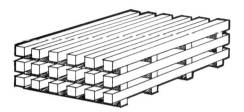

Figure 3-10
Stickered timber
pile.

Note: The stickers must be uniform in thickness, spaced every 5 feet, and be in line to prevent warping of the timbers. Cover the stack to prevent rain soaking but still allow for ventilation.

Timber Grades

Whether you are ordering timbers from a sawmill or cutting them yourself, the relative position of the heart determines the grade and cost. Figure 3-11 shows three basic grades.

Figure 3-11
Timber grades.

FREEHEART (GOOD)   CENTER HEART (STANDARD)   OFF-SET HEART (POOR)

Freeheart — This timber has been cut from a large log which eliminates the heart altogether. This lack of unequal stresses results in less checking, warping, or twisting of the timber. Freeheart is the most expensive grade.

Centerheart — This is the standard grade used by most builders due to its moderate price. The stresses created by the combined heartwood and sapwood are equally displaced with the heart in the middle.

Off-set heart — This is the poorest grade since unequal stresses caused by moisture differences between the off-set heartwood and sapwood cause unequal seasoning, resulting in distortion and twisting.

WOOD PESTS AND ROT

Wood boring insects and fungi help to keep forests clear of dead wood, which they reduce to valuable compost. You do not, however, want your home reduced to compost. The best defense against timber-destroying insects and fungi is steady warmth and ventilation which together reduce dampness and humidity. Bark adhering to wood is particularly vulnerable to insect attack, though most wood boring insects will go no deeper than the sapwood.

Dry rot (*Merulius Lacrymans*) is a fungus requiring a moisture content of 20% or greater to encourage spore germination. Unventilated spaces create stagnant areas where the damp encourages fungal growth. Affected wood has whitish, rubbery-looking growths or may, especially in older sites, show no symptoms at all. In the latter case, detecting dry rot is done by probing the wood beneath the surface with a screwdriver or knife to discover a spongy interior. All dry rot must be cut out and the remaining area treated with fungicides. Surface preservatives have limited effectiveness as they don't penetrate deep into the wood.

Storage Hut

A simple, inexpensive storage shelter for drying timbers or storing building components can be assembled in an afternoon by one person. If black plastic is placed as a ground cover and the ends are sealed (and control vented) the structure can double as a solar kiln.

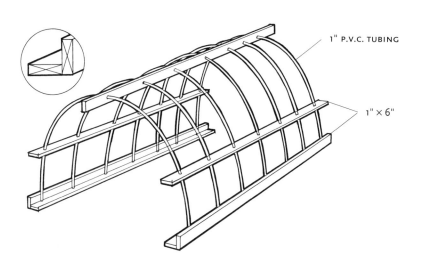

1" P.V.C. TUBING

1" × 6"

Figure 3-12
Storage hut.

Procedure:

1) Lay out and drill 1 1/8" diameter holes on 24" centers along the ridge and purlin boards.

2) Thread 20-foot lengths of 1" P.V.C. pipe through the ridge and purlin boards as shown.

3) Attach the sill plate to the P.V.C. ribs with wire, also on 24" centers. I find a protruding nail works well to position the rib prior to attaching with tie wire.

4) Bend the legs together and firmly stake to the ground.

5) Apply a layer of 6 mm poly vapor barrier (anti–U.V. type) and attach firmly to the sill plate. Ensure ridge support every 10 feet.

CHAPTER FOUR

Tools

The two basic categories of tools are hand tools and power tools. Working with hand tools lets one feel the wood—the difference between working with or against the grain, and the difference between species. We lose this feeling and therefore the close relationship it brings with the wood when we turn to power operations, but the hand tool cannot match the power tool in speed. One must choose between the intimacy of hand tool woodworking versus practical construction. It may be an effective compromise to use power tools for efficiency without a loss of quality workmanship, and reserve hand tools for the special tasks such as complex joinery and finish detailing.

SAFETY

Every woodworking procedure involving a cutting edge is potentially hazardous; when the edge revolves at 15,000 r.p.m. this potential is dramatically increased. Body protection devices for the hands, eyes, and ears make sense but they may not deflect all the dangers. Loose clothing, or dangling hair or jewelry can cause accidents, as can unstable footing or a cluttered work area. It is easy to become too involved with the process and allow your attention to divert from safety. No protective gear will be adequate if the operator does not maintain a safe attitude and develop good habits.

Safety should include periodic stretching of overused muscles as well as maintaining a good range of motion for all your major body joints. Remember, a tool is useless if your body doesn't work.

Mechanical Advantage

Using a mechanical advantage will allow you to save your back. To illustrate this mechanical advantage, refer to Figure 4-1. Diagram A shows no mechanical advantage whereas in diagram B an advantage is gained (equilibrium) when the distance of the pivot point changes to affect the length of the lever arm.

A block and tackle arrangement is a mechanical device which is used for lifting loads and hauling. It is comprised of two or more pulley blocks and a length of rope (tackle) that passes around the pulleys. With this aid it is possible to lift heavy loads using a relatively small force. For example, in diagram C there is no equilibrium since the left load is twice the weight

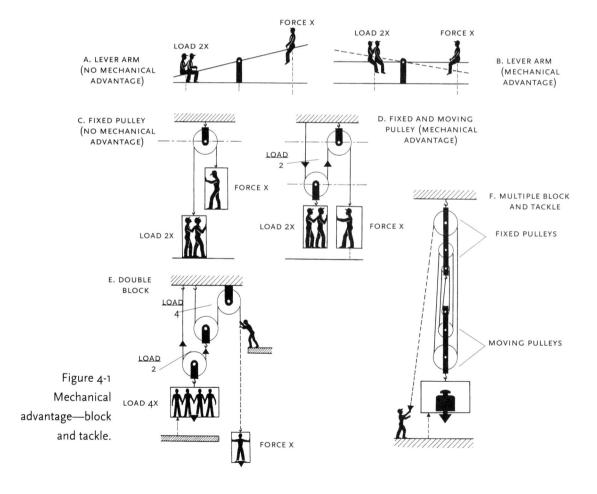

Figure 4-1
Mechanical advantage—block and tackle.

of the right load and the lever arm (equal to the radius of the pulley) is the same for both loads. Increase the length of the lever arm by adding another pulley, as in diagram D, and a mechanical advantage is gained (equilibrium). This arrangement enables a weight load to be raised by the application of a force only half as great as the load. In this case there is a top fixed pulley and a moving pulley, the latter being suspended by two "falls" of rope, each of which acts as a pull equal to half the load.

By increasing the number of pulleys and falls of rope, the mechanical advantage is increased. Each additional moving pulley block doubles the mechanical advantage. The sole function of the top, fixed pulley is to change the direction of the rope so that the force required is a downward pull. In diagram E a second moving pulley increases the mechanical advantage four times, requiring only one quarter the pulling force. A third pulley would require one-eighth, and if there were four moving pulleys it would be one-sixteenth the pulling force. Different arrangements are possible. For instance, in diagram F there are six falls of rope, enabling a load to be lifted by the application of a force only one-sixth as large.

The manual come-along and electric hoist are two lifting devices which replace pulleys with gears (Figure 4-2). While they work on the same mechanical advantage principle, their small gears must rotate many times to achieve any great amount of lifting distance. The log carrier and log tongs are two methods of gripping to lift the log, the former manual and the latter for power lifting (Figure 4-3). For lifting timbers, a

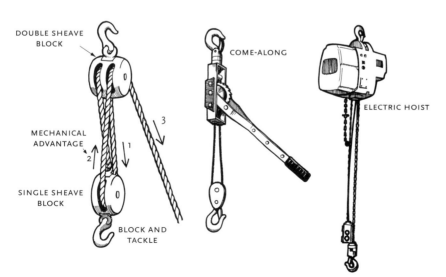

DOUBLE SHEAVE BLOCK

COME-ALONG

ELECTRIC HOIST

MECHANICAL ADVANTAGE

SINGLE SHEAVE BLOCK

BLOCK AND TACKLE

Figure 4-2
Lifting
equipment.

strong rope with two loops at either end or a length of heavy nylon webbing with two metal eyes works well to "choke" the timber with a couple of wraps.

Peavy: This tool will be needed to roll and move the logs or timbers around; you will use it often so have a couple on hand. A similar tool is the cant hook which is simply a peavy without a point.

Axe: An inexpensive 3¹/₂ lb (1.6 kg) axe for all-purpose use.

Peeling spud: Used to remove the heavy bark from trees. A narrow shovel of the type that is used to clean the tracks on bulldozers works very well when filed sharp.

Figure 4-3
Log and timber lifting tools.

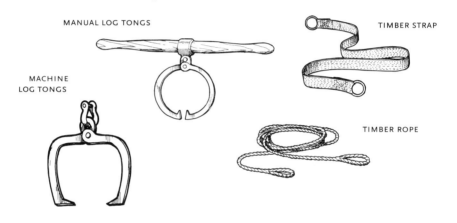

Figure 4-4
Log peeling tools.

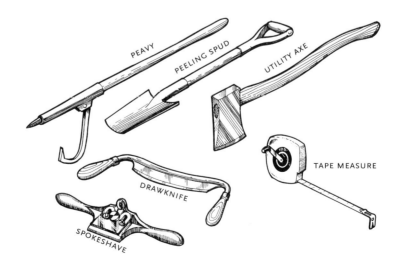

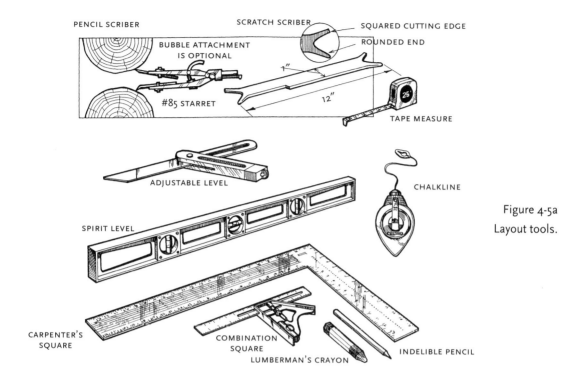

PENCIL SCRIBER
SCRATCH SCRIBER
SQUARED CUTTING EDGE
ROUNDED END
BUBBLE ATTACHMENT IS OPTIONAL
#85 STARRET
12"
TAPE MEASURE
ADJUSTABLE LEVEL
CHALKLINE
SPIRIT LEVEL
CARPENTER'S SQUARE
COMBINATION SQUARE
LUMBERMAN'S CRAYON
INDELIBLE PENCIL

Figure 4-5a
Layout tools.

Drawknife: Used for removing the inner cambium bark from the log, or for touching up damaged surfaces of logs. It is also used for decorative shaping and chamfering of wood.

Spokeshave: Similar use to the drawknife, primarily as decorative function.

Tape measure: A good tape, of 50'–100' (15–30 m) length will be needed.

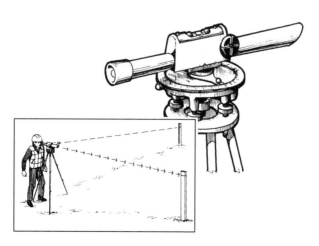

Figure 4-5b
Builder's level.

Layout Tools

To lay out is to arrange or display according to plan. The tools that we use in log and timber layout are indicated in Figure 4-5.

Scribers: Scribers are used to transcribe (duplicate) a curved or irregular surface. The insert shows two types of log scribers, the adjustable compass which uses a pencil to mark the surface and the rigid fixed-setting type which scratches the transcribed line. Note in each example a rounded bottom leg follows the primary surface. While the compass type is usually purchased (Starret Machine Co. #85), the rigid type is usually homemade from $1/8$" strap iron in a variety of sizes.

Tape measure: A 25'–50' (8–15 m) tape is required.

Spirit level: Used to indicate plumb (vertical) and level (horizontal) planes. A 24" (610 mm) and 48" (1220 mm) one is required.

Adjustable bevel: Used for copying and transferring angles and bevels.

Carpenter's square: Used for timber layout, and general carpentry.

Calculator: Used for mathematical problem solving.

Combination square: Used for 90° and 45° layouts, most frequently in timber construction.

Chalkline: A string wound in a case containing colored chalk dust. When it is unwound, pulled tight, and snapped against boards or logs, it leaves a straight guide line of chalk dust along its stretched position. This type of chalkline doubles as a plumb-bob.

Crayons and pencils: Lumberman's crayons and indelible pencils are used to mark the logs; the latter can be used for marking on wet surfaces.

*Builder's level: As the name implies, this tool is used for testing levelness, transferring points, and locating angles on a horizontal plane. It is extremely useful during foundation excavation when the foundation levels are to be determined and transferred. This tool can be rented for the period of time it is needed.

Joinery Tools

After measuring and layout is complete the joinery procedure is next. Removing the waste wood to the joint specifications is accomplished by boring, cutting, sawing, and shaping actions, each requiring different tools.

Hand auger: Used manually, comes in varying sizes.

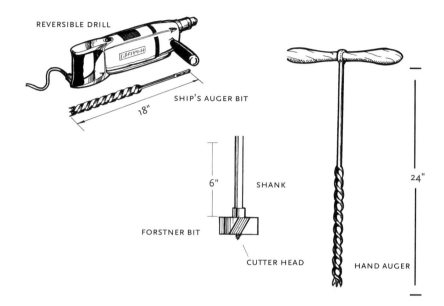

Figure 4-6
Boring tools.

Ship's auger bit: Used with a power drill to bore large, deep holes (i.e. electrical), various sizes.

Forstner bit: Used for mortises to produce a flat bottom surface, various sizes.

Electric drill: Heavy duty, reversible 1/2" drill required.

Utility knife: A general purpose razor knife, often used to score the layout line of a joint.

Axe: A 3¹/₂–4 lb. high-quality axe is required when building with logs.

Broad-axe (optional): An 8–10 lb (3.6–4.5 kg) broad-axe with a 12" (300 mm) cutting edge is used for hewing a log square. Its outstanding characteristic, aside from size and weight, is its flat face. This face initiates a chisel cutting action that produces a broad, flat surface. The handle is offset to provide clearance and avoid hitting the log as you hew. Used mostly for decorative work.

Adze: This is a tool especially suited for wood removal on wall channels where a frame partition joins a horizontal log wall. It is also used, though less frequently, for flat-siding log surfaces and for decorative work.

Figure 4-7
Cutting tools.

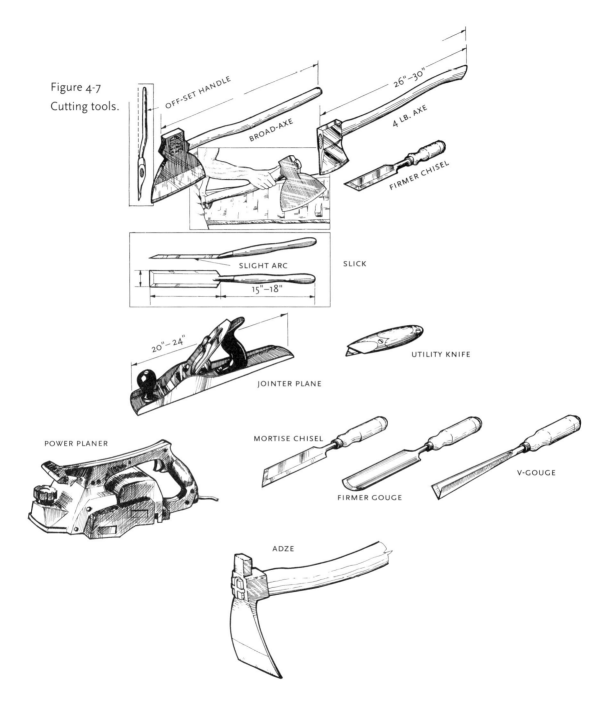

OFF-SET HANDLE

BROAD-AXE

26"–30"

4 LB. AXE

FIRMER CHISEL

SLIGHT ARC

SLICK

15"–18"

20" – 24"

UTILITY KNIFE

JOINTER PLANE

POWER PLANER

MORTISE CHISEL

FIRMER GOUGE

V-GOUGE

ADZE

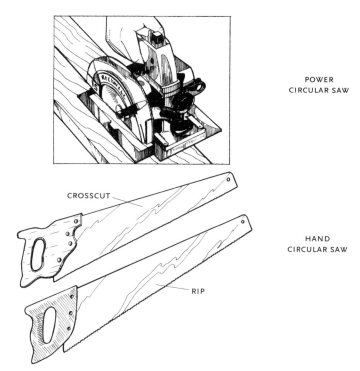

POWER
CIRCULAR SAW

CROSSCUT

HAND
CIRCULAR SAW

RIP

Figure 4-8
Sawing tools.

Chisels and gouges: Used primarily in timber construction, the firmer chisel is for removing wood and smoothing. The mortise chisel has an angled blade for working across the grain. The firmer gouge is for cutting grooves and the V-gouge is for edgework.

Slick: Just an overgrown chisel, the large 3" (75 mm) wide × 12" (300 mm) long blade works well for preparing and planing tenons or similar joints. If the blade has a very slight concave arc to its length, it will plane without lifting up on the handle. The socket handle should be angled upward slightly so knuckles will not get scraped.

Spokeshave: This tool, along with the following planes, holds the cutting blade in a fixed position inside a housing. The spokeshave is used primarily for decorative work.

Planes: The general hand plane and the longer jointer are the two hand planes most commonly used in timber construction. The longer the base (i.e. jointer) the better for flat-surfacing and truing long timbers. Power planers also come in a variety of sizes, and they are a quick and expedient way to finish and true long timbers.

Handsaws: Used primarily in timber construction, they come in Western and Japanese types. Western type handsaws are further classified as crosscut (sawing across the grain) or rip (sawing with the grain). The length of the handsaw stays roughly the same but the number of teeth per inch varies, for finer and coarser cuts. The Japanese handsaws vary in length while the number of teeth per saw remains the same. In this way the shorter saws have the most teeth per inch, hence a finer cut.

Power circular saw: The worm-drive circular saw is the most common for timber work because of its torque power. Interchangeable circular blades, for rip and crosscut procedures and more, are widely available. Quality blades have carbide teeth for longer wear. Common sizes for timber joinery are 8", 10", and 16".

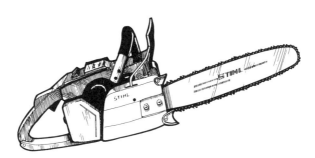

Figure 4-9
The chainsaw.

Chainsaw: On the whole, this is probably the most expensive, most used, and least understood of the log building tools. To begin with, the chainsaw should suit its function; trying to do serious log construction using a saw that is underpowered is a waste of time, while using an overpowered, overweight saw is unnecessarily fatiguing. But just buying any mediumweight, powered saw can be a waste of money if it's not a good one with the right options. Before describing what makes a good saw, let me drop a few names. During my years in log building I've noticed that the majority of professional log builders use either the Stihl, Husqvarna, or Jonsered chainsaws for their dependability and quality. Whether or not you choose one of these brands or opt for another may also depend on the available sales and servicing in your area. Whatever chainsaw you do finally decide on, make sure it is reasonably quiet and has antivibration rubber mounts protecting the operator from engine vibrations. Below is a checklist of things to look for in a log building chainsaw:

a) Medium size, between 3.0–5.0 cubic inches (50–80 cubic centimeters), capable of maintaining a high cutting speed for planing cuts.

b) Weight range of 15–20 lbs (7–10 kgs).

c) Good antivibration system.

d) Front mount exhaust to blow the sawdust away as you cut.

e) Adjustable automatic chain oiler.

f) Chainbrake.

g) 16–21" (400–540 mm) sprocket nose bar. This bar length is ideal for log construction as it will handle the majority of log sizes. The sprocket nose has a roller bearing which prevents excess heat buildup by reducing the amount of friction.

For the safe operation of a chainsaw, the operator should always wear the appropriate safety equipment, especially eye and ear protection. As with any cutting tool, a dull cutting chain has a greater chance of injuring the operator than a properly filed, sharp one. The operator must trust the tool to "bite" the wood at the intended point of contact. Should the tool slip, as a dull one will, control is lost and accidents can result. There are two basic cutter chains: the round gouge type and the straight chisel-edge type (the uses for each are explained later).

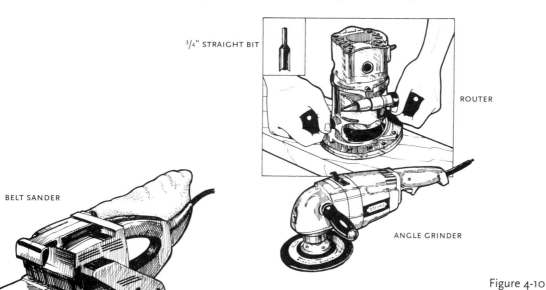

3/4" STRAIGHT BIT

ROUTER

BELT SANDER

ANGLE GRINDER

Figure 4-10
Shaping tools.

Router: A heavy duty commercial 1/2" power router with a 3/4" (19 mm) or 1" (25 mm) carbide "straight" bit is very useful for log and timber work. It can be used for post, wall, and window spline grooves, as well as for stair treads and other finishing jobs. Various styles of carbide cutter bits are widely available.

Angle grinder: Very useful for dressing up the ragged edges of logs, timbers, archways, and other embellishments. The sanding disks come in a variety of fine to coarse grits.

Belt sander: The sanding belt also comes in a variety of grits. Used to finish long timbers, sanding with the grain.

Log dogs: To prevent the log from moving while you are working on it, the dog is embedded into the log and the wood skid it is resting on. One or two log dogs are all that will be needed. Note the chisel points are at right angles to each other to facilitate easier entry into the wood grain.

Clamps: Used to hold timbers in a position to avoid movement when cutting the joint. Two types of adjustable, large throat bar clamps are shown.

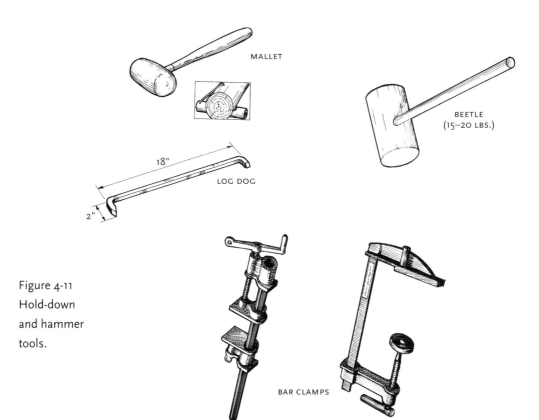

Figure 4-11
Hold-down
and hammer
tools.

Mallet: A hardwood 30 oz. mallet is required for timber joinery. Avoid using a metal construction hammer as it will damage the chisel handles.

Beetle: A 15–20 lb. mallet "big brother" used to persuade large timber
joints into position.

SHARPENING TOOLS

Working with a dull tool is both dangerous and frustrating, for the tool
cannot be trusted to bite into the wood; it will tend to glance off instead. It
is essential to work only with sharp tools. There are no absolute rules for
tool sharpening, only preferred ways. The novice who is confused by a
deluge of advice and a multitude of gadgets should follow the basic steps
outlined below, and find the style which suits him or her best.

The cutting edge

A new tool comes with a nearly useless factory edge, and it will be necessary to condition the edge for the type of cutting the tool will do. If an axe
is filed to a steep bevel it will function best for splitting, as the abrupt angle causes a wedging action. Conversely, a long beveled cutting edge is
better for carving, but it will also lose its sharp edge more quickly. For
most tools the best cutting bevel angle falls between 30° and 40°, or from
2 to 2$^1/_2$ times the thickness of the blade iron. This general cutting bevel
angle falls between the two extremes. You will find your own preference,
depending on the type of wood and desired cutting action (see Figure
4-12 for examples of the cutting angles).

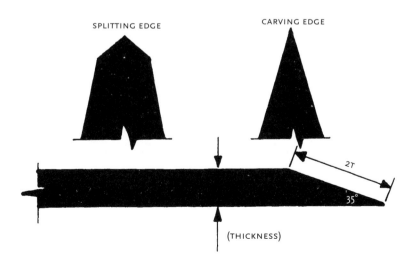

SPLITTING EDGE

CARVING EDGE

2T

35°

(THICKNESS)

Figure 4-12
Cutting angles.

On heavier tools which take a bigger bite into the wood, such as large chisels, or slicks and axes, a slight curvature of the edge will produce better results than a straight right-angled edge. Tools such as the broad-axe, drawknife, and plane irons are sharpened on one side only. This allows for the other, flat side to rest up against the wood and initiate a flat, planing type of action similar to a chisel's. Sharpening both sides of a tool may render it useless, so note the pre-sharpened surfaces when you purchase the tool. Despite the various cutting-edge bevels and curves, the procedures for attaining a sharp edge are the same: wet grinding, rough honing, and fine honing.

Wet grinding

Grinding on a grindstone or emery belt is the first step in conditioning the edge of the cutting tool. During this procedure the edge is first ground straight. Then, if a slight curvature is wanted, the corners are sloped in a gradual arc which crowns at the center, the same as an axe blade. Next, the desired bevel is ground. A pencil line for reference to show the length of the bevel from the edge works well. During this grinding stage it is important that the tool edge does not become too hot, for it will draw the hardness and ruin it. The safest method, therefore, is to wet grind or frequently immerse the tool in cool water as it becomes hot. If done correctly, a slightly concave bevel with a faint wire-edge will result (Figure 4-13). The wire-edge is the thin metal burr which forms on the back of the cutting bevel after wet grinding.

Grinding can be replaced by filing, first using a double cut file, followed by a single cut file. This is a more laborious method but will suffice

Figure 4-13
Wet grinding.

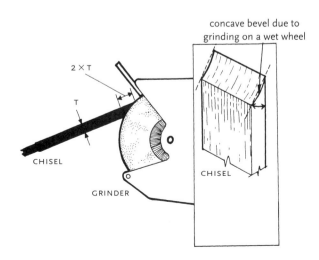

when a grindstone or emery belt is not handy. Filing is usually done for touch-ups at the worksite, followed by a quick honing—then back to work without too much time lost.

When filing, the procedure is to file into the cutting edge working from the bevel shoulder toward the edge itself. In this way you can follow the abrasive line created by the file as it nears the edge. Ordinary chalk rubbed into the file grooves will prevent the metal chips from clogging the file. Note that the tool should be firmly secured against movement. Also, never run your fingers along the filed surface of a fine tempered tool during sharpening, for the oily residue from your fingers will make it very difficult for the file to bite into the metal again.

Rough honing

Honing the tool with a soft, coarse oilstone is the next step after wet grinding. Oilstones come with a variety of grits and hardnesses—the harder the stone, the finer the grit. During the honing process the idea is to remove more metal with a soft, coarse grit stone. Then, as the edge becomes keener, change to a harder, denser grit stone that will not remove as much of the metal. On a microscopic level, the large scratches produced by grinding are being worn down and replaced by smaller scratches. Clearly, it would be fruitless to go directly from grinding, which removes a lot of metal and produces quite deep scratches, to a hard, fine grit stone, for it would take forever to wear these scratches down to produce a fine edge.

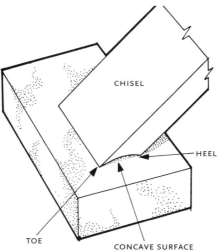

CHISEL

HEEL

TOE

CONCAVE SURFACE

Figure 4-14
Rough honing.

Oilstones can be natural or manufactured, but the manmade ones do not last as long, because the bonding agents which hold the stone particles together break down. Unlike a grindstone which uses water as a flushing lubricant, oilstones are made to be used with oil. A refined oil thinned with solvent or ordinary car brake fluid should be used for all honing, as common oil is too thick to remove the clogged metal particles from the stone surface. After use, a stone should be washed with soapy water, rinsed, and dried.

You will notice after wet grinding that a wire-edged burr has formed along the cutting edge; it will be necessary to remove this. The rough honing procedure begins by placing the blade bevel flat on the stone with the heel and toe touching. The slightly concave bevel surface created by grinding eliminates the need to raise the heel (Figure 4-14). Once this angle is attained, hold it constant and hone the tool using either reciprocating strokes or a figure eight motion. Check periodically to see if the concave surface has been ground flat from heel to toe, and add more honing oil. Continue rough honing, using the entire surface of the stone. To remove the wire-edge burr completely will require turning the tool on its back so it lies flat against the stone, then sliding it back and forth across the surface a few times.

Honing large chisels or slicks can be difficult; try using a 4" × 4" (100 × 100 mm) block as a guide (Figure 4-15). Axes, because of their weight, are best honed by moving the stone into the tool's cutting edge in clockwise, circular motions, while the axe is held motionless.

Figure 4-15
Honing large chisels and slicks.

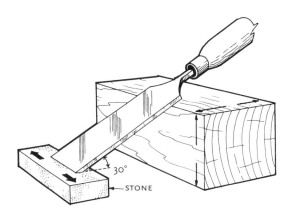

30°

STONE

Fine honing

Basically this is the same metal-removing procedure as rough honing but a harder, finer grit oilstone is used. The following tips may be useful for obtaining a "shaving" edge. When finishing up, the last few strokes should be made to align the minute scratches as shown in Figure 4-16. This alignment produces less surface drag as the tool enters the wood. For the ultimate edge and for those with access to a buffing wheel, buffing the entire bevel and sides will remove practically all surface scratches and abrasions. The difference made by buffing is amazing. You can see this in the axes used by professionals at competitions—their axes look almost chromed. A buffed blade not only looks good, but cuts well also.

To test the cutting edge for sharpness, gently run your thumbnail at a right angle across the edge. If your nail slides off the edge rather than biting into it, it is still too dull.

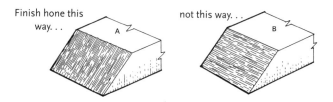

Finish hone this way. . .   not this way. . .

Figure 4-16
Finish honing.

How to sharpen auger bits

Auger bits are very important in solid wood post and beam construction. Their main uses are for drilling holes to pin or join wood members together, and for electrical wiring access holes. When drilling through solid wood the auger bit must be straight and sharp; a dull or bent bit can lead to undue stress on the electric drill. Figure 4-17 shows how to maintain an auger bit.

Sharpening the chainsaw's cutting teeth

The best advice for filing the cutting teeth of a chainsaw is to follow the basic instructions and always "pay attention." The cutting teeth on a chainsaw are like a multitude of miniature chisels. If they are not all filed correctly and evenly, some will cut more than others and some will not cut at all. There are filing guides available, but it is impractical and unnecessary to take the time and effort to set up a guide on the job site for only a

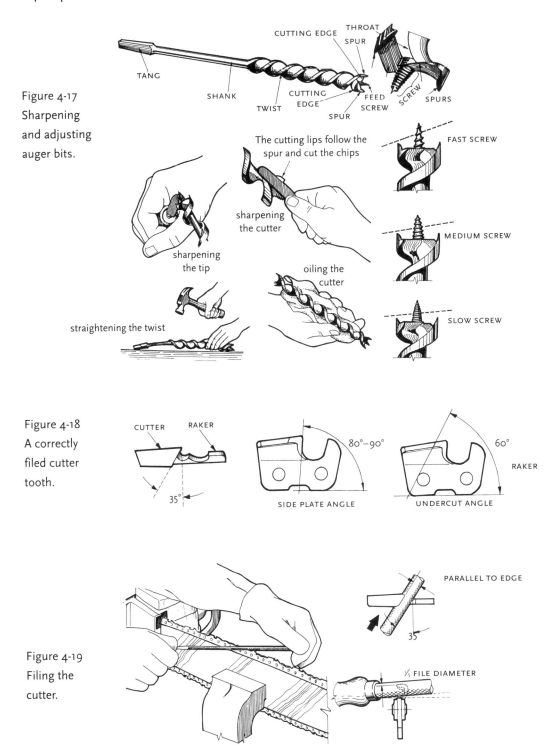

Figure 4-17
Sharpening
and adjusting
auger bits.

THROAT
CUTTING EDGE
SPUR
TANG
SHANK
CUTTING
EDGE
TWIST
CUTTING
EDGE
SPUR
FEED
SCREW
SCREW
SPURS

The cutting lips follow the
spur and cut the chips

FAST SCREW

sharpening
the cutter

MEDIUM SCREW

sharpening
the tip

oiling the
cutter

SLOW SCREW

straightening the twist

Figure 4-18
A correctly
filed cutter
tooth.

CUTTER   RAKER

35°

80°–90°

60°

RAKER

SIDE PLATE ANGLE

UNDERCUT ANGLE

PARALLEL TO EDGE

35

⅕ FILE DIAMETER

Figure 4-19
Filing the
cutter.

light touch-up. If there is not too much dirt or sand embedded in the wood, you need only touch up the cutting teeth by hand with a file right at the job site at the end of the day. After five or six such touch-ups it will be necessary to use a mechanical guide, which holds the file in a fixed position in relation to the cutting teeth, in order to realign all the teeth. This is usually done on a workbench with the chainsaw bar clamped in a vise.

The cutting teeth of a chain are made up of cutters and rakers. The cutters cut the wood and the rakers rake out the sawdust, and act as depth gauges. Generally, you check the height of the rakers after every third sharpening of the cutters, then adjust if necessary. If the raker is filed down too much, the cutters will bite into the wood and the chain will grab. Conversely, if the rakers are left too high, the chain will not cut to its capacity. To check the rakers you use a raker gauge. To check the sharpness of the cutters, as with any cutting edge, run the back of your thumbnail lightly into the cutting edge—if your nail slides along against the edge, then it is dull; if the edge bites into the nail, it is sharp.

The chainsaws described in this book use a $1/4$" (9 mm) diameter pitch chain and a $7/32$" (5 mm) diameter round file. Once the cutters have been filed back more than half their length, I suggest you use the next smaller file (Figure 4-18).

Filing the cutters

1) Secure the chainsaw bar in a vise and tighten the chain tension. Position the file in the cutter opposite your side as shown in the diagram and insets of Figure 4-19.
2) Apply three or four steady file strokes to each cutter, filing enough to remove any damage to the cutting edge. Keep all cutters at approximately the same length. (Check this visually.)

Filing the rakers

Check the raker height with the raker gauge after every third sharpening. Any projection should be filed level and rounded as shown.

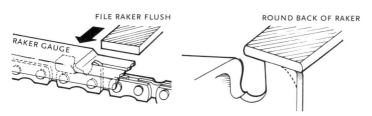

FILE RAKER FLUSH

ROUND BACK OF RAKER

RAKER GAUGE

Figure 4-20
Filing down
and rounding
the rakers.

CHAPTER FIVE

Hewing and Milling Methods

When working with round logs the first step is to know how to produce a flat surface. Included below are a few methods of hewing and milling, as an alternative for the builder who has neither access nor money nor desire for commercial milling.

1. Square-cutting the end of a round log.

If the ends of a post are not square it will sit on an angle when standing vertically. Outlined below is a simple method for squaring the end of a log.

Tools: Heavy tar paper (or similar material) cut square, pencil, chainsaw, eye and ear protection.

Procedure:
1) Secure the log on notched skids and dog it so it cannot roll.
2) Wrap the flexible square edge tar paper (or other material) around the peeled log $1^{1}/_{2}$ turns and match the edges together.
3) Scribe a pencil line using the material edge as a guide.
4) Remove material and cut the end square with a chainsaw.

2. How to lay out a log for squaring or flat-surfacing.

Unlike regular frame dimensional materials, a log has no flat surfaces. In order to create flat, squared surfaces a layout procedure must be done on

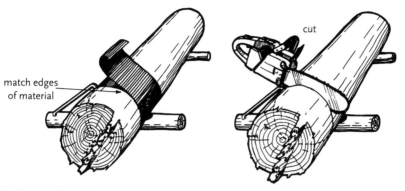

match edges
of material

cut

Figure 5-1
Square-cutting
the end of a
round log.

the log ends, after which these points can be matched together with chalked lines. The wise builder will group the same layout and cutting procedures and apply them to all the members he is working with so as to avoid duplication of steps. Note that when chalklining a log surface you always snap the chalkline in the same direction as the cutting plane. This is very important, for a log has an uneven surface and a line chalked from a horizontal angle will show differently than a line chalked from a vertical angle—or for that matter any other angle in between. This will become clearer as you progress.

Tools: Tape measure, chalkline, level, pencil, log dog.

Procedure:
1) Cut the log to the desired length.
2) Place notched skids under either end of the peeled log and secure with a log dog so that it will not move.
3) Working from the smaller end of the log, use a tape measure, level, and pencil to find the radius of the log end, and pencil a vertical plumb line (Figure 5-2a).
4) Repeat this procedure to find and mark the horizontal level line (Figure 5-2b).
5) Using these center dividing lines as references, mark out the width and height dimensions desired (Figure 5-2c).
6) Repeat this procedure on opposite end of log.
7) Join these two ends with chalked lines. See section 3, below, for cutting procedures.
   Note: Always pull the chalkline in the direction of the cutting plane. Any other direction will result in inaccuracy (Figure 5-2d).

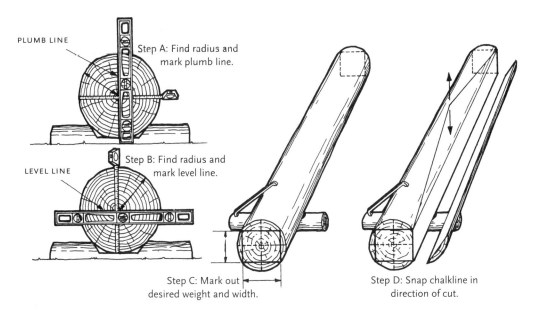

PLUMB LINE

Step A: Find radius and mark plumb line.

LEVEL LINE

Step B: Find radius and mark level line.

Step C: Mark out desired weight and width.

Step D: Snap chalkline in direction of cut.

Figure 5-2 (a–d) Layout and cutting procedures for flat-surfacing or squaring logs.

On longer logs a chalkline will droop due to gravity. Cut the span of the line in half by pressing it to the log surface at its midpoint, and then snap each length separately.

3. Wood removal:
Two methods showing how to flat-side a log freehand.

Quick jobs not needing an extremely accurate flat-side can be done freehand with the chainsaw. When only one flat surface is required it is sufficient to mark off the desired flat surface from each end using a level, and then join these with chalked lines, followed by cutting or sawing (Figure 5-3).

Tools: Eye and ear protection, level, pencil, chalkline, chainsaw, axe.

Procedure:

1) Secure the peeled log on a set of skids or on the ground so it will not move.
2) Determine amount of flat surface needed, then mark a level line on either end of log (see Layout, Figure 5-3a).
3) Join the level lines on either end of log with a taut chalkline and snap a line. Always snap the line on the same plane as that marked on the ends of the log (Figure 5-3).

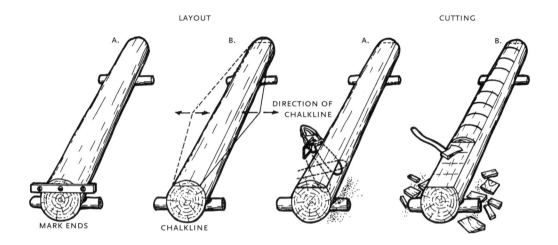

LAYOUT   CUTTING

DIRECTION OF CHALKLINE

MARK ENDS   CHALKLINE

4) Wood removal can be done using one of the two methods outlined below. Turn the chainsaw bar flat and enter the log at the plane shown in Figure 5-3, Cutting method A. While cutting use a pivoting action, digging the saw "dogs" (metal teeth at the base of the chainsaw bar) into the wood, then leaning over the log to observe the opposite cutting line. A chisel tooth chain works best for this ripping action. Use appropriate caution.

An alternative method is shown in Figure 5-3, Cutting method B, where successive cuts are made down to the line on both sides of the log. The waste wood can then be split off. Knots must be cut through, as they act like spikes holding the waste wood fast.

Figure 5-3 Procedure for quick flat-surfacing jobs.

4. How to hew with a broad-axe.

For the most part, hewing a log with a broad-axe is reserved for more decorative jobs such as overhead beams in a dining room, or for elaborate truss work. For quick accurate flat-surfacing it is best to stay with the chainsaw. But speed and efficiency are not always the axiom. The axe is deeply embedded in our heritage and I enjoy watching the wood pare off to reveal the inner grain patterns and to hear the crisp, clean bite of a sharp axe, rather than the high-pitched scream of a chainsaw.

Tools: 8–10 lb (3.5–4.5 kg) broad-axe, 4 1/2–7 lb (2–3 kg) scoring axe, steel toe boots, chalkline, level, log dog.

Procedure:

1) Place notched skids under end of the peeled log and secure with a log dog so it will not move.

2) Chalk a cut line. Using a level, mark the amount of flat surface desired by placing a plumb line at each end of the log and joining the two ends with a chalked line (Figure 5-4a). Remember to snap the chalkline in the direction of the cutting plane. In this case it is straight down.

3) Score the log as in Figure 5-4b. The aim is to create hinge-points that will allow the heavy slab waste wood to be hewn off with the broad-axe. Because a portion of holding wood is needed to hold the broad-axe in its kerf or cut, it is important to score to an approximate depth of 1/2"–1" (12–25 mm) from the cut line. Scoring right to the cut line would necessitate continual restarting of the broad-axe kerf, for the slab of waste wood would simply chip off as each score cut is reached. This would cause the loss of rhythm and swinging force so essential with hewing.

Scoring is usually accomplished with a special axe that has little blade curvature, however a regular heavy, sharp axe works well, too. The scoring is done perpendicular to the chalked cut line, with the feet spread apart as shown in Figure 5-4b. Make a series of these relief cuts down the length of the log at 8"–10" (200–250 mm) intervals, and wherever there is a large knot (acting like a

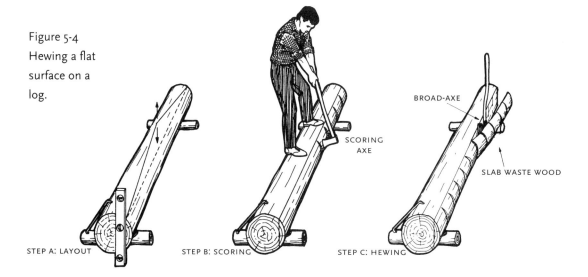

Figure 5-4
Hewing a flat surface on a log.

BROAD-AXE

SCORING AXE

SLAB WASTE WOOD

STEP A: LAYOUT   STEP B: SCORING   STEP C: HEWING spike). In cases where a large amount of slab wood is to be hewn off, a chainsaw may be substituted for the scoring axe, or else it will be necessary to repeat the scoring and hewing procedure a second time.

4) Figure 5-4c shows how to hew a vertical, flat surface using a broadaxe. Start from one end and step backward along the top of the log surface or beside the log while hewing. This is a dangerous operation, and care should be taken. (Wear steel toe boots.) Generally, a full swing is used for medium and heavy slab wood removal. Light-sized slabs need more axe control and a "choked up" grip on the handle facilitates easier handling.

As discussed earlier, buffing a cutting tool's surface so it is shiny removes a good percentage of the surface resistance, thus requiring less cutting effort. This technique works well on broad-axes with their large blades and (resistant) surfaces.

5. How to flat-surface a log using guide rails.

This portable method does an accurate job of milling shorter lengths of logs. It involves attaching a set of pads on the chainsaw bar which will slide along on parallel guide rails.

Tools: Eye and ear protection, level, tape measure, hammer, chainsaw, 1/2" (12 mm) socket wrench.

Materials: 3/4" (19 mm) plywood pads, 1/2" (12 mm) carriage bolts with nuts, 2" × 6" (38 × 140 mm) rails, nails, 2" × 4" (38 × 89 mm) stakes.

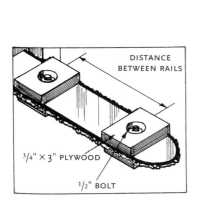

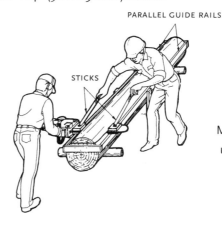

Figure 5-5
Milling a log using guide rails and chainsaw pads.

Procedure:

1) Secure and set up the log as shown in Figure 5-5, making sure the two side rails are an equal distance apart, down the length of the log.

2) Drill chainsaw bar and install plywood pads as shown in the diagram inset. For more adjustment mill two slots in the chainsaw bar.

3) Proceed to flat-side the log, having someone else apply a slight pressure on the pads (using two sticks) to keep them in contact with the rails.

   Note: Caution should be exercised when using a chainsaw in this manner.

6. How to flat-surface a log using a post and rail mill.

This mill is an expanded, more permanent version of the guide rails; it can accommodate longer log lengths.

Tools: Eye and ear protection, chainsaw, bar with pads, level, tape measure, hammer, shovel.

Materials: 2" × 10" (38 × 235 mm) straight lumber, posts, spikes, string line.

Procedure:

1) Determine length of material to be milled. This measurement will become the length of your mill.

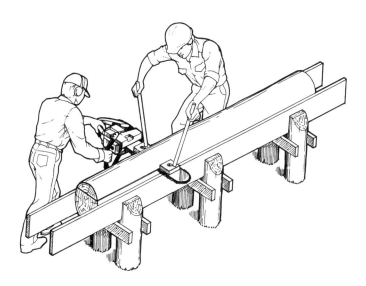

Figure 5-6
Milling a log
using a post
and rail mill.

2) Dig two parallel lines of holes and place 5" (255 m) log posts in each. The distance between the lines should be wider than the thickest log to be milled.

3) Inset the top rails and bases as shown in Figure 5-6. It is important to have the top rails parallel and at equal height. The bases which the log rests on must be an equal distance below the top rails. This distance between the guide rails must be greater than the thickest log to be milled.

4) Place the log into the mill, blocking where necessary to obtain a continuous flat surface down its length.

5) Proceed to flat-side the log, using a chainsaw with pads, with someone else to apply slight pressure on the pads to keep them in contact with the rails.

7. How to flat-surface a log using a frame and track mill.

For the serious builder a mill (such as the one described below) is a necessity. This mill works quickly to produce accurate, flat surfaces on short and long logs. With a variable vertical adjustment, planks can easily be milled by someone inexperienced with a chainsaw. This mill is less portable than the others described here.

Figure 5-7
A frame and
track mill.

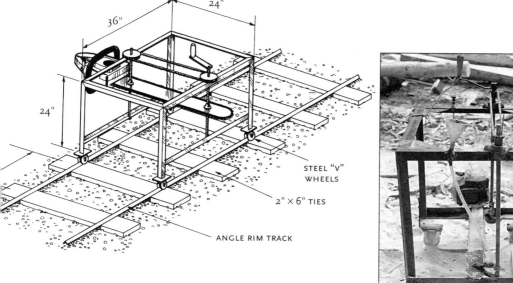

24"

36"

24"

24"

STEEL "V"
WHEELS

2" × 6" TIES

ANGLE RIM TRACK

Tools: Large chainsaw, 36" (1 m) bar with chisel tooth chain, builder's level, level, shovel, hammer, tape measure, eye and ear protection.

Materials: Angle iron, 3/4" (19 mm) threaded rod, connectors, steel "V" wheels for the angle iron track, bicycle chain and two sprockets, handle, 2" × 6" × 36" (38 × 140 mm × 1 m) plank-ties, gravel.

Procedure:

1) Construct the mill frame as shown in Figure 5-7.
2) Using a builder's level, level the ground and lay the track as indicated. Make sure the tracks are level and parallel to each other.
3) Roll the log into position, and secure it so it will not move. Adjust the chainsaw bar for depth of cut, and level it by placing a spirit level on the bar.
4) Milling can be done in both directions by simply pushing the carriage frame.

8. The mini chainsaw mill.

There are several portable mini mills available on the market. I have included this particular one because of its adaptability when used for

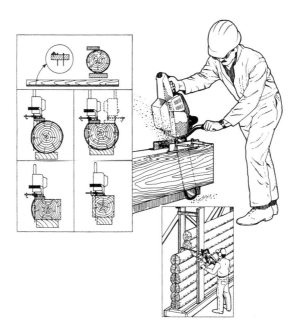

Figure 5-8
Cutting lumber
with a mini mill.

plumb-cutting prefabricated log/timber wall infill panels. Its method of operation includes a mechanical clamp which holds the chainsaw bar in a fixed position. The clamp then slides along a V-shaped metal rail which is nailed to a straight 2" × 8" (38 × 184 mm) plank. This apparatus can be used in a horizontal or vertical position. Figure 5-8 illustrates its operation in flat-surfacing a log and in plumb-cutting the ends of a log wall. Since the end of the chainsaw bar is not held firmly in place, there is a chance the cut could "wander" if the cutting chain is improperly filed (see chain-filing instructions in Chapter 4).

9. The mini bandsaw mill.

The mini bandsaw mill is a newcomer on the market and therefore pricey but with competition it has potential to be an affordable tool for the serious owner/builder in the future. Basically it is a horizontal bandsaw powered by a chainsaw. Operated by one person, the result is a smooth thin-kerf cut producing little sawdust, all with exceptional ease. It is wise to have an automatic blade sharpener for bandsaw mills (Figure 5-9).

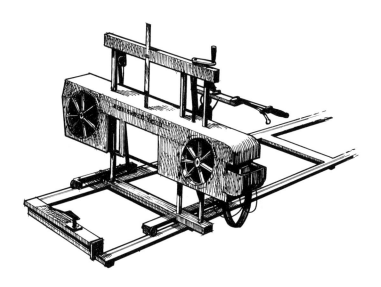

Figure 5-9
Chainsaw-
operated
bandsaw mill.

Joinery

Just as the joints of our bodies connect our structural bones and allow our limbs to move, the joints of a post and beam house also provide a connection between the structural members while allowing a slight degree of movement. Since our buildings are not mobile, as we are, a tight joint is required to maintain the strength of the union.

Joinery follows nature in its division of male and female, the male tenon fitting into the female mortise to form the united joint. All joinery begins with envisioning the joints—what they look like, and how they will fit together. This is then followed by layout and wood removal procedures. We begin therefore with various illustrations of notches and joints used in log and timber joinery. Note that templates are used in some of the following drawings; for more information on templates refer to Template Use, under Joinery Layout in this chapter.

JOINERY EXAMPLES

Log Notches and Grooves: A notch and lateral groove is used to join logs together. The two notches shown here are a round and a diamond shape, which are the most common in log corner joinery. When building with green logs, most builders use the diamond notch, since by removing most of the sapwood less shrinkage occurs. This results in a tighter notch after seasoning. In either case a "scribing" process is used for layout by duplicating the curved surface (refer to Joinery Layout). Note that corner notches and lateral grooves are cut on the underside of the log to allow moisture drainage and prevent rot. For information on Double-scribed Lock (square) Notch refer to Chapter 12, Roof Structures.

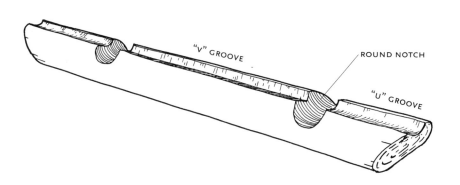

Figure 6-1
A log with completed notches and lateral groove.

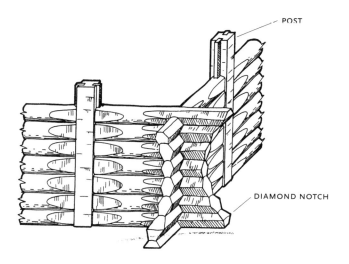

Figure 6-2
Shaping logs back from the joinery intersection.

Timber Joints

Note the timber dimensions illustrated are 8" × 8" (nominal 7^1/$_2$" × 7^1/$_2$") and 8" × 10" (nominal 7^1/$_2$" × 9^1/$_2$"). The actual nominal sizing allows for a match-up with conventional lumber nominal sizing (i.e. 2" × 8" is actually 1^1/$_2$" × 7^1/$_2$"). This is more a convenience than a necessity.

1. Full Mortise and Tenon: Used to join post to beam (Figure 6-3).

Figure 6-3
Full mortise
and tenon.

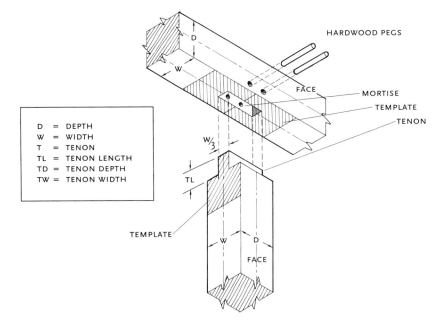

2. Peg Mortise and Tenon: Used to join post to intersecting beams (Figure 6-4a).

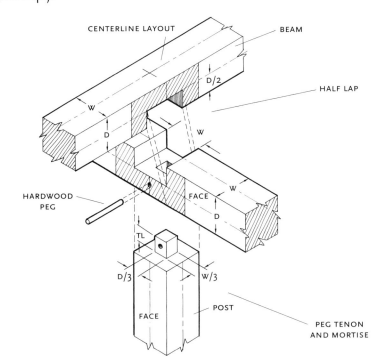

Figure 6-4a
Half lap corner
with a post
peg tenon.

3. Half lap: Used to join beams at right angles (Figure 6-4a). Variations shown in b, c, and d have more holding wood and are stronger. Example shows cantilevered ends—may be cut flush (Figure 6-4e). Halflap can be used to join two beams end-to-end but should be located over a post support.

Figure 6-4b
Housed lap.

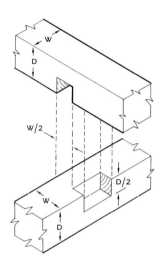

Figure 6-4c
Double
housed lap.

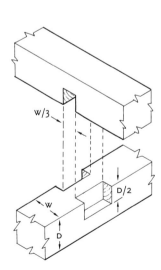

Figure 6-4d
Crossed lap. Layout
identical to half lap.
Cut on diagonal.

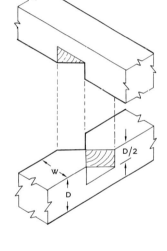

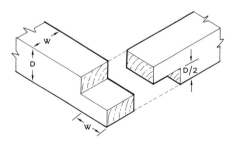

Figure 6-4e
Half lap.

4. Corner Dovetail: Used to join beams at corner right angles—locking joint (Figures 6-5a and b).

Figure 6-5a
Corner dovetail
(self draining).

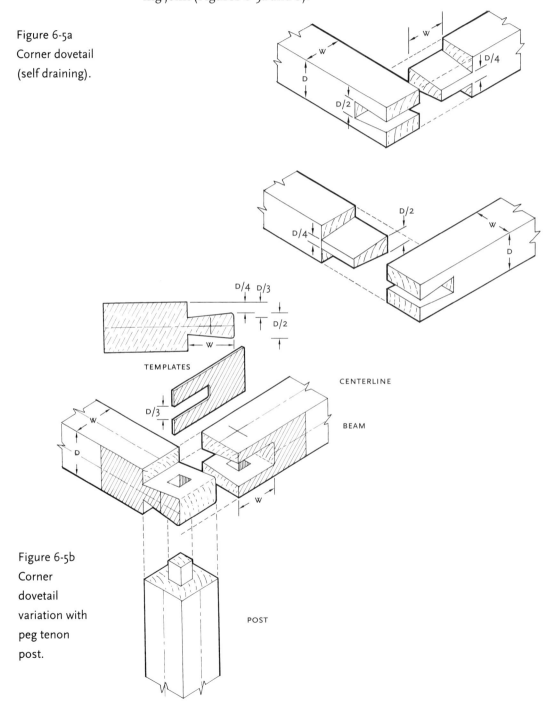

Figure 6-5b
Corner
dovetail
variation with
peg tenon
post.

5. Dovetail Half lap: Used to join and lock secondary structural beams (i.e. ceiling joists) at right angles (Figure 6-6).

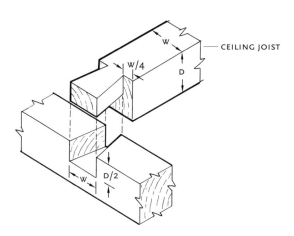

Figure 6-6
Dovetail half lap.

6. Housed Dovetail: Used to join beams at right angles, especially good for girders or tie-beams. Dovetail portion locks joint while housed portion retains beam strength (Figure 6-7).

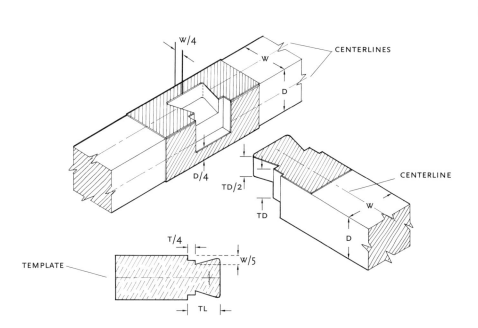

Figure 6-7
Housed
dovetail.

7. Scarf: Used to join two beams end-to-end to increase length. Should be located over post support—shear spline optional (Figure 6-8a; variations shown in b and c).

Figure 6-8a
Bladed splined
scarf.

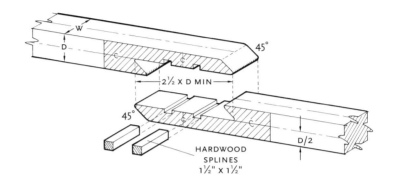

Figure 6-8b
Wedged and
locked splayed
scarf.

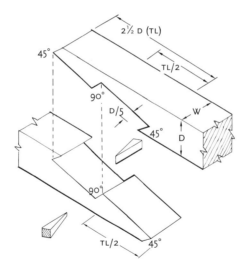

Figure 6-8c
Double
splayed scarf.

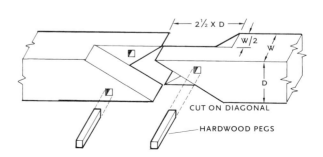

8. Shouldered Through Mortise and Tenon: Used to join a corner post to two intersecting beams—wedged and pegged (Figures 6-9, 6-10).

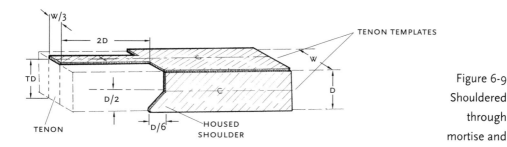

Figure 6-9
Shouldered
through
mortise and
tenon.

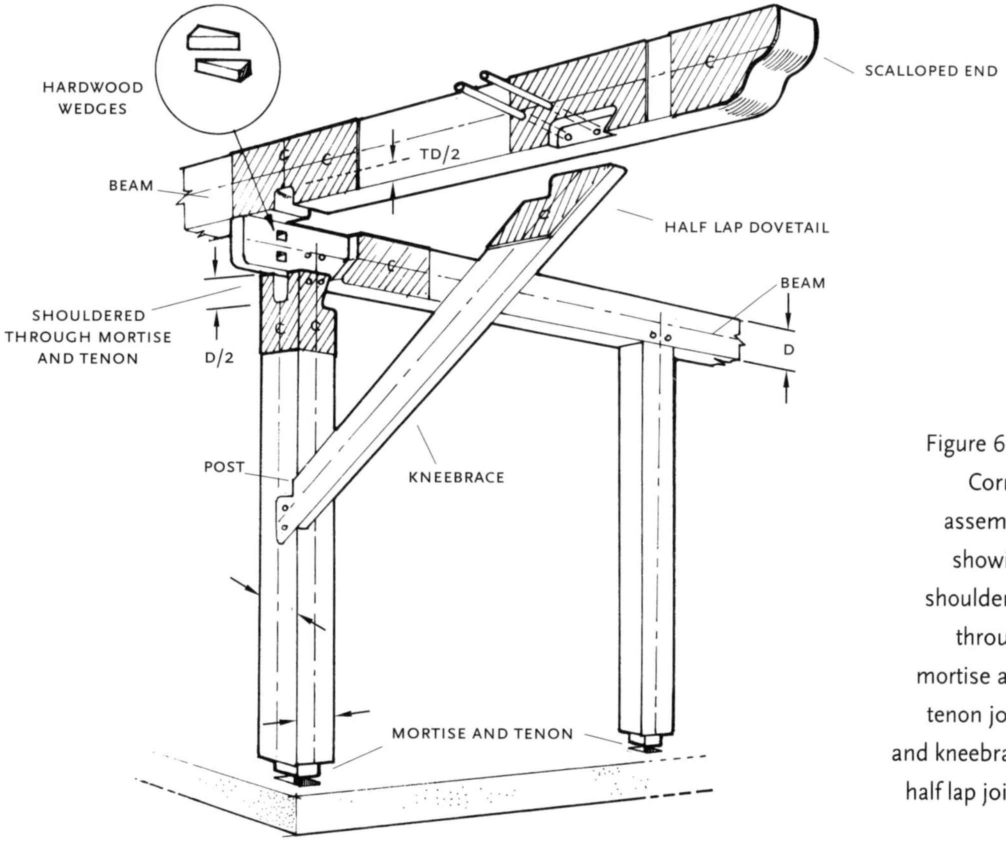

Figure 6-10
Corner
assembly
showing
shouldered
through
mortise and
tenon joint
and kneebrace
half lap joint.

9. Kneebrace Halflap Dovetail: Used to join kneebrace to post and beam. May be installed after assembly using this method (Figure 6-10). For more information, refer to Figure 7-12; see also Figures 12-33, 12-34.

10. Kneebrace Mortise and Tenon: Used to join kneebrace to post and beam. Must be installed during assembly (Figure 6-11). For more information, refer to Figure 7-11.

Figure 6-11
Tenoned
kneebrace.

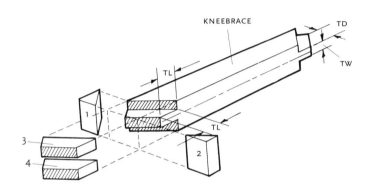

11. Post Truss: Used to broaden post support capability in order to eliminate the number of posts (i.e. interior supports) (Figure 6-12.)

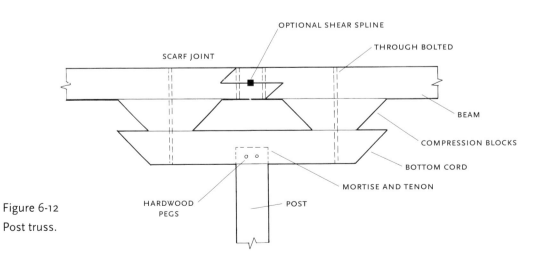

Figure 6-12
Post truss.

12. Fork and Tongue: Used to join roof rafters at peak. Adaptable to join rafters to kingpost (Figure 6-13).

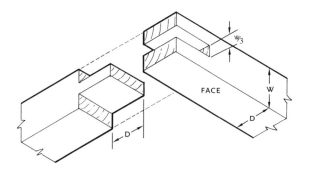

Figure 6-13
Fork and
tongue.

13. Birdsmouth: Used to join principal roof rafter to plate beam (2 types) (Figures 6-14a and b).

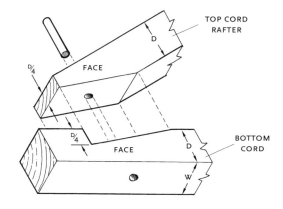

Figure 6-14a
Seated
birdsmouth.

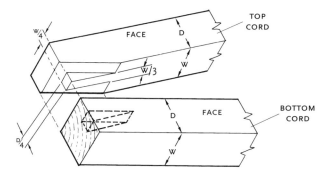

Figure 6-14b
Tenon birdsmouth.
For more
information refer to
Tenon Birdsmouth in
Roof Systems.

POST AND BEAM PREPARATION

A. Layout Plan

After you have a visual understanding of the joint, the layout must be planned before the physical layout on the wood begins.

1. Centerline Plan

When using materials that are not perfectly square, particularly logs which have no edges or flat surfaces from which to begin or end a measurement, layout work must originate from a centerline and progress outwards.

A centerline forms the point of reference and keeps joints in alignment even if the log or timber takes a slight bend.

Throughout this book we employ "center-to-center" layout, as opposed to "face-to-face" layout which is common to braced timberframe. Braced timberframe generally employs an external envelope of insulated panels nailed to the outside of the frame, which require the exterior timber faces to be in alignment. In post and beam construction, the logs, timbers, or other panel types are not applied to the outside but remain as an infill within the frame.

Centerline-layout eliminates the confusion of using face-layout and having to adjust and compensate for discrepancies between various timber thicknesses.

2. Grid Plan

The grid plan identifies the structural members of the post and beam frame, locating their position and the exact location of the required joinery. The grid plan in our example is based on a 10-foot grid module, with the building perimeter dimensions imposed on this grid. For demonstration purposes a simple 30" × 40" rectangle (center to center) is used with an intersecting tie-beam (Figure 6-15).

Note: In our grid plan the building is oriented north. The north wall is at the top of the plan with the south wall at the bottom, west and east walls facing left and right respectively.

Beginning at the bottom left hand corner of the plan, assign letters vertically A, B, C, D . . . , and numbers horizontally 1, 2, 3, 4, 5 . . . These

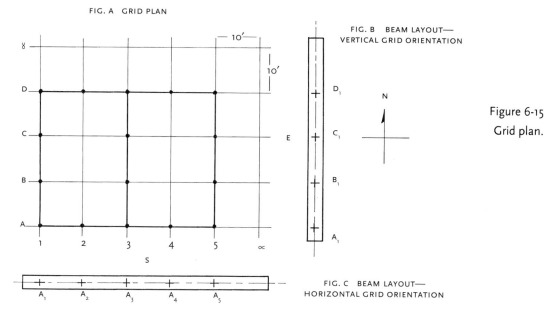

Figure 6-15
Grid plan.

letters and numbers will identify the location and directional alignment of the structural members, such as posts, beams, girders, and foundation weight-bearing points. At the intersection of these grid lines will be a post which can easily be identified by its letter and number designate. For example, A1 and D5 are corner posts located at the lower left and upper right of our plan. Posts B3 and C3 are midposts supporting a central tiebeam, and so on. These identification symbols are marked on the outside face of each post for easy orientation during assembly. In buildings with multiple floors, the floor number prefixes the post symbol, for example A1 becomes 2A1.

Horizontal structural beams and girders are identified in a similar way. A beam running vertically on the layout plan will have its post symbol and joinery location marked out vertically along its length, as shown in Figure 6-15b. In this example the beam spans posts A1 to D1.

Similarly, a beam running horizontally across the layout plan will have its corresponding post symbols and joinery location marked horizontally as shown in Figure 6-15c. This beam spans posts A1 to A5.

Note: Wherever an intersection of two beams occurs, the supporting post tenon will be reduced from a full to a peg tenon to prevent weakening of the joint. Thus, in our layout plan example, posts A1, A3, A5, D1, D3, and D5 would have peg tenons while the rest would have full tenons. The post height is determined by the ceiling height desired (refer to Golden Section, Chapter 2).

B. Joinery Layout

With the layout plan complete, and an understanding of the types and functions of the joinery required, you may begin layout of the posts and beams. Layout can be done manually using a carpenter's square, or by using a 3/8" plywood or 1/8" hardboard template (refer to Template Use, below). In either case all joinery layout initiates from the centerline chalked on the wood member.

Note: In order to gain a full understanding of the layout procedure, the builder must become familiar with the variances between log and timber methods.

1. Checking for Squareness.

Place a level or winding sticks (Figure 6-16a) at each end of the flat-surfaced log or timber and sight along its length to see if the tops are in alignment. If they are not aligned then the wood is warped and should be planed at the joinery locations. You can check for squareness using a carpenter's square (Figure 6-16b).

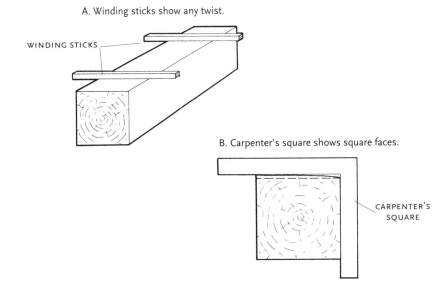

A. Winding sticks show any twist.

WINDING STICKS

B. Carpenter's square shows square faces.

CARPENTER'S SQUARE

Figure 6-16
Check for any
twist and square
faces.

2. Establishing Centerlines for Joinery Layout.

Position the post or beam so that the centerline marks on the ends are plumb (vertical). Connect the end marks with a taut stringline and chalk a centerline by pulling up and releasing the string (Figure 6-17).

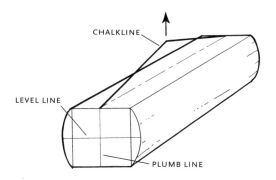

Figure 6-17
Establishing
joinery
centerlines.

3. Establishing Overall Length.

The overall length of a post or beam includes any tenons or projections required. This procedure of producing a right angle from a chalked centerline, using a carpenter's square as shown in the drawing, is used for both flat-surfaced logs and squared timbers. Mark and cut the right angle to produce a square end. Repeat procedure for the opposite end (Figure 6-18).

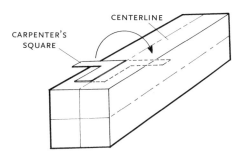

Figure 6-18
Establishing
overall length.

4. Template Use.

As mentioned earlier, joinery is divided into male tenon and female mortise joints. Traditionally the tenon is laid out with a carpenter's square and tape measure and its dimensions reproduced to create the mortise.

Layout in this manner however, is time consuming and often results in errors for the novice joiner.

A template is a pattern used for repeated accurate layout and can also be used for accurate shaping (refer to Wood Removal, below). For simplicity's sake, much of the joinery in this book uses template layout. Templates are cut from either 3/8" plywood (when used for shaping) or 1/8" hardboard to the exact dimensions of the timber joints shown earlier. When the post and beam components are to be prefabricated and stored, it is wise to pretest each joint with the template to avoid assembly complications. Note that the templates used have centerlines marked on them; these will align with the center and layout lines on the posts and beams. Refer to Joinery Examples, earlier in this chapter.

5. Example of Joinery Layout.

We are using, as an example, the top plate spanning A1 to A5 of our layout grid plan (Figure 6-15). According to the specifications of the blueprint (not shown), corner A5 will be joined with a simple half lap while corner A1 will be joined with a corner dovetail. The beam extends an additional five feet on the east end to support the extended gable eave. Since a 46-foot beam is too long, shorter lengths will be scarfed together.

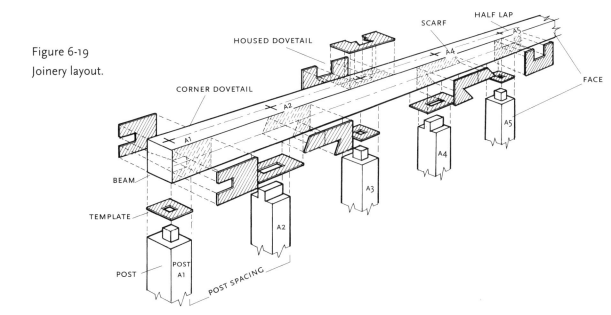

Figure 6-19
Joinery layout.

a) Begin by positioning the beam so that any camber (arch) faces crown up to counter the force of gravity.

b) Lay out the post spacings horizontally across the beam.

c) Position the joint templates so the centerlines match up with the beam centerline and layout marks (refer to Joinery Examples, earlier in this chapter).

d) Lay out joints and remove waste wood (refer to Wood Removal, below).

C. Wood Removal

It is at this early stage that good attitudes and habits towards working with wood must be formulated. Holderlin's words that "the spirit of the forest still lives in it" expresses exactly the type of approach to be taken when working with wood. Sometimes, because of the nature of the par-

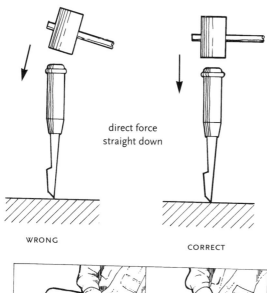

WRONG   direct force straight down   CORRECT

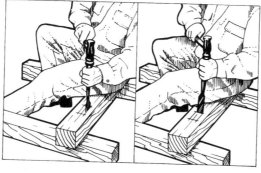

Figure 6-20
Wood removal:
comfort and
safety.

ticular species, the wood's moisture content and internal stresses—both embodiments of the forest's spirit—can cause a perfectly laid out and executed joint to simply not fit. Strive to understand why, and with this understanding will come the patience so needed when working with wood.

The tool that cuts the wood must be sharp and of good quality. But the tool alone will not cut a tenon or construct a house—it must be commanded by the body and mind of the person using it. The builder must develop a sense of the tool, feel comfortable with its grip and the way it cuts, adjust to its eccentricities, and develop rhythm and balance and a sense of which muscles are involved—the whole complex of factors needed to operate the tool. Knowing this, if at first you feel a little awkward, realize there is a significant degree of education required, and have patience (Figure 6-20).

To avoid mistakes, double-check the layout and visualize a logical assembly before beginning to cut. Remember, once removed, the wood cannot be put back, so let your motto be "Measure twice, cut once."

When you cut, leave the layout lines (if templates are not used). If these layout lines are removed, all reference to the shape and dimensions of the joint will be lost. Bisecting the layout line itself with a utility razor knife will sever the wood fibers, thereby defining the parameters of the joint as you cut while at the same time preventing splintering of the edges. Develop the practice of cutting only once in cross-grain situations; cutting close to the line and then trying to recut will only make a mess. As a general rule you shave the male to fit the female if a joint is too tight upon assembly. However, to be more accurate, the mating surfaces of the joint have both parallel grain and cross-grain respectively, and if the joint is too tight, it is easier to shave the parallel grain of the members to fit, as shown in Figure 6-21.

Figure 6-21
Male dovetail
tenon and
female dovetail
mortise.

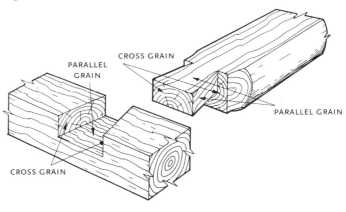

CROSS GRAIN

PARALLEL
GRAIN

PARALLEL GRAIN

CROSS GRAIN

1. Boring and Chiseling

Wood joinery is a union of female mortises and male tenons. A blind mortise of the type to fit a post tenon uses a combination of boring and chiseling to remove the waste wood and form the joint socket (Figure 6-22).

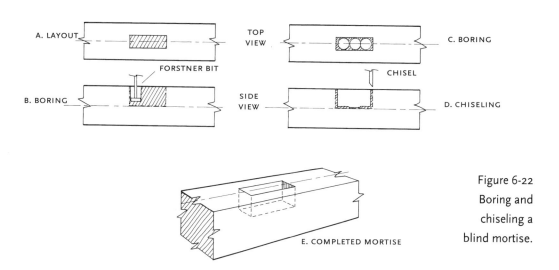

A. LAYOUT

TOP VIEW

C. BORING

FORSTNER BIT

CHISEL

B. BORING

SIDE VIEW

D. CHISELING

E. COMPLETED MORTISE

Figure 6-22
Boring and chiseling a blind mortise.

Tools: Eye protection, measuring tape, electric drill with forstner bit, mortise chisel and mallet, pencil, carpenter's square.

Procedure:
1) Lay out the mortise dimensions on the wood member (refer to Joinery Examples, earlier in this chapter).
2) Drill overlapping holes to depth of mortise.
3) Chisel edges to depth and clean.

2. Sawing

Sawing to remove joinery waste wood can be done using either an electric circular saw or a handsaw, of which there are two types: Japanese, which cuts on the pull stroke, and North American, which cuts on the push stroke. Sawing often involves a procedural order to remove the waste wood. The housed dovetail tenon shown is a good example of the steps one takes in sawing such a joint (Figures 6-23a and b).

Figure 6-23a
Sawing a
housed
dovetail, side
cuts 1 and 2.

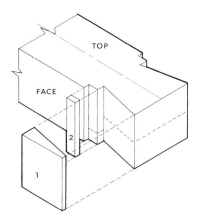

Figure 6-23b
Sawing a
housed
dovetail,
bottom cuts 3
and 4.

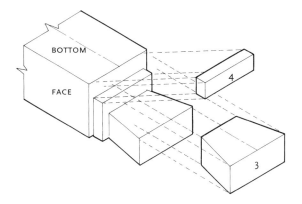

Tools: Eye protection, hand/electric saw, measuring tape, slick, pencil, carpenter's square.

Procedure:
1) Lay out the housed dovetail tenon on the wood member (refer to Joinery Examples, earlier in this chapter).
2) Drop layout lines vertically down using a carpenter's square.
3) Make vertical cuts and remove waste wood sections 1 and 2 on both sides of the tenon.
4) Roll timber upside down and remove waste wood sections 3 and 4. Clean up with slick. Chamfer the tenon edges for easier insertion.

3. Shaping

Templates also allow for "shaping" the joint using a milling process with the template as a guide. The example used is a housed dovetail mortise. Note how the outside corners of the template joint are rounded ($1/2$" radius). This is because the $1/2$" cutter bit cuts a round, not a square, corner. Needless to say, the male and female templates should fit tightly together to ensure a tight joint. Figure 6-24 shows how this milling process is achieved using a router and top-piloted cutter bit.

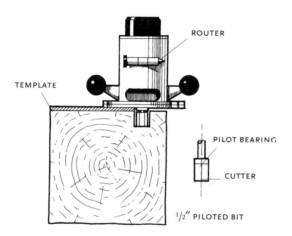

ROUTER

TEMPLATE

PILOT BEARING

CUTTER

$1/2$" PILOTED BIT

Figure 6-24
Shaping a joint
using a milling
process.

Tools: Eye and ear protection, router, $1/2$" top-piloted straight bit, $1/2$" long fluted straight bit, $3/8$" plywood template, $3/4$" brad nails, hammer.

Procedure:

1) Align the housed dovetail mortise templates to the beam centerline and joint center mark as shown in Figure 6-25. Note there are two templates which make up the mortise. Tack in place using brad nails.

2) Using the piloted cutter bit mounted in the router (as shown in Figure 6-24), mill the inside face of the joint.

3) Replace the piloted cutter with the long fluted straight bit. Using the milled groove as a guide, adjust the bit depth so that the smooth $1/2$" shank runs inside the groove with the cutter portion removing the waste wood below (refer to diagram 6-25b).

Figure 6-25a
Milling a housed
dovetail.

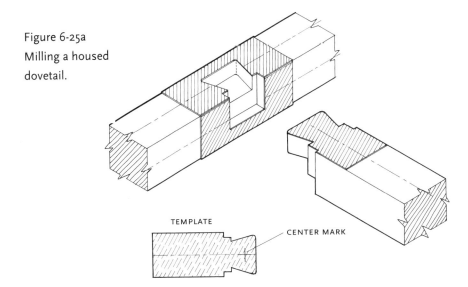

TEMPLATE

CENTER MARK

Figure 6-25b
Continuing the
milling process.

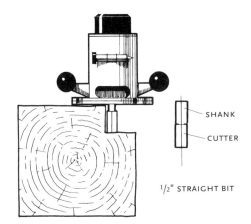

SHANK

CUTTER

¹/₂" STRAIGHT BIT

4) Successive passes may be required to reach the desired depth, lowering the bit each pass. Use this method to remove all waste wood of the top and side faces of the joint and pretest with male template.

Note: Exercise extreme caution in direction and feed speed of cutter.

D. Fasteners and Anchors

To fasten is to make secure. In a post and beam frame, the posts and beams are fastened together with various tight-fitting joinery. In turn, the male and female joints are fastened together with either pegs or pins, depending on the stresses present. The entire frame is fastened to the foundation with a method of anchoring. Throughout the book I indicate pegs, pins, or anchors in application but one must keep in mind that there is also a vast array of specialty anchors, holddowns, and such devices on the market.

For information on Shear Force refer to Chapter 13, Floor Systems. Refer to Figure 6-26b.

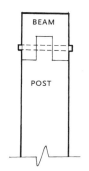 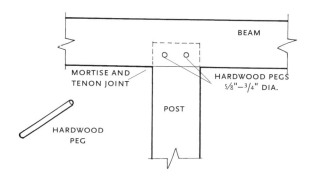

Figure 6-26a Mortise and tenon. The compression forces of the beam upon the post tenon allow for simple hardwood pegs/doweling.

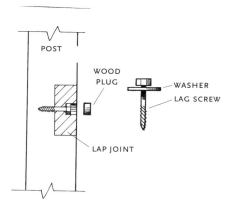

Figure 6-26b Metal lag screw and washer. With shear and torquing forces present, metal pinning is recommended for this half lap joint.

1. Pegs

Also called dowels or trenails, pegs are made of hardwood (oak, maple). Their purpose is to lock the tenon to the mortise. Most joinery requires simple pegging due to the low shear stress present. Peg diameters can range from ⁵/₈"–1" and larger, though I question the use of large pegs. Increasing the peg diameter causes a reduction in the amount of holding-wood on the tenon, causing possible tear-out of the end grain. Rather, two smaller-diameter pegs have more potential to bind (lock) than one larger peg. Pegs can either be purchased (these are called doweling) or handmade; either way a slightly undersized hole is required for a tight fit. Soaking the pegs in raw linseed oil causes swelling of the wood and will result in a tight fit as well. Square pegs in round holes are also used.

2. Pinning

In situations where there is a greater degree of shear stress present, or a compressive hold-down force is required, the use of a metal pin is recommended. Three types of pinning are outlined. The use of one over the other is relative to the fastening force required.

a) Galvanized Timber Spike: Moderate compressive and shear strength with moderate holding capacity, 8"–12" in length.

b) Galvanized Lag Screw: A screw affords better holding capacity and therefore better compressive and shear strength than a spike. Note that the spike and screw require drilling an oversized hole in the first member (to prevent binding) and embedding the pin into the second member. A lag screw with its head countersunk and plugged is an effective way of pinning a kneebrace halflap dovetail joint.

c) Galvanized Bolt: Bolting two members together should only be required where there is potential for excessive shear force. The hole should be drilled only slightly oversize to prevent binding. The heads of the nuts should be countersunk and plugged where visible. Through bolting in combination with a shear arrest (see below) would be recommended for an unsupported scarf joint.

d) Threaded Rod: Works the same as a bolt; can be cut to various lengths.

e) Shear Arrestors: There are two basic types: hardwood splines and metal split-ring connectors or shear plates. Splines are embedded (dadoed) halfway into each member, perpendicular to the grain. Split rings are sandwiched between the lapped joint and positioned so the bolt passes through the center. With shear plates the spikes are embedded into the members to resist movement. All of these shear arrestors depend upon a compressive force (bolted) to be effective.

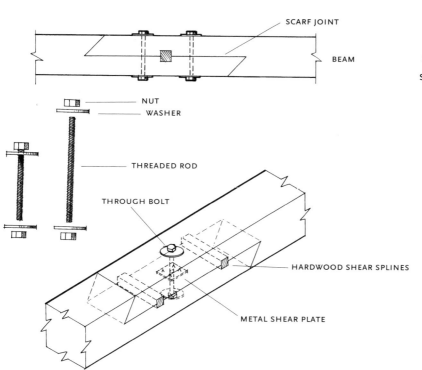

Figure 6-26c
Metal through-bolt, also showing wooden shear splines and metal shear plate. An unsupported scarf joint must be held firm to resist the compressive bending and pulling shear forces applied.

Figure 6-26d
Shear arrestors.

Anchoring the posts

During an earthquake or tremor irregular horizontal and vertical vibrational forces act on the structure. Depending upon the severity, mild to chaotic ground motions push and pull at the building's foundation, which causes the walls of the building to expand and compress (responding to vertical shockwaves) and to bend and sway from side to side (responding to lateral waves). The post and beam frame resists these forces by flexing at the joinery locations and through the resistance of the diaphragm infill and triangular kneebraces. It is crucial that the posts are securely connected to the foundation, either directly or indirectly

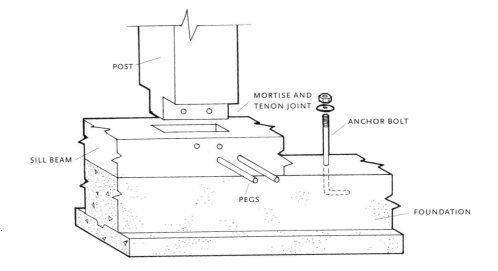

Figure 6-27
Anchoring
post to beam
to foundation.

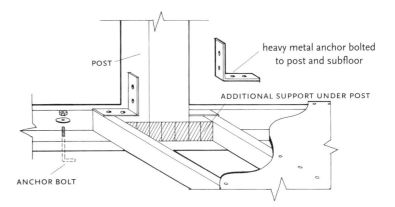

Figure 6-28
Anchoring post
to subfloor to
foundation.

through the subfloor. The following drawings show a few common methods of providing post to foundation connections; for more information refer to Chapter 13, Floor Systems. In addition, log and timber infills should be fastened to the subfloor as well (see applicable Wall Systems chapters).

Note: A high density, closed-cell foam roll should be placed between the wood and concrete as a moisture barrier.

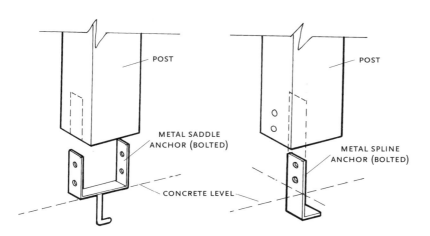

Figure 6-29
Anchoring
post to
foundation.

CHAPTER SEVEN

Modern Timber Post and Beam: Wall System

Like the pieces of a large jigsaw puzzle, the components of a modern timber post and beam house may be prebuilt, stored, shipped, assembled, and reassembled and are therefore recyclable. Figure 7-1 shows a diagram of the modular pieces which comprise a modest house. By concentrating on prefabricating the components of this house shell (i.e. lock-up phase) and ignoring the major costs of land purchase, excavation, foundation, subfloor, permit fees, and so on, resources can initially be focused on the primary goal—shelter. Rather than being forced into building a complex structure from ground to roof within a limited time (i.e. building season, bank financing, permits, insurance, etc.) one can build and assemble recycled materials at their leisure, as time and finances allow.

For example, Figure 7-2 is an illustration of my home on Gabriola Island, which I built using primarily recycled materials. While the entire building (4000 square feet) may appear complex and intimidating, the components of the framework and infill were completed and stored three years prior to purchasing the land. This design and structure is simply a continuation of the same modular pieces shown in the modest house design.

Devoid of infill walls and roof covering, the structural post and beam frame components in Figure 7-3 are examples of how various types of

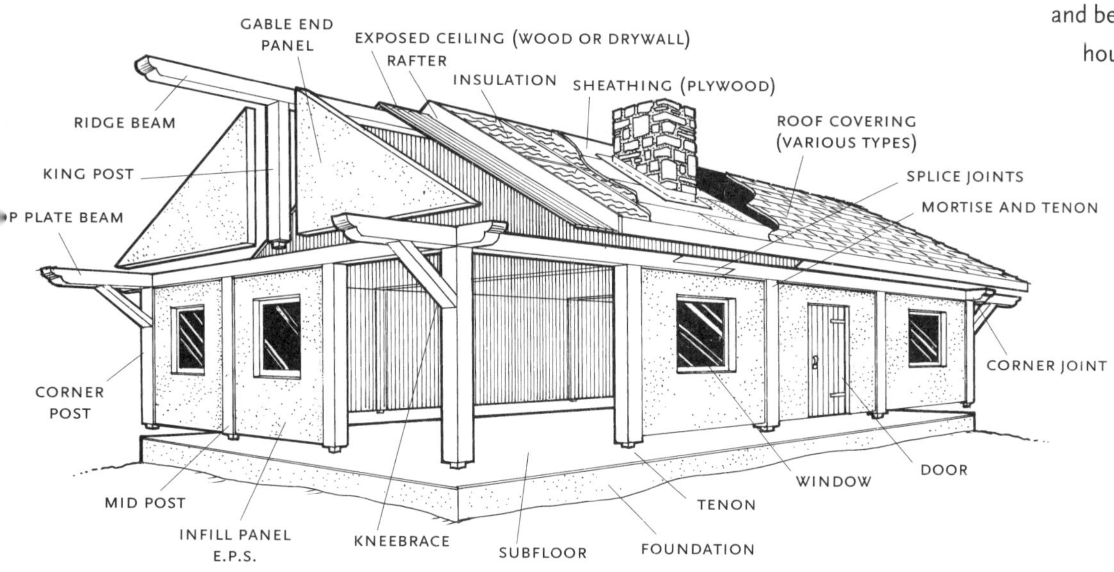

Figure 7-1
Components of
a timber post
and beam
house.

GABLE END
PANEL

EXPOSED CEILING (WOOD OR DRYWALL)

RAFTER

INSULATION

SHEATHING (PLYWOOD)

RIDGE BEAM

KING POST

ROOF COVERING
(VARIOUS TYPES)

SPLICE JOINTS

MORTISE AND TENON

P PLATE BEAM

CORNER JOINT

CORNER
POST

MID POST

INFILL PANEL
E.P.S.

KNEEBRACE

SUBFLOOR

TENON

FOUNDATION

WINDOW

DOOR

Figure 7-2
Author's owner-
built timber
post and beam
house.

R ENGLISH

Figure 7-3
Timber post
and beam
framework
(author's
home).

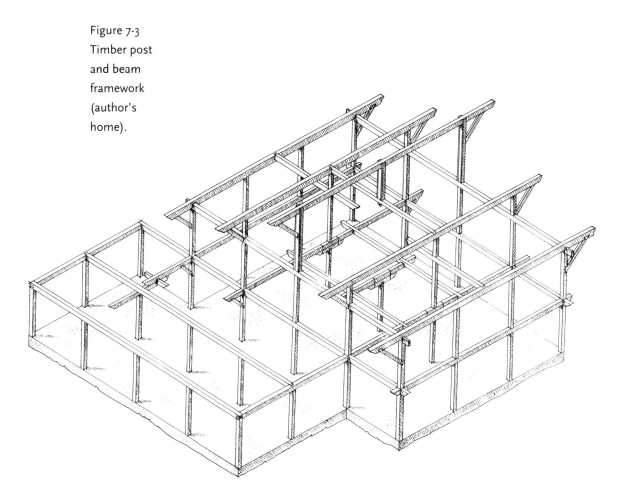

joinery go together. All of these structural timbers have a series of joints located along the centerline. The information as to the post spacings, wall heights, and the timber lengths is taken from the building plan. Because the frame is structural, the size of the timbers and allowable spans must be within accepted tolerances (Refer to Span Tables, Appendix III).

Figure 7-4 is an illustration of the smaller, modular "pagoda" building located on the deck of the house in Figure 7-2. When we continue to break this puzzle into yet smaller components we get a better understanding of how the pieces fit together to make up the whole. Refer to Figure 7-5.

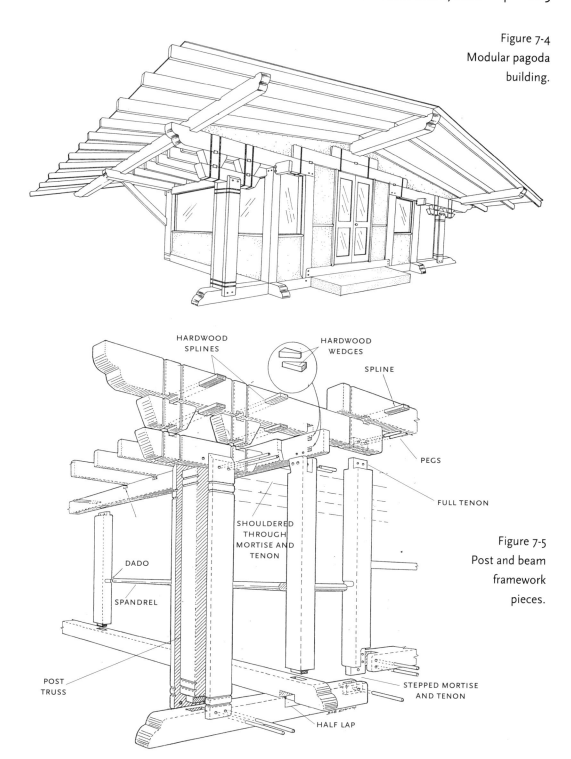

Figure 7-4
Modular pagoda
building.

HARDWOOD
SPLINES

HARDWOOD
WEDGES

SPLINE

PEGS

FULL TENON

SHOULDERED
THROUGH
MORTISE AND
TENON

Figure 7-5
Post and beam
framework
pieces.

DADO

SPANDREL

POST
TRUSS

STEPPED MORTISE
AND TENON

HALF LAP

1. Post and Beam Framework

Procedure:

1) Establish a cutting list. This is a drawing plan of the posts and beams indicating the lengths and joinery types and locations of each on the various timbers beginning at the ground sill and progressing to the top plate. Refer to Joinery Layout and Grid Plan, Chapter 6.

2) Lay out the timbers according to the cutting list. Visualize the framework and joinery as you progress. Remember the old saying "Measure twice, cut once." Layout can be accomplished using a template or by dimensioning; either way always originate from the centerline. Refer to Joinery Examples, Chapter 6, for joint specifications.

3) Cut the joints by removing the waste wood (refer to Wood Removal, Chapter 6).

4) Pretest each joint with the template and store the prefabricated posts and beams (refer to Storage, Chapter 3).

   Note: Consider prefinishing the wood members prior to storage to avoid dirt smudges.

2. Post and Beam Infill Panel

The infill wall panel described here is my own design in response to the need for low cost, minimal wastage, thermal efficiency, light weight, shipability, and storability. The infill panel is comprised of smaller 12" high by 8' long by $4^1/2$" thick interlocking unlimited sized panels made of rigid expanded polystyrene (E.P.S.) with grooves moulded every 16" on center. These are stacked vertically and joined together with 2" × 3" (nominal $1^1/2$" × $2^1/2$") studs glued into the grooves. Around the perimeter edge is a 1" × 3" ($^3/4$" × $2^1/2$") rabbeted into the panel. Refer to diagram Figure 7-6 and inset.

   Note: Some glues are not compatible with foam; read the label.

   Standard braced timberframe employs a "stress-skin" panel of styrofoam sandwiched between plywood sheathing. The huge waste normally associated with rough openings cut from such a panel is virtually eliminated with my system because the pieces can be reused in another wall panel by simply aligning the moulded grooves. The $4^1/2$" thick (R20 in-

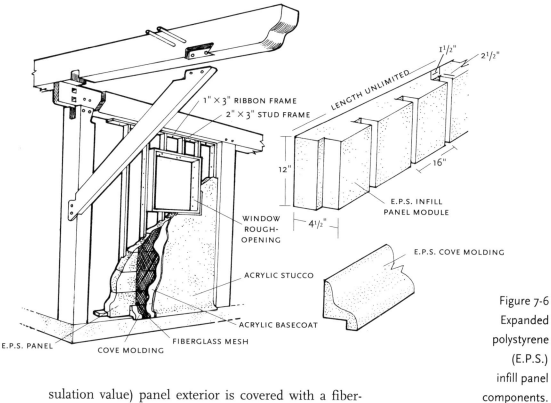

1" × 3" RIBBON FRAME

2" × 3" STUD FRAME

LENGTH UNLIMITED

1¹/₂"

2¹/₂"

12"

16"

WINDOW ROUGH-OPENING

4¹/₂"

E.P.S. INFILL PANEL MODULE

ACRYLIC STUCCO

E.P.S. COVE MOLDING

ACRYLIC BASECOAT

E.P.S. PANEL

COVE MOLDING

FIBERGLASS MESH

Figure 7-6
Expanded
polystyrene
(E.P.S.)
infill panel
components.

sulation value) panel exterior is covered with a fiberglass mesh after which a base coat of acrylic stucco is troweled on. After assembly, a finish color coat of acrylic stucco is applied, or any other type of finish material (i.e. rock faced). The wood studs on the panel interior are predrilled for electrical wiring and present a surface for drywall attachment.

The wall infill panel should be 1" less in height and width than the post and beam frame opening. Stack these infill panels on edge and store until assembly time.

Making the Panels

You can make your own panels by obtaining 4¹/₂" thick E.P.S. blanks from a manufacturer and cutting your own grooves to accept the 2" × 3" studs. These grooves can be cut using a "hot wire" tool and simple plywood

templates as shown in Figures 7-7a and b. Panels can be cut to width and length on a table saw with the blade mounted in reverse to prevent binding.

Figure 7-7a
Styrofoam hot
wire template.

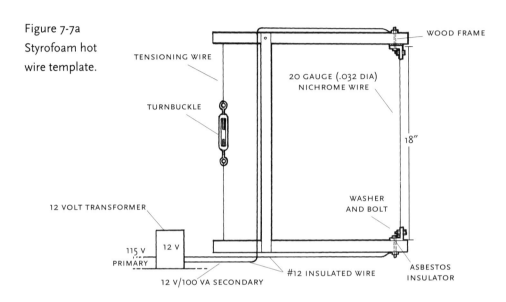

Figure 7-7b
Styrofoam
hot wire
with
plywood
template.

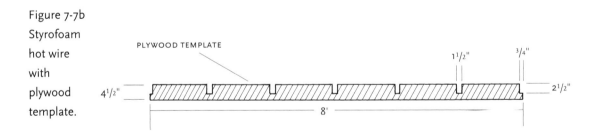

Electrical wiring runs along grooves cut in the E.P.S. panel interior face and through holes predrilled in the studs. This electrical groove (called chase) is cut with a "hot knife" which can be purchased through the E.P.S. manufacturer (Figure 7-8). As well, the drip cap molding shown in the drawing Figure 7-5 can also be purchased or fabricated out of E.P.S. using a similar profiled template. These and other components, templates, and jigs can be obtained through the Island School of Building Arts (see References).

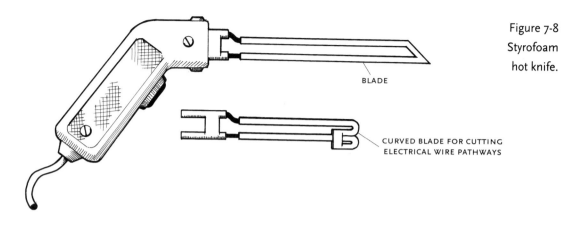

Figure 7-8
Styrofoam
hot knife.

BLADE

CURVED BLADE FOR CUTTING
ELECTRICAL WIRE PATHWAYS

3. Post and Beam Frame Assembly

The following assembly procedure is for the timber post and beam with
an E.P.S. (styrofoam) infill system. Refer to Figure 7-9 for an example of
frame assembly. The assembly method for log and timber post and beam

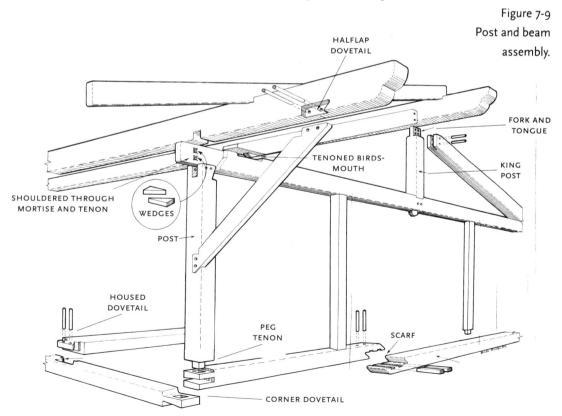

Figure 7-9
Post and beam
assembly.

HALFLAP
DOVETAIL

FORK AND
TONGUE

KING
POST

TENONED BIRDS-
MOUTH

SHOULDERED THROUGH
MORTISE AND TENON

WEDGES

POST

HOUSED
DOVETAIL

PEG
TENON

SCARF

CORNER DOVETAIL

infill is explained in its appropriate chapter. Prior to assembly, the jointed timbers should be grouped according to floors (first floor, second floor, roof) and sufficient cross-bracing should be on hand. Depending on the size and weight of the wood members a crew of four plus the owner should be sufficient for the job. Refer to the Mechanical Advantage section of Chapter 4, Tools.

Tools: Hammer, chalkline, tape measure, 4' level, beetle, come-along, $1/2$" electric drill, $5/8$" auger bit, scaffolding.

Materials: Timbers, 2" × 4" bracing, $5/8$" hardwood doweling, $3^1/2$" nails.

Procedure:

1) Chalk a centerline around perimeter of subfloor corresponding to the layout plan dimensions. Lay out the post centers along this chalked line.

2) Raise plumb and temporarily brace a corner section of the frame posts. Ensure proper anchoring of posts to subfloor (refer to Anchoring the Posts, Chapter 6). Place kneebraces now (see below).

   Note: Contact between wood and concrete should be separated with a moisture break (i.e. high density close-celled foam roll).

3) Erect scaffolding and position beams at the corner section where you've begun. Continue around the perimeter of building, placing interior posts and beams which intersect the outside walls. Any mortised kneebraces needed will be placed at this time. The oversized mallet (called beetle) is used to "persuade" the joinery into position. The come-along is used to snug-up any loose joints.

4) Once the first floor framework is complete then drilling and pegging/pinning the joints should be done. Chamfer the doweling by shaving the ends slightly before installing to allow for easier insertion. Chamfering of all tenons in joinery makes assembly easier.

5) Ensure the assembled frame is plumbed, squared, and braced as you proceed.

6) Continue assembly in the same manner for the second floor (if applicable) and the roof structural members. (Refer to Chapter 12, Roof Structures.) Infill walls can be installed as the framework assembly proceeds, or later after the roof is up.

Placing Kneebraces

A post and beam frame by itself is not rigid without some form of brac-ing. Log and timber infill gives the frame rigidity through the stability of its mass which provides a form of internal bracing.

The most common method of bracing a timber or log frame is to use kneebraces. These are short-length timbers which bisect the corner framed by a post and beam at a 45° angle. The resulting triangle will strengthen the corner against horizontal forces applied by wind. Three methods of installing knee bracing within a post and beam frame follow.

Tools: Eye and ear protection, circular saw and/or chainsaw, combina-tion square, tape measure, chalkline, electric drill with 5/8" (16 mm) auger bit, 1¹/₂" (38 mm) chisel and mallet, slick, pencil.

Materials: kneebrace material, 5/8" (16 mm) dowels.

Procedure:

    1 Figure 7-10 gives the mathematical equation for determining the hypotenuse length of a 45° triangle.

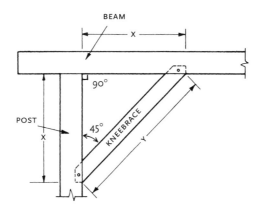

Figure 7-10
Determining
the length of
the kneebrace.

$$y = x \times 1.414$$

Example: Where distance x is 36" (1000 mm), find the length of the kneebrace needed (less any tenon allowance, if applicable).

Kneebrace length y = 36" (1000 mm) × 1.414 = 50.9" (1414 mm)

A. Butt joint kneebrace method (not recommended)
Figure 7-11 shows a simple butt joint kneebrace.

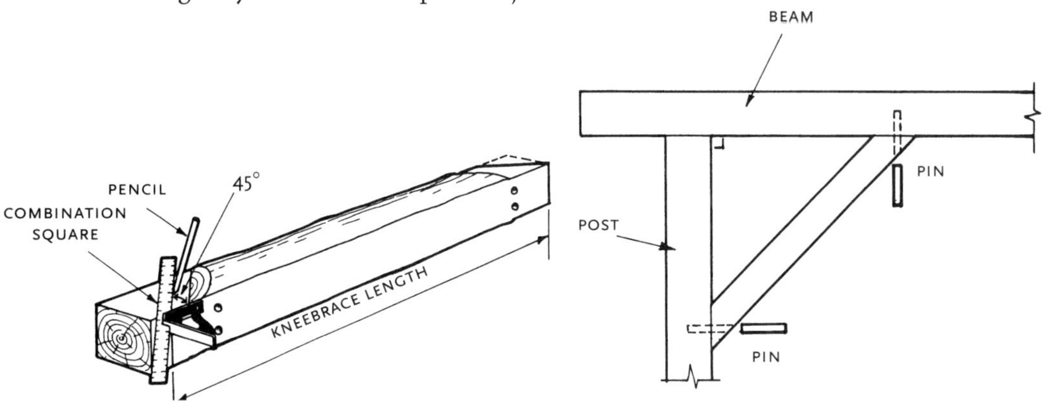

Figure 7-11
Butt joint
kneebrace
method.

After the butt joint kneebrace is cut it is fastened in place with lag screws which are countersunk and plugged.

1) Prepare the log or timber brace material and cut to rough length, including waste allowance.

2) Using a combination square, lay out the 45° angles as shown.

3) Cut the kneebrace and pin it in place.

B. Mortise and tenon kneebrace method

In the case of a free-standing frame, where the frame will not be housing diaphragm bracing infill material, the mortise and tenon joint is recommended to increase the holding capacity of the brace.

Note: This type of kneebrace must be installed during the framework assembly. Figure 7-12 shows the layout and cutting sequence for executing this joint.

1) Prepare the log or timber brace material and cut to overall length, including tenon allowance.

2) Lay out the kneebrace and tenons as shown in step A.

3) Cut the kneebrace tenon as shown in step B.

4) Lay out and cut the post and beam mortises as shown in step C. Make sure that the layout distance x is accurate. If it is not, the frame will be out of square. The kneebrace has a tapered tenon. Note that the distance TD represents the tenon depth at its widest portion, while Td represents its narrowest.

5) Assemble and peg the braces in place.

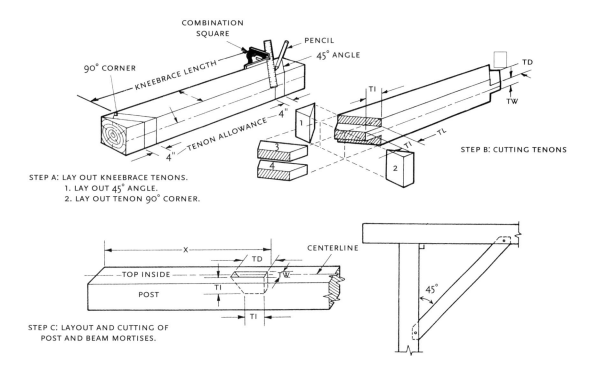

COMBINATION SQUARE
PENCIL
45° ANGLE
90° CORNER
KNEEBRACE LENGTH
TENON ALLOWANCE
4"
4"

STEP A: LAY OUT KNEEBRACE TENONS.
1. LAY OUT 45° ANGLE.
2. LAY OUT TENON 90° CORNER.

TD
TW
TI
TI
TL
STEP B: CUTTING TENONS

X
TD
TW
CENTERLINE
TOP INSIDE
TI
POST
TI

45°

STEP C: LAYOUT AND CUTTING OF
POST AND BEAM MORTISES.

C. Half lap dovetail kneebrace method

Another method of joining the kneebraces to the frame is to use a dovetail half lap joint. The advantage of this method is that the kneebrace does not require installation during the frame assembly but can be "let-in" after. For better holding capacity, pin the joint with a lag screw and countersink the head and plug (Figure 7-13).

1) Lay out the kneebrace and cut the male dovetail joints.
2) Position the kneebrace or template and trace out the mortise. Ensure the framework is square (90° corner) prior to this layout.

Figure 7-12
Mortise and tenon kneebrace method.

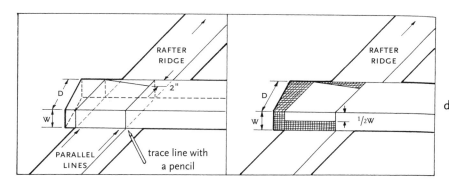

RAFTER RIDGE
D
W
2"
PARALLEL LINES
trace line with a pencil

RAFTER RIDGE
D
W
1/2W

Figure 7-13
Laying out and cutting the half lap dovetail tenon.

3) Cut the kneebrace mortises.

4) Fit into place and secure by pinning (refer to Fasteners and Anchors, Chapter 6).

4. Post and Beam Infill Assembly (Refer to Figure 7-6)

Installation of the infill panels can begin either during or after the framework has been assembled. For solid wood infill refer to appropriate chapters.

Tools: Screw gun, tape measure.

Materials: Exterior grade wood screws, cedar wedges, high density foam backer rod ($1/2$" and $3/4$" dia.).

Procedure:

1) Mark and predrill any required electrical service wire runs in the subfloor and/or posts. Panel studs are predrilled prior to assembly.

2) Install the infill panel within the frame bay. Wedge and screw the panel to the frame and subfloor.

3) Install a continuous backer rod around the exterior of the infill panel to form a tight seal to the frame (Figure 7-14). This foam rod takes up any seasonal expansion and contraction of the wood frame, which will be minimal after the wood has seasoned and providing the end grain of the joints has been sealed (coated with wax or painted) to prevent moisture absorption.

4) The interior shim space is now sealed with polyurethane spray foam.

With the wall panel shimmed and screwed into place and sealed

Figure 7-14
Panel sealing
backer rod and
foam.

POLYURETHANE
SPRAY FOAM

HIGH DENSITY
FOAM BACKER ROD,
VARIOUS
DIMENSIONS

to the frame, the exterior finish can now be applied. The finish shown in Figure 7-6 is acrylic stucco and is complementary to the mesh and basecoat already mentioned. However a rock, brick, or wood finish can also be applied over the existing basecoat by attaching directly to the embedded interior studs.

Note: After assembly and sealing of the panel within the frame, electrical wiring followed by an interior finish (gyprock) is screwed to the studs.

Note: According to the manufacturer, Expanded Polystyrene uses no C.F.C.s in manufacture.

5) Window and Door Openings

Refer to Chapter 11, Openings, for specification information.

Windows are placed into a rough opening, shimmed, and trim applied as in any conventional construction, since there is no shrinkage to contend with. The advantage with this post and beam method is the ease of installing curved and round windows into the nonstructural infill. Simply cut out the shape with a reciprocating saw and fasten the window frame to the interior studs and apply the trim as usual.

Doors can either be installed between posts or within the infill panel. In the latter case, additional support for the side jambs is required, therefore the rough opening will be widened to accommodate the extra studs.

Figure 7-15
Assembled
timber
framework and
infill panels.

CHAPTER EIGHT

Traditional Timber Post and Beam: Wall System

This chapter is intended for those who prefer the appearance of hewn timbers to that of round logs. The following procedures describe methods of joinery commonly practiced hundreds of years ago. However, with simplified template and jig construction these methods become more realistic for today's builder (Figure 8-1).

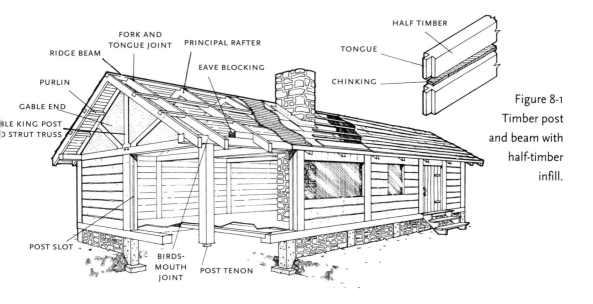

Figure 8-1
Timber post
and beam with
half-timber
infill.

1. Preparing the post tenons and grooves.

Traditionally, the squared timber posts were fashioned with a tenon on either end which mated into mortises in the foundation sill and top plate. Generally, the male portion of a joint is prepared first, and the female portion is cut to match the male piece's dimensions. Cut the mortise for a tight fit, then shave the tenon if necessary.

The traditional method for joining the infill wall half-timbers to the posts is by tenon and groove. The half-timbers have a tenon which fits into a groove or slot in the posts. Below are diagrams and procedures showing how to prepare a corner post. The procedure will be the same for a midpost, except for the placement of the groove.

Tools: Eye and ear protection, chainsaw, carpenter's square, tape measure, chalkline, hammer, crosscut handsaw, chisel or slick, pencil.

Materials: Posts.

Procedure:

    1) Hew or mill the post materials until they are of equal dimensions; they can be square or rectangular. Test for a right-angled surface on

the corner posts by using a carpenter's square. By using two squares, as shown in Figure 8-2a, any twist in the post will be revealed. If possible, the posts should be dry and without any spiral grain.

2) Cut the post to overall length. If the wall height is to be 8' (2440 mm) then the overall length should be 8'8" (2642 mm) to include the 4" (100 mm) tenons.

3) Lay out the tenons on the post ends. Chalk a centerline down both sides of the post, as shown in Figure 8-2b. Working from this centerline lay out the tenon length, thickness, and width, using a carpenter's square. The 2" (50 mm) body of the square works as a template for the tenon's thickness. Alternatively, use the template described in section 2, below.

Figure 8-2
Laying out the post tenon and grooves.

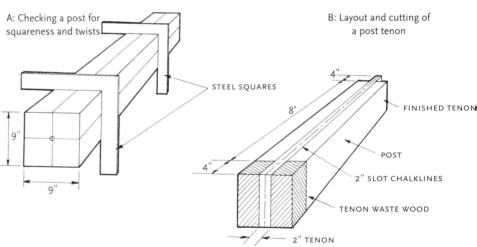

A: Checking a post for squareness and twists

STEEL SQUARES

9"

9"

B: Layout and cutting of a post tenon

4"

8'

4"

FINISHED TENON

POST

2" SLOT CHALKLINES

TENON WASTE WOOD

2" TENON

4) Remove the waste wood of the tenon layout. The result is a full shoulder tenon, which can be left as it is or narrowed, if desired.

5) Lay out a 2" × 2" (53 × 53 mm) deep groove down the midline of the timber, using the chalked centerline as the reference. Since the completed post shown in Figure 8-3 is for a corner, the grooves are at a right angle to each other. If this were to be a midpost the grooves would be on opposite sides of the timber.

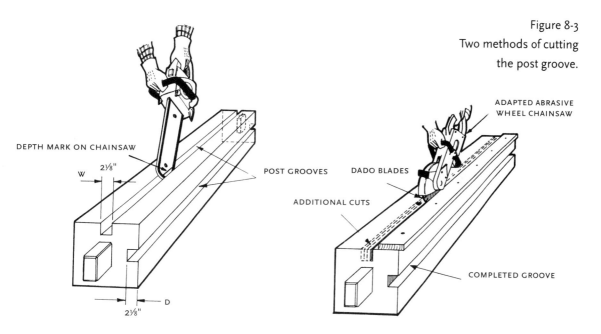

Figure 8-3

Two methods of cutting
the post groove.

ADAPTED ABRASIVE
WHEEL CHAINSAW

DEPTH MARK ON CHAINSAW

W   2⅛"

POST GROOVES   DADO BLADES

ADDITIONAL CUTS

COMPLETED GROOVE

D

2⅛"

6) With a pencil mark on the side of the bar to serve as a depth gauge, use a chainsaw to carefully cut the post grooves. Another method involves the use of a router and straight fluted bit to cut the groove.

Note: New tools are brought onto the market regularly. There is currently a new generation of portable log and timber cutting tools in the way of planers, groovers, mortisers, and tenoners. You should be aware of the products, but for the owner/builder on a budget these tools can be an extravagance. For this reason I endeavor to outline simple, inexpensive jigs as alternatives.

Note: There is a new power tool on the market which is similar to a power planer with the exception that it cuts an adjustable groove depth.

2. Laying out the post mortises on the sills and top plates.

In traditional post and beam construction the posts are raised into position on the sill, and the top plate is left off until the wall infill half-timbers are in place. This procedure is necessary to place the wall half-timbers from the top and slide them down, which could not be done if the top plate were in position. However, initial fitting of the top plate mortises to the post tenons requires much less effort than doing so once the walls are up. The procedures below show how to lay out the post mortise locations on the sills and top plates.

Tools: Chainsaw and mortising jig (optional), brace and $^3/_4$" (19 mm) bit, $1^1/_2$" (38 mm) chisel, mallet, tape measure, knife, pencil.

Materials: Posts, sills and top plates, hardboard.

Procedure:
1) Start on the gable wall end and position the top plate so that it is parallel to the sill, with its bottom side facing up. It will be the same length as the sill (Figure 8-4), less any overhang allowance.
2) Lay out the sill and top plate mortises using either Method A or B below. Refer to Joinery Layout, Chapter 6.
   a) Tracing the tenon end on a piece of hardboard, cut it out, and test by slipping it over the post tenon. Slip it up to the bottom of the post, trace the post dimension on the hardboard, and cut it out. The resulting template will give the post image and the mortise position. Use this template to lay out the mortises (Figure 8-5).
   b) Transfer the dimensions of the post and tenon onto the sill and top plate location. Note that this method is not as accurate as the first.
   Note: The post should bear directly on the solid sill beam; therefore it is necessary to remove the flooring at these post locations.
3) Remove the mortise waste wood by drilling and chiseling as described in Chapter 6, or use a slightly modified electrical cavity mortising jig as described in Chapter 15.
4) Repeat these procedures for the side wall sills and top plates, making sure to extend the top plate to provide a roof overhang.
5) Lay the subfloor decking and expose at the post locations.

3. Raising the posts.

Raising the posts does not require a lengthy procedural outline. It merely takes a few extra strong backs to help with the work. Make sure the numbered posts are located in their respective sill mortises or you may have to

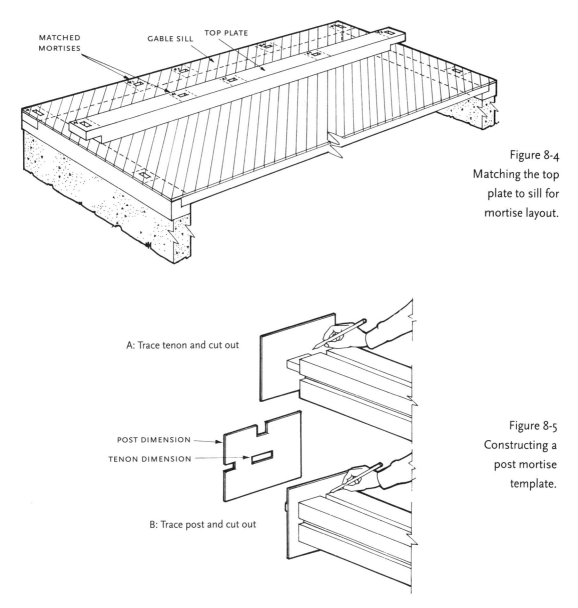

MATCHED
MORTISES

GABLE SILL

TOP PLATE

Figure 8-4
Matching the top
plate to sill for
mortise layout.

A: Trace tenon and cut out

POST DIMENSION

TENON DIMENSION

B: Trace post and cut out

Figure 8-5
Constructing a
post mortise
template.

do some adjustments later (unless a template has been used to lay out the post tenons) (Figure 8-6).

Once the posts are in position, make sure they are plumbed and braced to prevent any movement. After each half-timber wall panel is

Figure 8-6
Positioning,
plumbing, and
bracing the
posts.

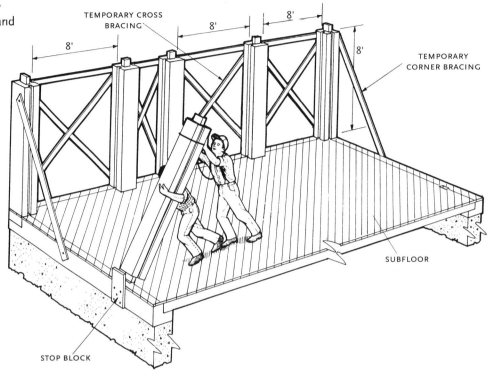

TEMPORARY CROSS BRACING

TEMPORARY CORNER BRACING

SUBFLOOR

STOP BLOCK

complete a temporary 2" × 6" (38 × 140 mm) tie may be nailed on the tops of the posts as shown in Chapter 9.

To prevent any spreading of the posts it is recommended that the wall infill half-timbers be constructed in a jig. This jig is described in sections 4 and 5, below.

Tools: 4' (1220 mm) level, hammer, tape measure.

Materials: 2" × 6" (38 × 140 mm) bracing, nails.

4. Constructing the half-timber infill walls using a jig.

Custom cutting and fitting each wall half-timber in place between the vertical posts can be a difficult and lengthy procedure. If the walls are to be scribe-fitted, a jig like the one described in Chapter 9 would do the job. However, since here the walls will be chinked and not scribed, another type of jig must be constructed to simplify the job. Now, instead of cutting a groove in each end of the wall to be keyed with a spline to the posts (as outlined in Chapter 9), you would instead fashion a "tongue" at either end. Below is an inexpensive jig, with a method for mass-producing half-timber infill panels. The example given is for an 8' × 8' (2440 × 2440 mm) infill wall with a 2" (50 mm) tongue. For an illustration of an alternative jig type, see section 5, below.

Note: Refer to Chapter 9 for methods of pinning and pegging wall infill pieces.

Tools: Eye and ear protection, chainsaw, tape measure, chalkline, hammer.

Materials: Wall timbers, 2" × 6"s (38 × 140 mm), 2" × 4"s (38 × 89 mm), 1" × 4"s (19 × 89 mm), nails.

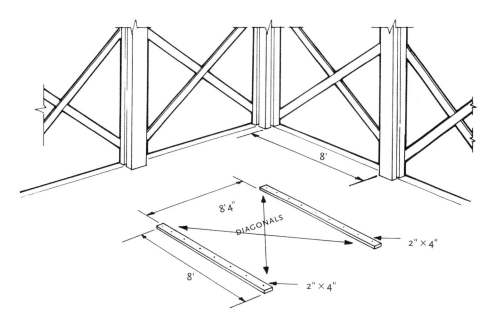

Figure 8-7
Jig layout.

Procedure:
1) Working on the flat subfloor surface nail two 8' (2440 mm) long 2"× 4"s (38 × 89 mm) to the subfloor. They should be parallel to each other and 8'4" (2540 mm) apart to include the tongue lengths. Check their parallel spacings by taking diagonals (Figure 8-7).

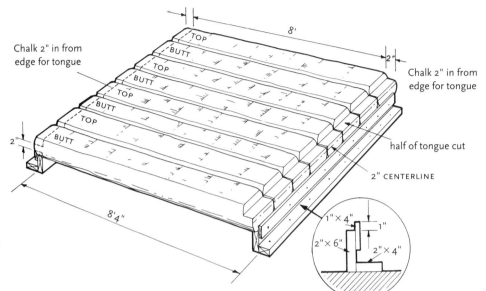

Chalk 2" in from edge for tongue

8'

TOP

BUTT

2"

Chalk 2" in from edge for tongue

TOP

BUTT

TOP

BUTT

half of tongue cut

TOP

2"

BUTT

2" CENTERLINE

8'4"

1" × 4"

1"

2" × 6"

2" × 4"

Figure 8-8
Jig in use.

2) Nail a 2" × 6" (38 × 140 mm) to the inside of the 2" × 4"s (38 × 89 mm) and a 1" × 4" (19 × 89 mm) ledger strip, as shown in Figure 8-8 inset.

3) With the jig complete, the wall half-timbers (hewn on two sides) can be cut to overall length. In an 8' (2440 mm) wall the overall length would be 8'4" (2540 mm) to include the 2" (50 mm) tongues.

   Note: Longer tongues are optional.

4) Place the wall half-timbers on the jig as shown in Figure 8-8. The ledger 1" × 4" (19 × 89 mm) will hold them in position while the 2" × 6" (38 × 140 mm) suspends them off the floor. The butts and tops should be alternated as shown.

5) Trim any high spots between the half-timbers with an axe so that they lie close to one another.

6) Lay out the tongue lengths by chalking a line 2" (50 mm) in from each end. Chalk another two lines on the ends to give a 2" (50 mm) wide tongue.

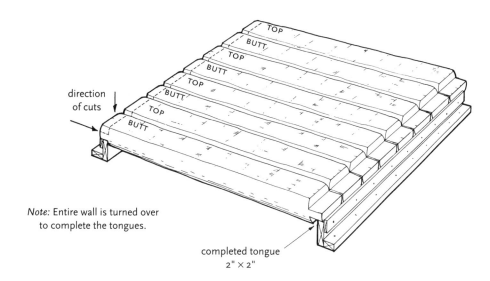

direction
of cuts

Note: Entire wall is turned over
to complete the tongues.

completed tongue
2" × 2"

Figure 8-9
Completed half-
timber wall
tongues.

7) Make vertical and horizontal cuts with the chainsaw to remove half
of the tongue's waste wood.

8) It will be necessary to turn the members to complete the tongues.
Repeat the layout and cutting procedure, referring to Figure 8-9.

9) Set the completed wall half-timbers in place between the vertical
posts. The bottom log should be flat-surfaced to sit on the floor,
with a layer of foam roll between.

5. An alternative wall construction jig.

Figure 8-10 is an illustration of a jig that some builders have used in the
past to test the fit of wall pieces before they are carried to the building.
The diagram speaks for itself. Essentially it is a model of a sill and two
vertical posts. The posts are slotted to receive the wall half-timber
tongues, and the entire assembly is adjustable to accommodate wall panels of different lengths. Notice that a section exposing part of the slot has
been cut away on both verticals. This is to facilitate stacking the wall half-
timbers while allowing for the bottom one to be removed. This is advantageous if the walls are to be scribed. This jig is included here largely as a
point of interest, or in case a reader might wish to adapt or improve on it.

Figure 8-10
Alternative wall jig.

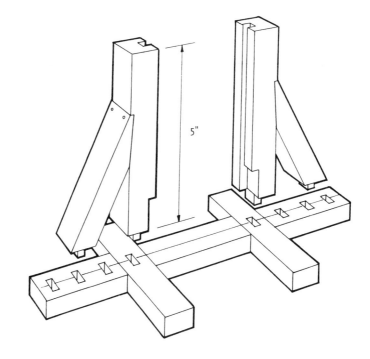

6. Placing the top plate.

Now that the wall half-timbers are placed and leveled to an even height (i.e. 8' or 2440 mm), the top plate can be positioned. Since the mortises of the top plate members were laid out and cut at the same time as the sills, this procedure needs no explanation (Figure 8-11). Once the top plate is in position and level, it can be drilled and pegged to the vertical posts. Any settling that does occur can be concealed by chinking or by the installation of a skirting board as described in Chapter 9.

7. Applying chinking to the wall half-timbers.

The term "chink" refers to a small crack or fissure. In the context of timber or log construction it refers to the gap between any two horizontal wall members. The term "chinking" loosely describes the entire process of filling this opening, which is part of a dual process: chinking with a material to form the bulk fill between wall members, and caulking to provide a weather-tight seal. There are also available commercially prepared foams specially formulated for chinking purposes.

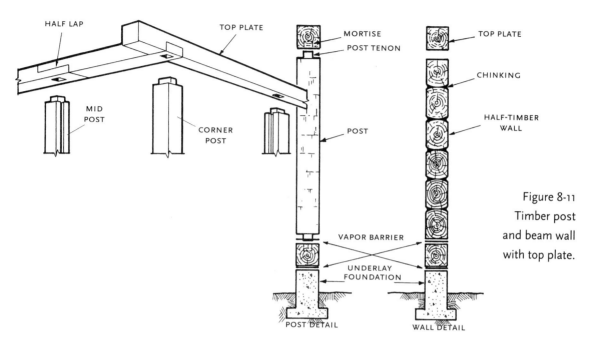

Figure 8-11
Timber post
and beam wall
with top plate.

In Chapter 9 the construction of the walls involves a scribing process to eliminate the gap and preclude any chinking. The identical scribing process may be used for half-timber wall members as well.

A chinked building has both advantages and disadvantages. The construction process will be easier and faster if the wall members do not have to be scribed and custom fitted together. Also, the contrast of tan or grey timbers with white chinking between may be considered attractive. The major drawback with a chinked wall is that any runoff water can become trapped between the chinking materials and the wood, eventually resulting in rot. For this reason it is wise to have plenty of roof overhang to prevent chinked walls from becoming rain-soaked.

For some I suggest a combination quick-scribe and chink. Refer to Chapter 9 for scribing details. This method is for those individuals who do not have the patience or inclination to do a perfect scribing job, as well as for use with very uneven logs which would require a lot of time to scribe. The aim here is to make a quick scribe and lateral groove so that the wall members will lie close to each other. The remaining minor gaps would then require a minimal amount of caulking material.

The chinking process is described below.

Tools: Handsaw, knife, hammer, large spoon, caulking gun (optional), 1¹/₂" (38 mm) paint brush.

Materials: Oakum (tar-impregnated hemp rope), poles or wood or metal lath chinking, shingle nails, barbed wire (optional), stucco mortar, powdered acrylic, whitewash, caulking compound (optional).

Procedure:
1) Figure 8-12 shows three ways to chink half-timber infill walls. In A, sapling poles are nailed on the inner and outer surfaces with oakum insulation (or a substitute) sandwiched in between. In B, the sapling poles are replaced with wood quarter round material. In C, wood or metal lath material is used. The metal lath should be used in conjunction with a mortar caulking mix.

Figure 8-12
Chinking
with poles or
lath.

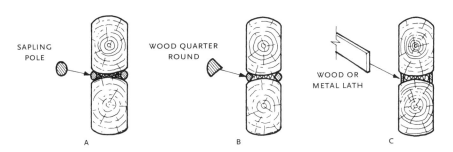

SAPLING POLE

WOOD QUARTER ROUND

WOOD OR METAL LATH

A   B   C

2) Wherever needed, apply some form of anchorage. If metal lath is used during the chinking process, the mortar or caulking will have sufficient holding surface. But if poles or wood laths are used some sort of anchorage will have to be secured to the chinking before the mortar can be applied. Methods of anchorage include shingle nails, barbed wire, or metal lath nailed to the chinking material down the length of the opening both inside and out.
3) Figure 8-13 shows how the stucco mortar mix is applied with a spoon. The rounded back of the spoon makes a slightly concave surface. As mortar mixes are brittle and will crack as the wood ex-

pands and contracts, it is important to make the mix as plastic as possible. For this purpose acrylic powder combined with the dry mix works well. Trial experimentation will discover the best proportions for providing the most plastic mix. Alternatively, there are synthetic caulking compounds available which remain pliable.

4) Figure 8-13b shows a quick-scribing method which eliminates pole or lath chinking by closing the gap enough so that a bead of caulking compound can be used. The shallow lateral groove is then stuffed with insulation or oakum, and the gap is caulked with a petroleum-based compound. These compounds retain their elasticity and can be purchased in a variety of colors. Application is usually done with a caulking gun which extrudes the mixture from a tube. If the weather is cold it may be necessary to warm the caulking tubes before application can begin.

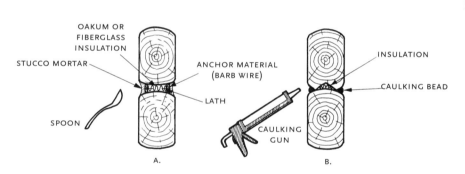

Figure 8-13
Applying
mortar.

8. An alternative method of timber infill wall construction.

When saving time is a factor the builder may forgo the infill wall pieces and construct the roof directly on the building's frame. These wall infill pieces may then be placed between the posts and keyed to them by means of a "pieced spline." The methods already described have required that the top plate be placed after the wall infill pieces are in position and completed.

When using the pieced-splined method it is recommended that the wall infill pieces be scribed rather than chinked. This is because a segmented spline does not afford the degree of lateral shear strength provided by a full length one. Furthermore, a chinked wall does not afford the degree of lateral strength of a scribed and pinned wall. Combining these two weaker elements would create a weaker wall. Refer to Chapter 9 for details on scribing log walls.

Figure 8-14
Assembling timber
wall infill pieces
after the roof is in
place.

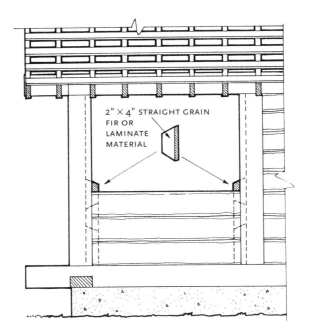

2" × 4" STRAIGHT GRAIN
FIR OR
LAMINATE
MATERIAL

It is intended that these wall infill panels will be constructed in a prefabrication jig like the one described in Chapter 9. A jig is recommended because a log is a tapered cylinder. If logs are fitted individually they will sit on a slight angle, causing a gap at either end where the horizontal half-timbers meet the posts, while an entire panel can be plumb-cut to the dimensions imposed by the vertical posts. During assembly a framework must be temporarily braced until the infill wall material and top plate is in place.

Tools: Eye and ear protection, chainsaw (or router with ³/₄", or 19 mm, straight bit), handsaw, tape measure, chalkline, hammer, level.

Materials: Post, wall timbers, spline material to be straight grain fir or laminate material.

Procedure:

1) Mill the posts then lay out and cut a spline groove so a 2" × 2" (38 × 38 mm) or 2" × 4" (38 × 89 mm) spline will fit. The groove can be cut with a chainsaw or router.

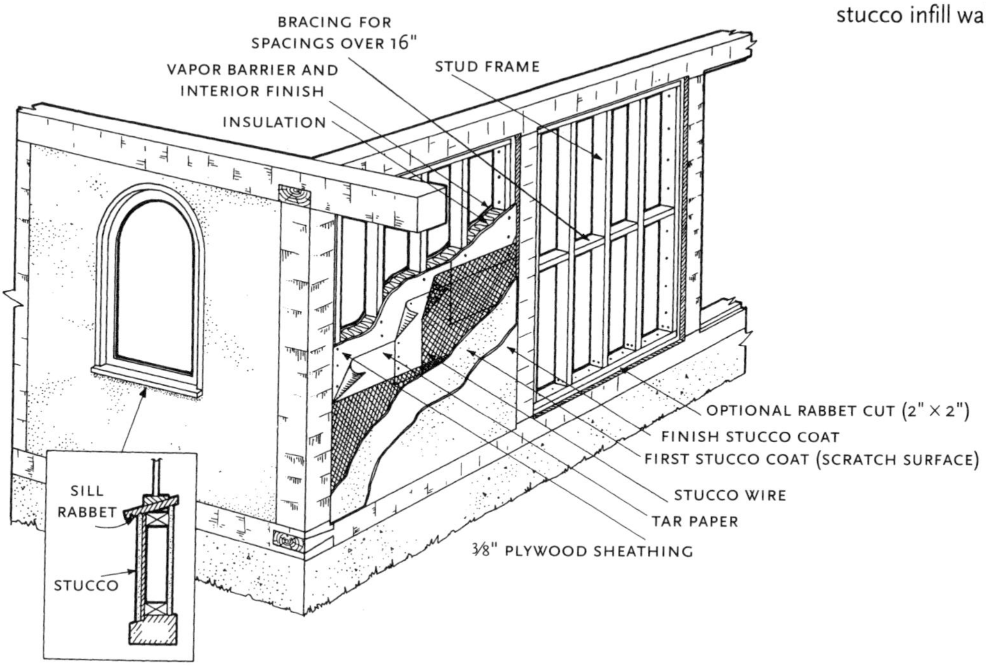

Figure 8-15
Stud framing with
stucco infill walls.

Labels in figure:
BRACING FOR SPACINGS OVER 16"
VAPOR BARRIER AND INTERIOR FINISH
STUD FRAME
INSULATION
OPTIONAL RABBET CUT (2" × 2")
FINISH STUCCO COAT
FIRST STUCCO COAT (SCRATCH SURFACE)
STUCCO WIRE
TAR PAPER
⅜" PLYWOOD SHEATHING
SILL RABBET
STUCCO

2) Erect all posts and top plates; plumb and brace them securely. The roof may be constructed at this point if desired.

3) Build the wall panels in a jig, then plumb-cut them to fit between the posts. Cut the spline grooves, disassemble the panels, and erect the pieces between the posts.

4) Insert the spline in the matched grooves, locking the post and wall timbers together. The spline should protrude part way into the next wall timber as shown in Figure 8-15, and should fit tightly into the groove.

5) Insulate the timbers, pin, and drill for electrical wiring as required (see Chapter 9 for detailed instructions).

9. Stud frame infill with stucco finish.

Another type of wall infill utilizes a stud frame with a stucco exterior finish. Although many other exterior materials can be applied to a frame wall, stucco is described here because of its attractiveness, simplicity of application, low cost, and its suitability for areas where wood materials are scarce. Moreover, the plastic nature of stucco allows for easy finishing to contoured surfaces such as around curved windows. A stucco surface can also be finished in a variety of ways: smooth, rough, brushed, sculptured in relief, or set with mosaic patterns or glass inlay. It can also be colored. Inside the building, to obtain the same effect a skim-coat of building plaster is coated over drywall.

The surfacing described below is known as a "California finish." It is smoothed over textured facing and is slightly off-white or yellow so as to highlight the wood frame.

Tools: Chainsaw (optional for rabbet cut), level, tape measure, hammer, handsaw, circular saw (optional), chalkline, combination square, wire cutters, utility knife, pencil, mortar trowel, shovel, cement mixer, darby float (48", or 1220 mm, board or metal blade with two handles), hand scrub brush, dash brush.

Materials:

Frame: Stud frame materials, 3/8" (9 mm) plywood sheathing, tar paper, stucco wire (16 gauge galvanized 2" (50 mm) mesh × 50" (1270 mm) wide roll), interior finish materials, vapor barrier, insulation, nails.

First coat stucco mix for 25 sq. yd (21 sq. m) coverage:

20 shovels fine sand; 1 bag (88 lb, or 40 kg) type 10 cement; 1/2 bag (25 lb, or 11.3 kg) type S lime.

Combine these and add water until the mix spreads easily and readily adheres to a vertical surface and the underside of a horizontal surface.

Second coat stucco mix for 50 sq. yd (42 sq. m) coverage:

4 bags white sand (353 lbs, or 160 kg) (For white-colored stucco use "China White 00"; for yellow-colored stucco use "Valley Yellow 00." Additional colors may be obtained with colored oxide agents. Instead of white sand you can use a mix of #20 and #30 dolomite coarse and fine sand.); 1

bag white cement (88 lb, or 40 kg) "Federal White" or "Onada" brands; 1 bag Type S lime (50 lb, or 22.7 kg).

Combine and add water until the mix spreads easily and readily adheres to a vertical surface and the underside of a horizontal surface.

Procedure:

1) Construct the stud frame wall infill as shown in Figure 8-15. Cutting a 2" × 2" (50 × 50 mm) rabbet groove around the exterior face of the post and beam frame will ensure a more airtight seal. However, if the stud frame is properly nailed to the framework and caulked this will not be necessary.

    Note the installation of horizontal bracing of the stud wall where spacings are greater than 16" (400 mm). This is a precaution against warpage of the plywood sheathing, which provides the actual bracing.

2) Sheath the exterior surface to the stud wall. Apply tar paper and then stucco wire, as shown in Figure 8-15. Stucco wire is nailed to the wall with roofing nails every 12" (300 mm) to supply the anchorage for the stucco.

3) Apply the first coat of stucco with a trowel. Work in one direction without allowing the stucco to dry at the edge. Wherever possible, work the full width of the wall at one time. Any joining should occur at a natural division of the surface, such as a window or door. The first coat should cover the stucco wire to a depth of approximately 1/4" (6 mm), and must be thoroughly troweled to ensure a good bond. Use the darby to aid in leveling and smoothing the surface. Scratch the surface with a scrub brush to provide a good mechanical bond for the second stucco coat. Then let the wall cure for four days. It is best to cure each coat with periodic water sprinkling, together with protection against the elements with tarpaulins. Stucco should never be applied in freezing weather as it is likely to fail.

4) Just before applying the second finish coat, saturate the first coat completely with water.

5) Trowel on the second finish coat mix to a depth of approximately 1/4" (6 mm) and then smooth out. To obtain a textured appearance

Figure 8-16
Stud framing
with wood
siding infill.

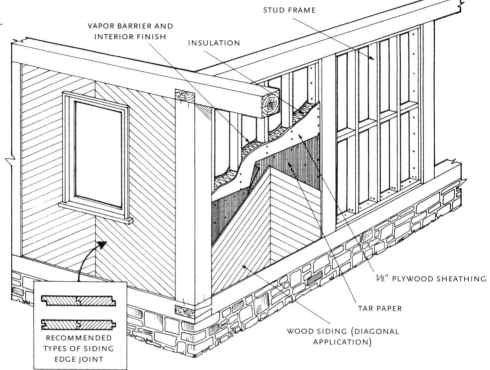

VAPOR BARRIER AND
INTERIOR FINISH

STUD FRAME

INSULATION

³⁄₈" PLYWOOD SHEATHING

TAR PAPER

WOOD SIDING (DIAGONAL
APPLICATION)

RECOMMENDED
TYPES OF SIDING
EDGE JOINT

use a 6" × 6" (150 × 150 mm) square dash brush. Dip the brush into a pail of mix and use it to "throw" a facing over the second coat. Complete the entire wall, then very lightly smooth over with a trowel. Cure and protect this final coat as described above.

6) Complete the wall by insulating, then applying a vapor barrier and an interior finish, as shown.

10. Stud framed wood exterior siding.

If wood siding is preferred for the exterior, the same stud frame infill method described for a stucco finish would be employed here. Application of the wood siding is a simple matter of nailing it to the face of the plywood sheathing with a layer of tar paper stapled between (Figure 8-16). The style of application can be designed to suit the taste of the builder. Exterior wood siding should be cut with a tongue and groove or lapped edge joint, since a butted joint is likely to leave gaps between the boards as a result of shrinkage during hot, dry weather and/or buckling during wet weather expansion.

11. Window and door openings.

Refer to Chapter 11, Openings.

CHAPTER NINE

Log Post and Beam: Wall System

Log post and beam requires a minimum of material preparation and purchase, and for this reason it is a favored technique for both professionals and owner/builders. The outlined construction procedures entail scribe-fitted wall log joinery prefabricated on a remote jig. Such a jig can be either on the building site or entirely separate from it. A practical method of wall storage and shipment is described so that a builder may store or transport the disassembled component parts across the country, if desired. Also included in this chapter are instructions for a post and beam walk-in basement wall. Many builders of long-log notched corner buildings will choose to use a post and beam basement access wall to avoid settling problems while still maintaining the log theme. For those building with half-timbers, it will still be necessary to refer to this chapter from time to time, as many aspects of the construction procedures are identical.

1. Parts of a log post and beam building.

Figure 9-1 shows a post and beam log house with its various components identified, so the reader may become familiar with these terms and parts.

2. Constructing a wall panel jig.

A jig is a device used to hold work during manufacture or assembly; in this case it will enable prefabrication of log infill wall panels as separate from the building foundation. Such a jig allows one to pre-build all the

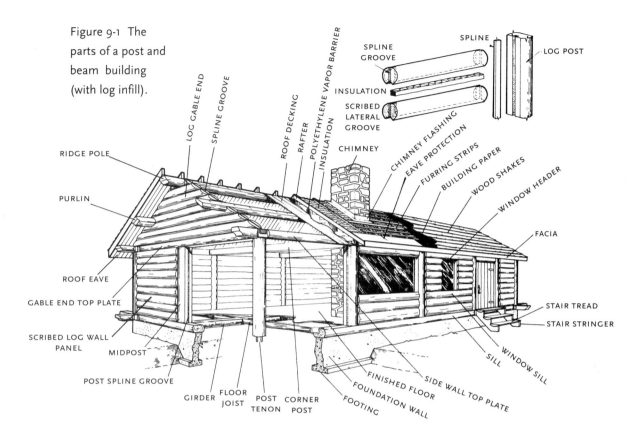

Figure 9-1 The parts of a post and beam building (with log infill).

wall parts for storage or later shipment, as well as assembly onto a foundation which has limited worksite room. It allows construction and storage of the building components inside a barn, shed, or in the shelter described earlier. Above all it is a more accurate method of wall construction. With this jig an entire wall can be pre-built and the ends plumb-cut to a specific width. With the wall still in place on the jig the ends can now be grooved to receive the spline which keys it to the post. The alternative is to fit each log individually between stationary posts—difficult, for a log is a tapered cylinder and inevitably a gap results between the post and in-fill log.

The wall panel jig is comprised of two pieces: a base and a back-brace. The base represents the building's subfloor; it must be level and securely staked to prevent any movement. It is wise to check its position with a builder's level from time to time. The back-brace serves to stabilize the wall as it is being built and also forms part of the plumb-cutting jig outlined in section 6, below. If a "mini" mill such as the one described in Chapter 5 is used to plumb-cut the wall sections then the positioning of the back-brace is not as important. The jig described below is dimensioned for 8' (2440 mm) long wall panels, using logs with approximate 12" (300 mm) mid-diameter. It can be scaled for longer or shorter panels, or to suit your own log sizes.

Tools: Builder's level or water level, hammer, handsaw, tape measure, carpenter's square, chalkline, sledge hammer, axe, chain hoist (optional), pencil.

Materials:
   Base:
        2" × 6" × 13" (38 × 140 × 330 mm) (5 pieces)
        2" × 6" × 108" (38 × 140 × 2743 mm) (2 pieces)
        2" × 12" × 108" (38 × 286 × 2743 mm) (1 piece)
   Back-braces:
        2" × 6" × 114" (38 × 140 × 1895 mm) (6 pieces)
        2" × 6" × 94$\frac{1}{2}$" (38 × 140 × 2400 mm) (1 piece)
        1" × 4" (19 × 89 mm) crossbracing
   Stakes:
        2" × 4" × 15" (38 × 89 × 380 mm) (10 pieces)

Procedure:
   1) Construct the base as shown in Figure 9-2. Ensure that the 2" × 12" (38 × 286 mm) is centered on the base frame and the chalked centerline is also centered. Accuracy here will pay off, especially if you plan to use a mini mill to plumb-cut the wall panel ends.
   2) Level the base and stake securely.
   3) Nail the back-braces to the base as shown. Accuracy here can be disregarded if you plan to use a mini mill. Cross-brace and stake securely.
   4) Build any number of these jigs, depending on how many wall panels you want to build simultaneously.

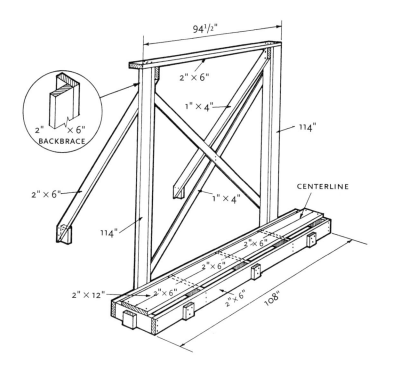

Figure 9-2
Wall fabrication jig.

3. How to place and scribe a wall log.

Before the scribing and fitting of wall logs can begin, the first bottom log must be placed. Since this bottom log will sit on the subfloor it should have a 8"–10" (200–250 mm) flat surface. Make a chalked centerline on the underside of this log to align with the centerline on the jig base. This bottom log should be quite large so that it will slightly overhang the subfloor edge to provide a drip cap. If an 8' (2440 mm) finished wall panel is desired, the logs should be 9' (2743 mm) long to allow for wastage (Figure 9-3).

After the bottom log is placed, additional logs will be scribed, one upon the other, to build the wall. The scribing procedure transfers the contours of the top surface of the log below onto the undersurface of the log placed above it (Figure 9-4). The resulting two scribe lines will appear on the undersurface of the log placed above it in the form of a scratched line if using a scratch-type scriber, or a pencil line where a pencil-type scriber is used. The wood between these two lines is then removed to

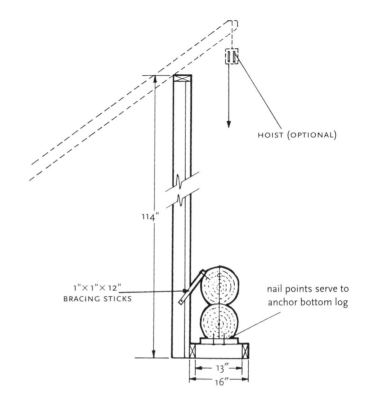

Figure 9-3
Side view of a jig
with first and
second wall logs
in place.

HOIST (OPTIONAL)

114"

1"×1"×12"
BRACING STICKS

nail points serve to
anchor bottom log

13"

16"

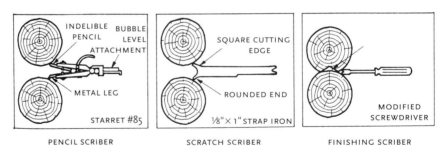

Figure 9-4
Types of
scribers.

INDELIBLE BUBBLE
PENCIL LEVEL
ATTACHMENT

METAL LEG

STARRET #85

PENCIL SCRIBER

SQUARE CUTTING
EDGE

ROUNDED END

⅛"×1" STRAP IRON

SCRATCH SCRIBER

MODIFIED
SCREWDRIVER

FINISHING SCRIBER

make the lateral groove, taking care not to cut away the scribe line. If the scriber is held level and the lateral groove has been cut properly, a tight fit joins the two logs together, entirely eliminating the need for exposed chinking material. It is always best to keep the scriber setting to a minimum, as accuracy is lost when the scriber setting is widened. (Refer to Chapter 10 for additional scribing information.)

The wall logs will look much better if they are on the same parallel plane along the entire length of the building's wall. That is, if the second, fourth, sixth, and eighth logs up from the bottom are set at the same height in all of the wall panels, this uniformity is more attractive than if these logs were at different heights on the various walls (Figure 9-5). To accomplish this, simply place reference marks on the back vertical braces of each jig at equal heights to correspond to each even-numbered wall log (Figure 9-6). Build up one wall panel and use it as an example for the height measurements.

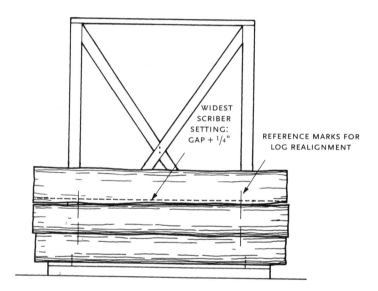

WIDEST SCRIBER SETTING: GAP + $1/4$"

REFERENCE MARKS FOR LOG REALIGNMENT

Figure 9-5
Constructing a log wall panel on a jig (front view).

As you build up the wall make sure that it does not become bowed. This can be done by marking a vertical plumb line on the log ends.

Tools: Scriber, tape measure, level, hammer, pencil.

Materials: Wall logs, nails.

Procedure:
1) Place the second log directly over the first so that it is aligned along the center of the wall, and brace-nail into the vertical back-brace supports. Alternate butts and tops.

   Note: It is possible to "stack" up to two or three logs and then scribe them all at the same time.

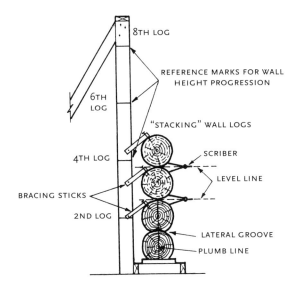

Figure 9-6
Constructing a
log wall panel on
a jig (side view).

2) Scribe the log(s) using either the pencil- or scratch-type scriber shown in Figure 9-4. The modified screwdriver is only used to re-scribe troublesome logs which are poorly fitted. Set the scriber to the widest gap between the logs and add $1/4$" (6 mm) to this setting (Figure 9-6). Remove any knots beforehand so the log rests close to the log below. Scribe both sides of the log. A light spray of water to dampen the path of the indelible pencil produces an easily read-able line.

3) Pencil a reference mark for easy realignment (Figure 9-5).

4) Remove log(s) to ground skids and cut the lateral groove. Refer to section 4, below.

5) Reposition the log(s) and check for fit. Adjust if necessary.

6) Brace-nail the log(s) to the back-brace and extend a plumb line up the logs ends (Figure 9-6).

4. Cutting a lateral groove to fit the wall logs.

The lateral groove, when properly scribed and cut, allows for moisture to drain away and provides a chinkless fit between wall log members to prevent wind and weather from entering and heat from escaping the building.

Tools: Eye and ear protection, chainsaw, indelible pencil, axe.

Procedure:

1) Turn the log upright and pencil clearly over any lightly scribed lines. Also pencil the desired angle of cut (whether a normal or wide scribe) on the log end (Figure 9-7).

2) Position and wedge or dog the log so the saw blade enters at the proper angle and depth.

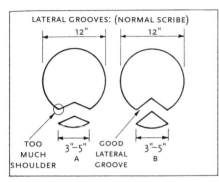

LATERAL CUT: NORMAL SCRIBE
SHOULDERED: THE LOG WILL NOT FIT PROP-
ERLY. TOO MUCH INNER SHOULDER RATHER
THAN EDGE IS RIDING ON THE LOWER LOG.
GOOD SCRIBE WIDTH AND DEPTH. STRONG
EDGES WITH GOOD BEARING.

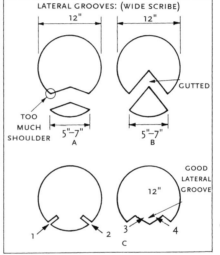

LATERAL CUT: WIDE SCRIBE
SHOULDERED: SAME AS NORMAL SCRIBE.
TOO MUCH WOOD REMOVED CAUSED EXCESSIVE
CHECKING AND WEAK EDGES.
GOOD PROCEDURE FOR A WIDE SCRIBE, WITH
SHARP, STRONG EDGES YET NOT GUTTED.

Figure 9-7
Lateral
grooves for
normal and
wide scribes.

3) Keeping the blade $1/8"-1/4"$ (3–6 mm) inside the line, cut down the length of the log. Repeat for the opposite scribe line and remove the waste wood.

4) Using an axe, pare with the grain down to the scribe line. Do not remove scribe line. The finished lateral groove cut should resemble the "good" grooves shown in Figure 9-7.

Hints for cutting the lateral groove:

1) When you cut the lateral groove walk backwards pulling the saw as you go. It is wise to clean your pathway of debris (Figure 9-8).

Figure 9-8
Finished lateral
groove on a wall
log.

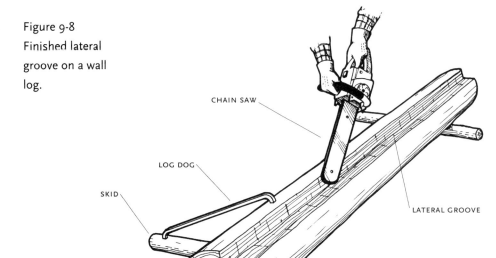

CHAIN SAW

LOG DOG

SKID

LATERAL GROOVE

2) Dry logs tend to splinter. Cut further inside the line if this happens.

3) On a curvy scribe line, lifting the bar and working more with the nose does a better job.

5. Leveling the walls.

A log is a tapered cylinder. By alternating butts and tops on each course much of the leveling problem will be taken care of. However, it will be necessary to take accurate readings and make appropriate adjustments so that the wall comes up level, especially when approaching the top. Level readings can only be taken on even-numbered courses with equal numbers of tops and butts at each wall end.

Wall construction progresses rapidly up to about the sixth course, after which it becomes increasingly difficult to lift the logs. To overcome this problem, included in this procedure is a simple method of separating the wall into two sections, using the sixth log as the starter log for the top section.

Tools: Tape measure, level, scriber, pencil, wooden wedges, hammer.

Procedure:

1) Position and align the sixth log on the wall, and brace it securely to the vertical supports. Note that you can only check for level when there is an "even" number of logs on the wall.

2) Place a level on each end of the wall (Figure 9-9a) and measure the distance down to the jig base. Then note the difference between the two ends of the wall.

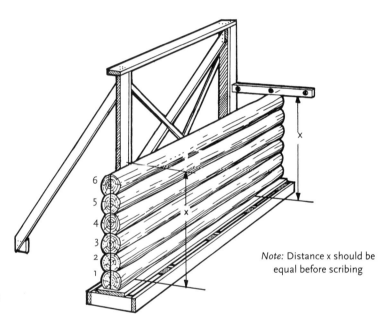

Figure 9-9a
Leveling the log
wall.

A: Leveling the
sixth log course

Note: Distance x should be
equal before scribing

3) If there is only 1"–2" (25–50 mm) difference, block the low end up so the log sits level and scribe the log. Then remove the log to cut the lateral groove.

4) If there is more than 2" (50 mm) difference, replace this log with one that is more suitable, bringing the wall near level. Then block the low end and scribe the log in place. Do not readjust or move the log while scribing.

5) Once the sixth log has been fitted into place on the wall, remove it and position it on a second jig as shown in Figure 9-9b. Match the center plumb lines on the ends of this sixth log with the centerline on the jig base.

6) Since the entire length of the top surface of this sixth log was an

equal distance from the jig base prior to its removal, it should be blocked so that its top surface is again on a level plane with that of the base (Figure 9-9b). Using a level, plumb the log ends so they are vertical and in alignment with the jig base centerline.

Figure 9-9b
Leveling the log wall and constructing it in two sections.

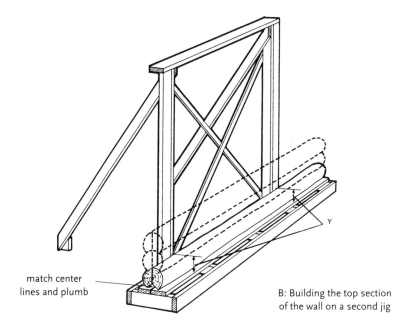

match center lines and plumb

B: Building the top section of the wall on a second jig

7) Nail-brace this sixth log securely to the back-brace supports and complete the wall. The wall height will be 1" (25 mm) lower than the post length. In the examples used here the posts are 8' (2438 mm) long, thus the wall panel will be 7'11" (2413 mm). The top log of this wall will require flat-surfacing and minor preparation. It is easier to accomplish this at this stage rather than when the walls are in place. Refer to section 17 or 18, below, for details, depending on the type of top plate chosen.

8) Replace this top wall section to its lower portion in preparation for plumb-cutting the ends.

6. How to plumb-cut a wall panel using a jig.

This procedure outlines how to use a jig to cut the ends of the wall panel so they are perfectly straight and vertical. This jig is simply an upright version of the post and rail mill shown in Chapter 5. Should the builder wish, the mini mill illustrated in the same chapter also works well for plumb-cutting, and has the advantage of being more portable. Whichever device is chosen, a guide of some sort is necessary to make an accurate vertical cut. It is also equally important to have the cutting chain of the chainsaw filed correctly to avoid a "wandering" cut.

Tools: Eye and ear protection, chainsaw with 26" (660 mm) bar and chisel chain, bar pads, hammer, 4' (1220 mm) level, tape measure.

Materials: Jig.
   2" × 6" × 114" (38 × 140 × 2895 mm) (2 pieces)
   2" × 6" × 94¹/₂" (38 × 140 × 2400 mm) (1 piece)
   2" × 4" × 19" (38 × 89 × 482 mm) (2 pieces)
   1" × 4" (19 × 89 mm) bracing
   nails

Procedure:
   1) Erect the 2" × 6" (38 × 140 mm) plumb-cut jig according to Figure 9-10. Make sure that the uprights are:
   • parallel to each other
   • exactly plumb
   • braced securely to prevent flexing.
   2) Fit a sharp, properly filed chisel chain to a 26" (660 mm) bar. Improper filing will cause a curved cut.
   3) Attach ³/₄" (19 mm) plywood pads to the bar. Carriage bolts should be recessed into the wood pads (see Figure 9-11 for correct pad placement). For more information refer to Chapter 5, section 5.
   4) Start the cut from the top, making sure that the pads are always in contact with the 2" × 6" (38 × 140 mm) rails. Have someone else place moderate pressure holding pads against the rails by using two sticks.
   5) Complete the cut.
      If the saw starts to cut crookedly STOP!
      Turn the saw upside down, cutting with the back of the bar, and the cut will correct itself. If the cut does not correct itself, move the guide rails back 3" (75 mm) and cut again. Add 3" (75 mm) to the opposite end.
   6) The plumb-cut log infill panel will appear as in Figure 9-12.

Figure 9-10
Plumb-
cutting a
wall panel.

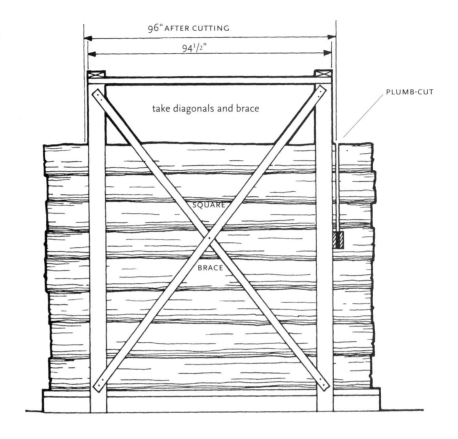

96" AFTER CUTTING

94½"

PLUMB-CUT

take diagonals and brace

SQUARE

BRACE

Figure 9-11
Plumb-
cutting a
wall panel
(side view).

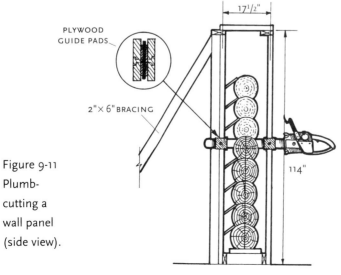

PLYWOOD
GUIDE PADS

2" × 6" BRACING

17½"

114"

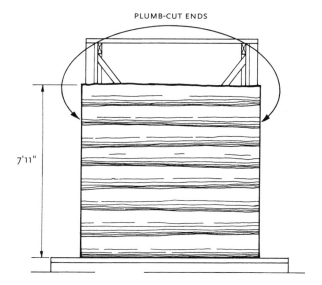

PLUMB-CUT ENDS

7'11"

Figure 9-12
Log wall infill
panel with plumb-
cut ends, ready
for spline
grooving.

7. How to spline-groove a wall section.

The aim is to produce a straight, uniform groove in the wall panel to match a similar groove in the post, so that a spline can be used to key with the wall panel to the vertical post. This method replaces the tenon and groove method. The directions for this task describe the groove being made with a router. Less strain is placed on the router if relief cuts are made with a circular saw or chainsaw.

Tools: Router, eye and ear protection, 3/4" (19 mm) straight bit, level, hammer, circular saw or chainsaw.

Materials: 1" × 4" (19 × 89 mm) straightedge, nails.

Procedure:
1) Fasten a 3/4" (19 mm) straight bit to a router.
2) Nail a straight length of 1" × 4" (19 × 89 mm) against the outer edge of the log ends. Make sure it is plumb. This will serve as a guide to rout a groove down the center of the log ends.
3) Make relief cut(s) with a chainsaw or circular saw.

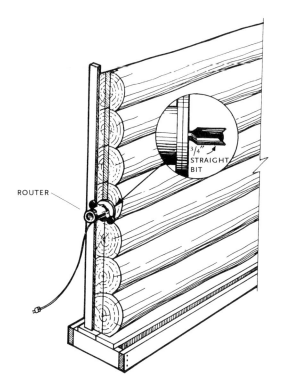

Figure 9-13
Routing a spline
groove in the log
wall panel.

ROUTER

STRAIGHT BIT
³/₄"

4) Make two passes with the router, extending the bit each time to get the 1⁵/₈" (41 mm) maximum depth (Figure 9-13).

5) Repeat for the opposite end of the wall. Figure 9-14 and its inset show a keyed wall and post.

   Note: This groove will accommodate a ³/₄" × 3" (19 × 75 mm) marine plywood key strip which has a great deal of shear strength. Due to the tight fit against the post no other materials are necessary. However, if a 2" × 2" (38 × 38 mm) spline is desired, simply move the guide over to accommodate the extra width. As any other replacement spline material must be resistant to shear stress, use such woods as a clear grain Douglas fir or a laminate material.

6) Number the individual logs in each panel before disassembly. The post need not be connected to the wall panel at this time.

   Note: Placing the top plate onto the walls requires a certain amount of advance preparation on the wall panels. It is easier to do this work while the wall is still in its construction jig by making the necessary measurements, removing the top log, and then making

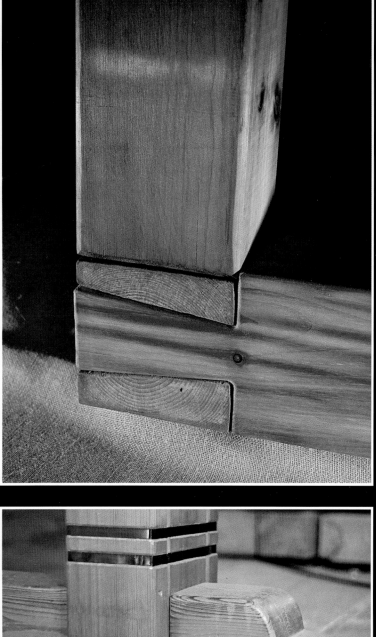

The function of a corner dovetail is to connect the end of bottom sill beams and/or top plate beams together to form a right angle corner when no extension or cantilever is required. Apart from the front entry and side entry variations, it is the sloping sides of the dovetail flare which form the wedge against removal. The peg tenon of the post enters the joint to complete the locking connection. In contrast to the strong, dominant framework is the recessive, passive, infill wall.

Extending a beam past an intersecting connection may be required structurally (as for cantilevers) or simply desired visually. Projecting beam extensions give a feeling there is more to come, a potential for growth which is the opposite of box-like stagnation. The scalloped double curve on the end of the beam gives interest to the blunt, square end.

Big timbers allow cantilevers and projections in roof and balcony designs. The strength of a post and beam corner connection used to support the cantilevered weight is accomplished with the shouldered-through mortise and tenon. Here the tenon of the anchor beam passes through the vertical post. The beam strength is maintained with its full dimensional loading shouldered on the post rather than on just the reduced tenon. The cantilevered top plate beam sits squarely on the post while straddling the anchor beam tenon with a housed/shouldered lap joint. The entire joint is wedged and pegged. A dilution of sulfuric acid causes a photoreactive response, creating a natural patina the color of redwood on the white pine timbers. Softened edges transform the rectilinear timbers back into a more organic form.

The function of the post truss is to support a greater beam load area through the additional use of compression blocks and a bottom cord. When these members are through-bolted with shear splines, a truss is created. Post trusses reduce the number of posts required to support a timber span. As well as serving a functional role, the post truss also gives a visual sense of strength. Through-bolts are hidden while the brass ties, oak splines, and pegs are enhanced.

The housed dovetail is a practical method of joining two major structural beams at right angles. The flared dovetail portion locks the male tenon to the female mortise to prevent the joint from pulling apart, while the housed portion retains the strength of the beam connection. The combined weight and compressive force on the beams eliminates the need for additional fastening or pegging. This joint is most suitable in girder to sill and tie-beam to plate locations or in other areas where maximum locking strength is required.

Apart from the purely functional role of the housed dovetail, it is, like all of the dovetails, an attractive form. Here the clean, simple wedge is accented by the curves created in the shaping process. The result is visually stimulating, practical, and functional. Like a ship's deck, the housed dovetail presents an eased edge for a caulking seal against the elements.

The transition of natural round log into the rectilinear dimensions of squared timber provides new design potential. In the blockwork corner example, the student gradually tapered the log into a diamond shape, personalized with carvings on the log/timber ends.

Exposing flat, square surfaces on a round log enables modular proportioning. Layout methods involving custom scribing of irregular round surfaces is replaced with exact measurements of square surfaces. This allows for multiple layout procedures, template use, and prefabrication of modular components. This log second story floor system and spiral staircase illustrate how the joists and treads can be measured, reproduced, and stored for future use.

The owner/builder of this pièce-en-pièce home sought to mirror the grain pattern of the cedar half-timber walls on the gable and ceiling using cedar boarding. The resulting rich, honey-colored tones absorb reflective light, giving a muted, intimate atmosphere.

The lower photo shows the front porch of a half timbered post and beam (pièce-en-pièce) ranch house. The rural landscape, with its combination of boots, kids, mud, and dogs demands practicality and durability in building design.

Red, orange, blue and green go well with the natural golden hues of wood here and the drywa (gyprock) reflects light from outside into the interior of a room. Post and beam construction allows for large window and door areas as well as a multitude of infill types

A whimsical reversal of function following form, here the author's master bedroom pagoda is suspended above a reflective pool built on the deck of his house which is, in turn, poised over the edge of a rock escarpment. This room gives the impression of sleeping in a tree house or an eagle's aerie. Roof rafter tails cast shadows like wings over the shimmering pools.

Symmetrical composition and modular construction make this house design reminiscent of the early pièce-en-pièce style of the Hudson's Bay forts built across Canada during the 17th and 18th centuries. Extended roof overhangs ensure a longevity that will span centuries and provide housing for generations to come.

Inside the formal tradition continues, with reflected light from the drywall/plaster ceiling brightening and highlighting the woodwork and preventing the room from becoming too dark.

flat the top of the wall
panel at 7'11"±

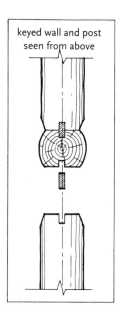

keyed wall and post
seen from above

Figure 9-14
Wall panel
and posts,
grooved
and keyed
together
with a
spline.

the necessary cuts. Refer to section 17 or 18, below, for the type of
top plate provisional work.

8. Two ways to store and ship intact log wall panels.

The metal clamping devices described below allow the removal of the entire wall from its construction jig in one complete unit. This permits the
walls to be stored indefinitely, ready for assembly, without danger of the
individual logs twisting. Such a procedure would be very advantageous
for the person wishing to build in stages as he or she can afford it, for
those wishing to get a head start for the spring by constructing the walls
during the winter, and for the contractor needing to ship to a distant
client.

Included here are two slightly different options for this metal clamping device. The first requires disassembly of the wall logs for insulating,
then predrilling for wiring and pinning. This option is sufficient if there
will be no lifting device available at the foundation site and the logs will
have to be individually placed piece by piece.

The second option involves some minor changes to the hardware and the wall panel itself, but the time saved in wall assembly is significant. With these alterations it is possible to completely finish the wall panel to include insulation and predrilled holes for wiring and pinning, then to ship, and finally place each of these panels on the building's subfloor.

Option A:

Materials:

$1/4" \times 5" \times 5"$ (9×125 mm) HRMS plate iron (2 pieces)

$1/4" \times 5" \times 8"$ ($9 \times 125 \times 200$ mm) HRMS plate iron (2 pieces)

$3/4" \times 8'6"$ (19×2590 mm) CRMS bar (2 pieces) threaded 8" (200 mm) at each end

$3/4"$ (19 mm) washers (4)

$3/4"$ (19 mm) nuts (4)

Procedure:

1) Fit the threaded rod into the routered groove at each end of the log wall.

2) Slip the two 5" (125 mm) square pieces of plate iron under each end of the wall so that the threaded rod passes through a hole in the plate iron. Then attach a washer and nut (Figure 9-15). Alterations will have to be made to the jig base in order to fit the metal plate iron in position.

3) Slip the remaining pieces of plate iron over the threaded rod at the top of the wall. Place a washer and cinch down with a nut.

4) To remove, slip a hook into each eye at the top and winch clear of the ground. A trolley, overhead crane, or derrick truck will be required to move the wall unit for storage.

Note: As the wall shrinks, cinch nuts down.

Option B:

Materials:

$1/4" \times 5" \times 5"$ ($9 \times 125 \times 125$ mm) HRMS plate iron (2 pieces)

$1/4" \times 5" \times 8"$ ($9 \times 125 \times 200$ mm) HRMS plate iron (2 pieces)

$1/2" \times 8'6"$ (12×2590 mm) CRMS bar (2 pieces) threaded 8" (200 mm) at each end

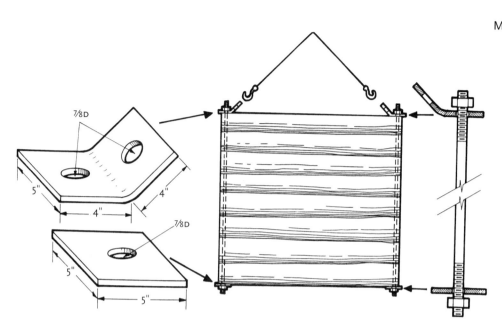

Figure 9-15
Metal clamping
devices to
facilitate
storage and
shipping.

$^1/_2$" (12 mm) washers (4)

$^1/_2$" (12 mm) nuts (4)

Rented metal banding machine (optional)

Procedure:

1) On the bottom log cut a groove $1^1/_2$" (38 mm) deep by $5^1/_2$" (140 mm) wide by $5^1/_2$" (140 mm) long on the underside (Figure 9-16). This groove is necessary to recess the plate and nut of the bar clamp, so that it will not prevent the wall panel from sitting flat on the subfloor.

2) Construct and finish the wall on its jig, insulating, predrilling for electrical wiring, and pinning each log as you work. (Refer to sections 14 and 15, below, for insulation and pinning.)

3) Plumb-cut the wall ends as previously mentioned and rout the spline groove. Though it is possible to use this groove for the threaded bar, it is better to deepen the groove another $^3/_4$" (19 mm) and recess the $^1/_2$" (12 mm) bar into this further groove. In this

Figure 9-16
Finished wall
panel ready for
storage,
shipping, and
assembly on
building's
subfloor.

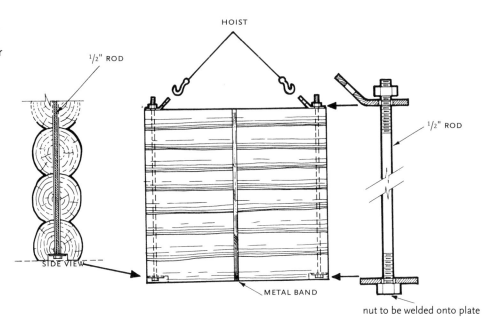

HOIST

1/2" ROD

1/2" ROD

SIDE VIEW

METAL BAND

nut to be welded onto plate

manner the wall can be firmly joined to the post before the bar is removed.

4) To remove the wall from the jig insert the bar clamps and, as an additional precaution, band the wall at its midsection. Use the same metal bands as those used for banding lifts of lumber or cedar shingles together. The entire machine can be rented or purchased from a tool distributor.

5) Refer to section 16, below, for assembly instructions for the finished wall panels onto a subfloor.

9. Constructing mid and corner posts.

The posts, like the wall panels, can be milled and stored ahead of the actual building assembly. They should, however, be stored in a manner which will minimize twisting or warping. For this reason it is best to use dry, straight-grained log material.

Tools: Tape measure, level, square, pencil, hammer, nails.

Procedure:

1) Select straight-grained, sound logs (dry, if possible).

2) Flat-side the logs using one of the mills described, and remove equal waste from each side of the log. All posts must be milled to the same thickness (i.e. 9", or 228 mm). Accuracy is essential. Posts with uneven flat surfaces will lead to gaps between the posts and log infill panels.

3) To obtain a corner post, mill a flat side, then rotate 90° and mill this surface (Figure 9-17). Check the right angle with a carpenter's square.

4) If a mortise and tenon joint is intended at the sill and top plate, allow for the increase in post length.

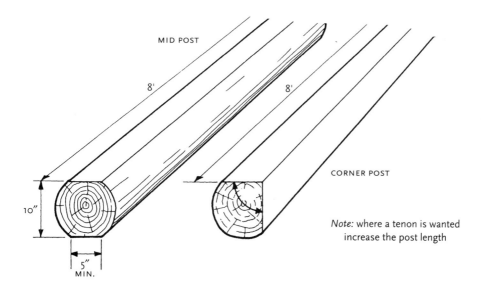

MID POST

8'

8'

10"

5"
MIN.

CORNER POST

Note: where a tenon is wanted increase the post length

Figure 9-17
Mid- and corner
posts ready for
spline grooving.

10. How to spline-groove a post.

To spline-groove a post is to rout a groove down the midline of the post. When matched to the wall panel's groove a spline can be inserted to key the two together. This method replaces the tenon and groove method. An alternative method for cutting a groove is shown in Chapter 8. There is a power tool available (Makita, Hitachi, Mayfell) for cutting grooves. Check with a supplier.

Tools: Eye protection, router, ³/₄" (19 mm) straight bit, chalkline, tape measure, hammer, chainsaw or circular saw.

Materials: 1" × 4" (19 × 89 mm) straightedge, nails.

Procedure:

1) Measure the log diameter and find the center at each end of the log (Figure 9-18).
2) Chalk a line joining these points.
3) Offset a 1" × 4" (19 × 89 mm) straightedge to one side of this line, the distance of the router base radius. Be sure it is parallel to the centerline. This will act as a guide to rout a groove down the center of the log.
4) Make relief cut(s) using a chainsaw or circular saw.
5) Make two passes with the router, extending the bit the second time to the 1⁵/₈" (41 mm) maximum depth.
6) Repeat this procedure for all posts. See Figure 9-18 for a top view of a corner post with the log wall panels keyed in place.

Figure 9-18
Routing a spline
groove in a post.

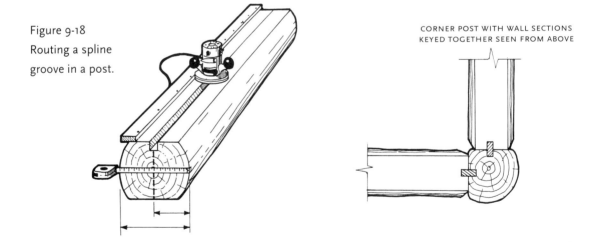

CORNER POST WITH WALL SECTIONS
KEYED TOGETHER SEEN FROM ABOVE

11. How to place the prefabricated log wall on the subfloor.

It is very important that the log sill, or subfloor, on which the log wall will sit is level and even. Distortions in the subfloor can cause gaps between posts and wall panels. Where a standard subfloor is used remember to provide additional support blocking under the posts, although it is preferred that the posts bear directly on the concrete foundation. Refer to Chapter 13, Floor Systems.

The information given here and in sections 12 and 13 describes assembly of individual wall pieces. For information on placing the completely finished wall panels onto a subfloor refer to section 16, below.

Tools: Tape measure, chalkline, 4' (1220 mm) level, come-along, hammer, 3 lb (1.5 kg) sledge, drift pin.

Materials: Posts and wall logs, 2" × 6" (38 × 140 mm) bracing, nails, spikes, rope.

Procedure:

1) Chalk a centerline at the building's perimeter to correspond with the wall panel midline. Square off by taking diagonals. If the log work is planned to provide a drip-cap allowance, offset this centerline 1'–2" (25–50 mm) closer to the foundation edge (Figure 9-19).

Figure 9-19 Work sequence for placing the fabricated walls and posts.

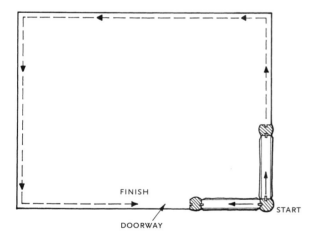

2) Erect and firmly brace a corner post that is nearest a doorway. (Refer to section 12 for methods of attaching a corner post to a log sill.) Work simultaneously toward the door and around the building, aligning the routered grooves on the centerline. A post is followed by a panel of horizontal filler logs, another post, then another

Figure 9-20
Wall
assembly.

panel, and so on around the building until the door is reached again. The wall logs will be drilled for electrical wiring, insulated, and pinned during this assembly procedure.

Note: Until the final top plate is in place, it is important to brace the walls firmly (Figure 9-20).

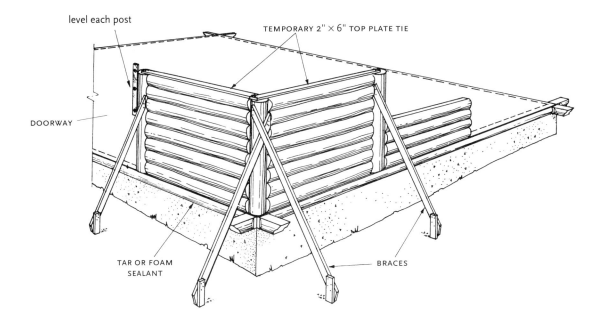

3) Large windows, like doors, are usually placed between posts. Consult the procedures for top plate placement in section 17, below, and openings, in Chapter 11, before actual assembly of the walls.

4) The last log wall panel before reaching the door should be left with only one end plumb-cut. Then, before placing the last door post, the panel can be custom cut to the correct length to adjust for any discrepancies that have arisen. Alternatively, the door opening can purposely be left wider than the required width, allowing the doorway to be framed in later.

5) When assembling a wall panel to sit tight against a post, be careful not to knock the post out of plumb.

6) To keep the assembled walls from spreading apart at the top, a temporary 2" × 6" (38 × 140 mm) tie should span and be nailed to each post, as shown in Figure 9-20.

12. Three methods for joining posts to a log sill.

The posts can be joined to the log sill in a number of ways. A few methods with varying degrees of difficulty are described below. While each of these methods will adequately anchor the posts to the floor, the mortise and tenon method should be used at least for corner posts. Refer to Fasteners and Anchors, Chapter 6, for metal anchors.

Figure 9-21
Three
methods of
post
anchorage to
a sill.

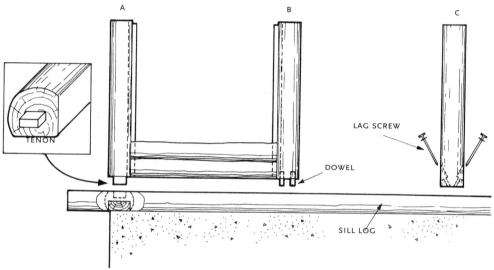

A. Mortise and tenon for joining posts to a log sill (Recommended).

Tools: Eye and ear protection, chainsaw, carpenter's square, slick, $1^1/_2$" (38 mm) chisel and mallet, 4' (1220 mm) level, electric drill with $1^3/_4$" (45 mm) auger bit, tape measure.

Procedure:
1) Cut all the posts to length, measuring from sill log to plate log plus a 4" (100 mm) tenon. If a similar joint is intended to the top plate include the additional tenon length as well (see Chapter 8, section 1).
2) Lay out all tenons using the 2" (50 mm) wide body of a carpenter's square as a template and the centerline of the post.
3) Cut the tenon and chamfer all edges and corners.

4) Lay out only the first corner mortise. The other mortises will be laid out as the wall panels and posts are positioned on the building.

5) Cut the mortise to fit the dimensions of the tenon, using the drill and bit and cleaning with the chisel. Alternatively, construct a modified electrical box cavity jig as described in Chapter 15.

6) Apply a wax-type sealer to the end grain of the tenon and mortise to prevent moisture absorption.

7) Position, plumb, and brace the post securely.

B. Doweling for joining posts to a log sill.

Tools: Electric drill with 5/8" (16 mm) bit, tape measure, hacksaw, file, 3 lb (1.5 kg) hammer, 4' (1220 mm) level.

Materials: 5/8" (16 mm) CRMS round bar.

Procedure:

1) Cut all posts to length, measuring from sill to plate.

2) Bore two 5/8" (16 mm) holes 3" (75 mm) into the bottom of the posts.

3) Insert two pointed 5/8" × 31/2" (16 × 89 mm) steel pins into the holes, so the points protrude.

4) Place post in final position and hammer down on the top of it. The pins will indicate the drilling spots on the sill log.

5) Drill two 5/8" × 3" (16 × 75 mm) holes into the sill log, using the indicated marks as guides.

6) Insert two 51/2" (140 mm) lengths of CRMS round bar into the post holes.

7) Apply a sealer to the underside of the post followed with a layer of moisture barrier foam roll.

8) Position, plumb, and brace the post securely.

C. Joining posts to a log sill with lag screws.

Tools: Electric drill with 1/2" (12 mm) and 3/4" (19 mm) bits, tape measure, 4' (1220 mm) level, crescent wrench.

Materials: 12" (300 mm) lag screws, 1/2" (12 mm) washers, waterproof glue, 3/4" (19 mm) wood dowel.

Procedure:

1) Apply a layer of high density foam roll to the underside of the post for a moisture break.

2) Position, plumb, and brace post securely.

3) Drill two ³/₄" (19 mm) countersink holes 2" (50 mm) diagonally into the post base.

4) Change bits and bore a ¹/₂" (12 mm) hole into each of the countersunk holes diagonally through the post base, but not into the sill log.

5) Secure the post to the sill by placing a lag screw with a washer into each hole, embedding it into the sill log. Countersink the head.

6) Plug the hole, using a wooden dowel and glue.

13. How to join infill logs to posts.

With the first corner post nearest to a door positioned, plumbed, and braced, the assembly of plumb-cut infill pieces can proceed. Insulating the lateral grooves of the infill logs, pinning the logs, pre-drilling for electrical wiring, and cutting of window headers will all be done as the numbered wall logs are placed. Detailed instructions for these steps follow.

Tools: Electric drill with ⁵/₈"(16 mm) extended auger bit, hammer, 4' (1220 mm) level, sledge hammer, drift pin, come-along, lumberman's crayon.

Materials: ³/₄" × 3" × 8' (19 × 75 × 2440 mm) marine grade plywood key strips cut from 4' × 8' (1200 × 2400 mm) plywood, 12" (300 mm) spikes with washers, ¹/₂" (12 mm) nylon rope, lag screws, tar or foam roll (foam roll serves as an air and moisture seal and can be purchased at any lumber store).

Procedure:

1) Fit the plywood key strips into the groove of the posts. Infill logs are then free to slide down the keyed spline strips during settling.

2) Apply a layer of foam roll to the underside of the first flat-surfaced infill log, and snug up against the post. The spline will fit into the spline groove of the infill log (Figure 9-22).

3) Drill a ⁵/₈" (16 mm) hole through the bottom log, then lag screw

this first log to the subfloor. The holes will be covered by the lateral groove of the following log.

4) Predrill for electrical wiring where appropriate (see Chapter 15).

5) Place the next infill log, snug it up against the post, and then check for fit. The ends should be flush. To keep these ends in alignment fit a temporary spline into the grooves of the infill panel (Figure 9-22).

Figure 9-22
Placement of prefabricated walls on the building's subfloor.

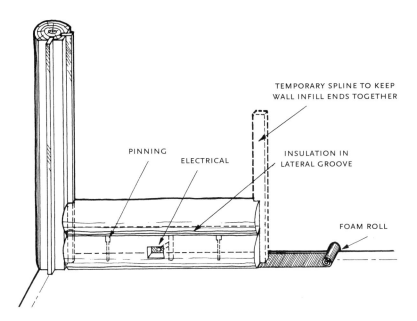

TEMPORARY SPLINE TO KEEP
WALL INFILL ENDS TOGETHER

PINNING

ELECTRICAL

INSULATION IN
LATERAL GROOVE

FOAM ROLL

6) Lift the free end of the infill log and insulate the lateral groove (see section 14, below).

7) Reposition the log and pin it securely (see section 15, below), and mark lightly with a crayon to indicate where pins are. Do not pin where a window will be placed. Most large windows, however, will be flanked by posts (see Chapter 11).

8) Continue placing the infill logs. Check periodically to make sure the post is not knocked out-of-plumb.

9) Continue to construct the wall to top plate height. Place another post, then another wall infill panel and so on until the building walls are erected. Remember to number all the infill logs. This is done so that they do not get misplaced in the wall, since once the wall logs are dismantled from the construction jig they can easily be mixed up.

14. Insulating the lateral groove.

Although the insulation in the lateral groove is not visible, it plays an important thermal role and care must be taken to ensure that it fills the entire groove. Substances as technical as polyurethane foam (injected), and as basic as moss have been used for insulation. However, as the most commonly used material is fiberglass, this is the material that is discussed below.

Tools: Sharp, long-bladed knife.

Materials: 3" (75 mm) thick fiberglass batts.

Procedure:

1) Cut the batts into 3" (75 mm) strips (depending on the average depth of the lateral grooves).
2) Check the fit of the log and then raise it a couple of inches, using a block of wood.
3) Place the insulation into the groove by hand. As shown in Figure 9-23, in order to fill the groove completely turn the batt on edge.

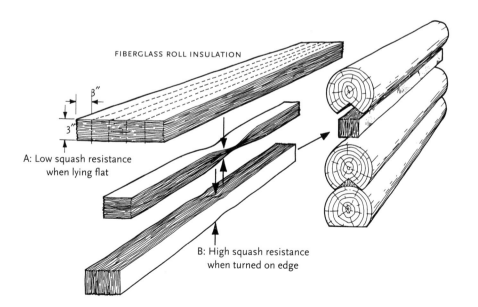

FIBERGLASS ROLL INSULATION

3"

3"

A: Low squash resistance when lying flat

B: High squash resistance when turned on edge

Figure 9-23
Insulating the
lateral groove.

15. How to dowel or pin a wall log.

Doweling and pinning are two mechanical means of arresting distortions in the wood members. Doweling uses hardwood dowels or pegs (usually 1", or 25 mm in diameter) which are hammered into holes which have been drilled down the midline of the log and into the log below. Doweling is usually reserved for those long-length log walls which do not have intersecting partition walls. Primarily they function to prevent the logs from twisting out of position, but they also add strength to the whole wall. Dowels should be staggered (i.e. not aligned one above the other in the wall).

In pinning, 1/2" (12 mm) steel pins or spikes are used instead of wood dowels. They function in the same way as dowels unless they have a head (i.e. 12", or 300 mm spikes). When enlarged with a washer the head of the spike serves to create downward pressure, effectively pressing the pinned log into the log below. This is advantageous for log infill as the shorter, lighter logs often "float" due to the fiberglass insulation within the lateral groove. Thus spike pins, while aiding in the prevention of any twisting, will also produce a tighter fit between log wall members than will dowels.

The builder should be warned, however, that unless spike pins are correctly installed, problems can result. Merely spiking one log to another without careful pre-drilling will eventually cause gaps to appear between the logs when they have completed their drying process. It is essential, therefore, to drill a slightly oversize hole completely through the log to be pinned. After this is done, insert the spike and washer, then sledge hammer the spike firmly into the log below. The spike head and washer will compress the wood of the top log (Figure 9-24) but it is free to undergo its seasonal expansion and contraction while still being firmly pinned. A similar procedure is used in cabinetmaking, when two pieces of wood are fastened together with screws.

Tools: Electric drill with 5/8" (16 mm) ship's auger bit (for pins), 1" (25 mm) auger (for dowels), tape measure, 3 lb (1.5 kg) sledge hammer, drift pin.

Materials: 12"–14" (300–350 mm) spikes with washers or 1" (25 mm) hardwood doweling.

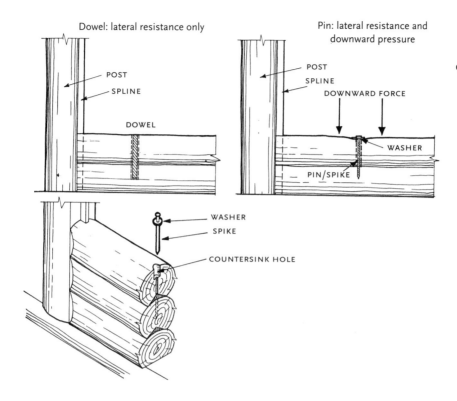

Figure 9-24
Pinning or doweling the infill logs.

Procedure:

1) Identify all the logs where openings will be situated, and keep well away from these spots when positioning steel pins.

2) Pinning/doweling is to be done as each log is insulated and placed in its final position in the wall.

3) Pins/dowels should be placed on the midline of the log spaced approximately 5' (1.5 m) apart so that the lateral groove of the following log will conceal the hole (Figure 9-24).

4) Doweling a log

   Drill a 1" (25 mm) hole completely through the log and half way into the lower log. Then hammer the dowel in place and cut it flush with the top surface of the log.

5) Pinning a log

   Drill a ⁵/₈" (16 mm) hole completely through the top log but not into the lower log. Countersink the spike head, where necessary. Then drop the spike (with washer) through the top log and sledge hammer it into the log below, pressing the head into the log surface.

6) Continue the process of insulating, predrilling for electrical, and pinning or doweling each log until all the walls and posts are up. When this has been done the top plate is ready to be placed.

16. Erecting finished wall panels on the subfloor.

When the wall panels are constructed and finished on the building site, there is not much more work involved in placing them onto a foundation subfloor. But placing entire panels requires a crane truck and as such it is important to be as thoroughly prepared as possible. You will need at least four people: one to handle the wall sections on the truck ,and three to handle the wall sections on the subfloor. The clamping mechanism for such a unit assembly is described earlier (Figures 9-15, 9-16).

Tools: Sledge hammer, crescent wrench, hammer, 4' (1220 mm) level, tape measure, chalkline, electric drill with 1/2" (12 mm), 3/4" (19 mm), 1" (25 mm) auger bits, come-along, rope.

Materials: Foam roll, 2" × 6" (38 × 140 mm) bracing, nails, 12" (300 mm) spikes with washers, 6" (150 mm) lag screws, lumberman's crayon.

Procedure:
1) Label all the wall panel and post pieces and keep a written record of their assembly sequence on the foundation subfloor.
2) Start by positioning and bracing the corner post closest to a doorway. Apply a foam roll moisture barrier to its bottom and fasten it to the subfloor using one of the methods previously described.
3) Chalk a centerline around the perimeter of the subfloor.
4) Place the wall panel so its spline groove mates with the spline of the post. Make sure that there is a foam barrier between the wall and the subfloor; that any electrical access hole on the wall panel has been marked on the subfloor; and that the wall is aligned on the chalked centerline, and is plumb and well braced.
5) Fasten the wall panel to the subfloor by lag screwing it to the floor.
6) Remove the bar clamps (Figure 9-16, above).
7) Position, plumb, and secure the next post so that its spline mates with the panel groove.

8) Attach a temporary brace across the tops of the posts, as shown in Figure 9-25.

9) Repeat this procedure until all the walls are up.

10) When this has been done, place the top plate and roof members (see sections 17 and 18, below).

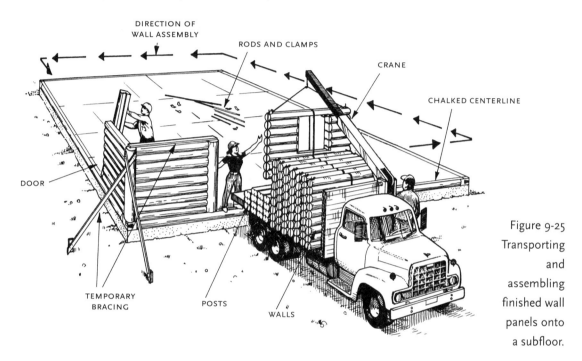

Figure 9-25 Transporting and assembling finished wall panels onto a subfloor.

17. Constructing and fitting a dimensional top plate.

Once the walls are in place, the top plate ties them together and provides a level surface on which to support the roof. The procedure outlined here is for a dimensional frame top plate. Its primary advantage over a heavy log or timber top plate is in the simplicity of construction and placement. However, if a second storey with exposed log or timber joists is desired, a solid log or timber top plate is recommended to allow for joinery while still retaining the top plate strength. This type of top plate particularly suits a conventional frame roof system as it provides flat surfaces for truss and soffit work (Figure 9-26).

Basically, this top plate uses structural frame trim boards which sandwich, and are bolted to, the posts. The top infill wall log is recessed into the cavity. The settling space created after shrinkage of the horizontal

Figure 9-26
Constructing
and placing a
dimensional
top plate.

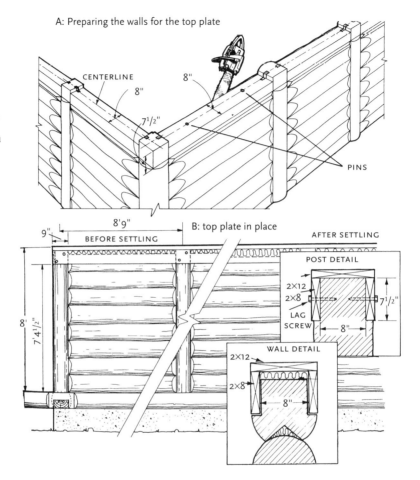

filler logs is concealed by the trim boards, and a weather-tight seal is still maintained. It is important to have trim boards wide enough to maintain this seal after the walls have settled (usually a 2" × 8" (38 × 184 mm) will suffice). An 8' (2440 mm) wall built of green logs will have an estimated 4" (100 mm) settling.

Since the posts and structural trim boards support the weight of the roof, it is important that they are sound, and that the span between vertical posts will not exceed Building Code specifications. A span of 8' (2440 mm) between posts is recommended.

Tools: Eye and ear protection, chainsaw, chalkline, tape measure, hammer, handsaw, drill with ⅝" (16 mm) auger bit.

Materials: 2" × 8" (38 × 184 mm) and 2" × 12" (38 × 286 mm) rough fir, ⁵/₈" (16 mm) lag bolts, glue, insulation, nails.

Procedure:
1) All the posts should be at a level height from the floor (e.g. 8', or 2440 mm).
2) The height of all the wall panels should be 1" (25 mm) lower than the top of the posts, with the top log pinned to the log below.
3) Square off and chalk a line along the center top of the log walls. It should strike the top center of each post as well (Figure 9-26a).
4) Chalk a parallel line 4" (100 mm) on either side of this center line, leaving a space of 8" (200 mm) between the inner and outer lines. If your logs are not very large 6" (150 mm) will suffice, but in that case you must make similar adjustments to the top plate.
5) Using the inside and outside lines as guides, cut a ledge equal to the trim board depth around the inside and outside walls of the building.
   Note: These lines can be marked out and the ledge cut while the wall panel is still in its construction jig.
6) Bolt or lag screw the structural trim boards to the posts. Do not attach the trim boards to the filler logs, as this will prevent their settling.
7) Run a bead of glue along the top surface of the filler logs, place an 8" (200 mm) strip of insulation in the space, then run a bead of glue on the underside of a 2" × 12" (38 × 286 mm) top plate and nail this plate to the trim boards. As the filler logs settle, the insulation will be pulled down to fill the void.

18. Preparing and fitting a log top plate.

A log top plate is used for houses which have second storey log floor joists, and where cantilevered strength is needed. The integration of notched corners in Chapter 10 requires a log top plate for just this reason. The problems associated with handling a long, heavy log can be overcome by splicing shorter lengths together. However, such splices must be made over a post.

The log top plate will bear directly on the vertical posts and will support a portion of the weight of the roof between the post span. The infill wall logs do not support any roof weight but are free to settle on their own. Because this top plate is a structural beam it must conform in size to the amount of roof weight it supports over a given span.

Consider a 32' × 40' (9.75 × 12 m) building, with a 4/12 roof pitch, and with only one ridge pole roof support, built in an area subject to 40 lbs per sq. ft. snow load. According to the information for calculating beam sizes in Appendix III, the minimum size of the top plate needed for an 8' (2440 mm) span between posts would be 6" × 6" (150 × 150 mm) or 4" × 8" (100 × 200 mm). We would, however, be using a large log to match the infill logs and post sizes (Figure 9-27).

Tools: Eye and ear protection, chainsaw, tape measure, chalkline, electric drill with 5/8" (16 mm) auger bit, handsaw, hammer.

Materials: Plate logs flat-surfaced on two sides to 8" (200 mm) thickness, 5/8" (16 mm) steel pins, insulation, 1" × 8" (19 × 184 mm) skirting boards, nails.

Procedure:
1) All the posts should be at a level height from the floor (e.g. 8', or 2440 mm).
2) All the wall panels should be at a level height of 1" (25 mm) lower than the top of the posts with the top logs pinned to the log below.
3) Square off and chalk a line along the center top of the log walls. It should strike the top center of each post as well.
4) Chalk a parallel line 4" (100 mm) on either side of this centerline, leaving a space 8" (200 mm) between the inner and outer lines. If the logs are not very large, 6" (150 mm) will suffice.
5) Using the inside and outside lines as guides, cut a ledge equal to the skirting board depth around the inside and outside walls of the building (Figure 9-26a).

    Note: These steps can be marked out and the ledge cut while the wall panel is still in its construction jig.
6) Prepare the flat-surfaced top plate logs by cutting a 1" (25 mm) deep rabbet groove down each side as shown in the inset diagrams of Figure 9-27. There should be 8" (200 mm) between the rabbet grooves and remember to always work from a centerline.

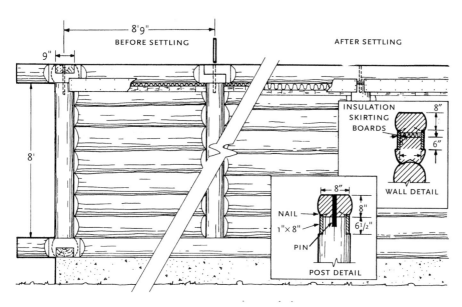

Figure 9-27
Constructing a
log or timber
top plate.

7) Place the sidewall top plate logs on the building first, making scarf splices over every second or third post where necessary. Allow projection at both the front and back of the building for roof overhang support.

8) Place the gable wall top plate logs on the building and join these at the corners, splicing where necessary (see Chapter 6 for joinery instructions).

9) Pin the top plate securely to each post with $^5/_8$" (16 mm) pins as an alternative to mortise and tenon. (Mortise and tenon is recommended.)

10) Insulate the space between the top plate and infill logs, and nail the skirting boards to the top plate—never to the infill logs.

Note: Walls exceeding 16' (5 m) in length and without interior partitions for bracing should include the beams to tie the walls together. Tie beams also provide support for second storey floor joists. They are placed before the roof system, in the same manner as girder beams, as described in Chapter 13, "Housed Dovetail."

19. Log post and beam method for a basement wall.

Basements do not have to be dark, damp holes, rarely used except as storage areas or laundry rooms. Building a house into a gentle hillside, or grading to provide a slope, allows a basement to be constructed so that one wall—usually facing south for maximum solar benefit—has a fully exposed ground access. Such a ground access wall provides a separate entrance into the basement, as well as good ventilation and illumination.

A long-standing problem for log homes with notched corner construction has been how to build this basement wall while keeping within the natural log theme. The notched corner construction method could not be employed because of settling problems, and the difficulty of joining the log work to the concrete walls. A conventional frame wall would alter the appearance of the house.

The answer, not only for a post and beam house but for notched corner construction as well, is to build this wall using the post and beam method. It serves the purpose of providing aesthetic continuity without the worry of settling problems. Described below are the steps for constructing a log post and beam basement wall with an open timber ceiling (Figure 9-28).

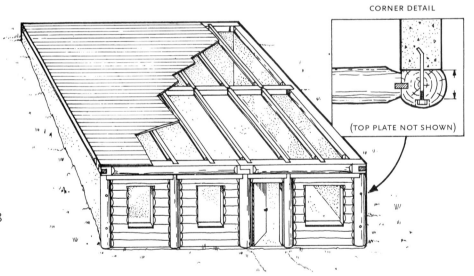

CORNER DETAIL

(TOP PLATE NOT SHOWN)

Figure 9-28
Basement
post and
beam.

Tools: Electric drill with 3/4" (19 mm) and 1" (25 mm) auger bits, crescent wrench.

Materials: Foam roll, 5/8" (16 mm) threaded anchor bolts (for posts), 1" (25 mm) wood dowels, glue.

Procedure:
1) Construct the concrete foundation walls to a height of 8' (2440 mm). While the concrete is still wet embed two 5/8" (16 mm) threaded bolts in each wall, as shown in Figure 9-28. In this diagram, where the corner posts are 10" (250 mm) thick, the anchor bolts project 9" (225 mm) from the concrete face.
2) Apply a layer of foam roll to the wall face and bolt the corner posts as shown.
3) Assemble the wall panels as previously described.
4) Place the top plate as previously described. Here a log top plate is shown supporting a log girder and floor joists.

20. Window and door openings.

Refer to Chapter 11, Openings.

Log Blockwork: Wall System

Note: The procedures described in this chapter can be directly applied to long log, notched corner building (blockwork).

An attractive option in post and beam building is the addition of round notch corners. In this chapter are described procedures for constructing and integrating these graceful corners, using the log wall infill method described in the last chapter. It is important to be aware of the wood's shrinkage factor here, since ignorance of this can lead to failure in combining the notched corners with the vertical posts.

If the log materials used for these notched corners are green (with a high moisture content), the roof overhang must have its weight supported by the strength of the top plate. If the roof weight were to rest directly on the corners, the roof would sag at its corners after settling. To prevent this, every effort should be made to obtain dry log materials for the corners. However, this chapter will describe the steps for corner construction when using green materials.

First, the wall system for this sample building will be placed on the subfloor as explained in Chapter 9, section 11. However, there will be no corner posts, and the walls will stop 4' (1220 mm) short of the chalked centerline. This is done to accommodate the notched corners. The chalked centerline refers to the perimeter line inset 4" (100 mm) from the edge of the subfloor. The walls will be centered on this line and provide an overhang of approximately 3" (25 mm) for a drip cap. The notched corners will be taken from a small 8' × 8' (2440 × 2440 mm) square building (walls only) constructed in the center of the subfloor (or elsewhere). The log materials will be 14' (4.25 m) lengths to allow for the curved log ends. The logs described here have a 12" (300 mm) mean diameter, but may be either larger or smaller, to match the size of the other wall logs. The directions for construction of the notched corner building follow. These procedures described can be applied to any size of notched corner building without integration into a post and beam building (Figure 10-1).

Figure 10-1
Log post and
beam building
with round
notch corners.

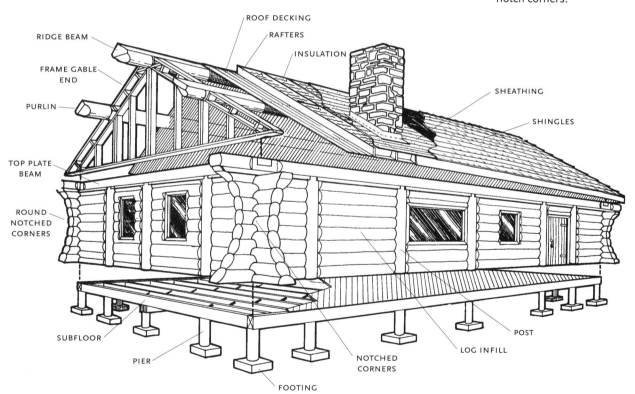

ROOF DECKING
RAFTERS
INSULATION
RIDGE BEAM
FRAME GABLE END
SHEATHING
PURLIN
SHINGLES
TOP PLATE BEAM
ROUND NOTCHED CORNERS
SUBFLOOR
PIER
NOTCHED CORNERS
LOG INFILL
POST
FOOTING

1. How to prepare and place the first logs.

The objective here is to flat-surface the bottoms of the first logs so they will sit flat on the subfloor. Since we are working with an average of 12" (300 mm) logs (butt size), simply cut one log in half lengthwise to form the first two sill logs. The next two logs, which notch over the top and form the first "round," should be large enough to have a 5"–6" flat surface and still be 12" (300 mm) thick. For this reason, use 14" (355 mm) logs. Before notching these first logs together, chalk an 8' square (2440 × 2440 mm) on the subfloor deck. The centers of the first logs will be positioned on these lines, as shown in Figures 10-2 and 10-3.

Figure 10-2
An 8' square
chalked onto
the subsurface.

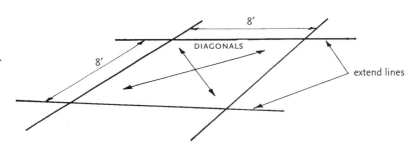

Figure 10-3

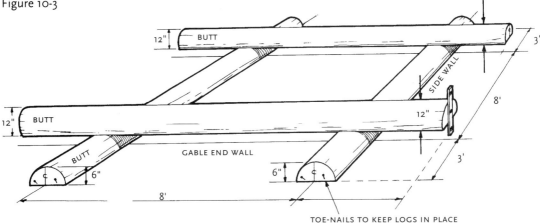

Tools: Chalkline, tape measure, level, hammer.

Materials: Flat-surfaced logs, nails.

Procedure:

1) Using one of the methods described in Chapter 5, flat-surface the first logs to approximately the sizes shown in Figure 10-3.

     Note: The dimensions may vary, depending on the size of the logs in your building, but the procedure remains the same.

2) Mark chalklines on the subfloor to form an 8' square (2440 × 2440 mm), taking diagonals. Leave the extended lines to aid in placing the first logs, as shown in Figure 10-2.

3) Chalk centerlines on the flat undersurface of each log.

4) Position the two "halved" sidewall logs on the centerlines, and toe-nail them to the subfloor to prevent movement.

5) Position the next two wall logs on top of the first two, so that their centerlines are directly over the chalked lines on the floor (Figure 10-3).

6) The butt ends of the logs should be aligned as shown.

7) This first round is now ready to be scribed and notched together.

2. Scribing and cutting the first bottom log notches.

It will be necessary to notch the two top logs down over the logs below so that their undersurfaces lie flat on the subfloor. The process of scribing and cutting out the notch waste wood can be done in either one or two steps, depending on the accuracy of your scribing technique. Since there is no lateral groove to contend with at this time the process can usually be accomplished in one step.

A good chainsaw, when handled correctly, becomes a precision cutting tool. With a little practice you will find it no great feat to actually split the wood along a pencil line, and cut out an entire round notch using only the saw and no chisels. The trick to cutting out a round notch with a chainsaw is to first "knife" the scribe line with a utility razor knife, and then use a chipper chain rather than a chisel-tooth chain. The former can cut and plane a curved surface, while the latter will only bite into the wood and rip in a straight line.

However, if the scribing was inaccurate, accurate cutting will not correct the error. Remember, increasing the scribe width results in less ac-curacy.

Tools: Scriber (a #85 Starret divider with a bubble attachment is recom-mended), eye and ear protection, chainsaw with chipper chain, razor knife, level.

Procedure:

Figure 10-4
Scribing and
cutting the
bottom log
notches.

    1) Set the scriber to match the distance between the floor and under-surface of the log to be scribed (Figure 10-4a).

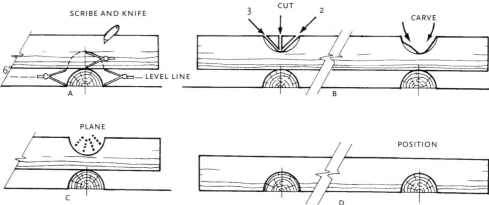

    2) Keeping the points of the scriber vertical (one above the other) and the body level, scribe the contours of the log below onto the log above, as shown in Figure 10-4a. Do both sides of the log.

    3) Repeat this procedure for all four corners.

    4) Once all the corners have been scribed, turn the logs and secure them so that the scribed notches are facing up.

    5) With the razor knife, make an incision ⅛"–¼" (3–6 mm) deep around the notch outline. Knifing the scribe line will sever the wood fibers along this line. As you plane down to this line with the chainsaw the wood will suddenly peel away, indicating that you have reached the limit of the notch. Knifing will also help to pre-vent the wood from splintering at the edges of the notch.

    6) Remove the waste wood of the notch by cutting, carving, and plan-ing, as shown in Figures 10-4b and c. Refer to the procedures for

rough and finish notching detailed in sections 4 and 5, below. All notches should be slightly concave so that the edges only will bear the weight of the log.

7) Repeat the cutting procedure on all the notches, and position the logs so that their chalked midlines align with the centerline on the subfloor.

8) Toe-nail these two logs to the subfloor to prevent movement (Figure 10-4d).

3. Placing the wall logs.

The visual impression of a building will be better if each course of horizontal logs is on the same plane. (For example, if the third log in one wall is set at the same height as the third log and so on, in all the wall panels of the building.) The builder should strive to match wall logs so that they are on the same plane for each entire wall of the building.

If your log materials are fairly uniform in diameter, and you remain aware of the need to maintain levels as you work, there will be no difficulty in doing so. A method of checking and maintaining equal wall log heights on the construction jig was described at the beginning of Chapter 9. But as these notched corners are not prefabricated in a jig, it will be necessary to take measurements and make the appropriate adjustments.

As the walls are going up, always alternate the direction of butt ends on every course round (Figure 10-5). When positioning a log on the wall always place it over the center of the wall. Remember that markedly bowed logs should be placed with the bow facing outside the building. It is unlikely that with such short-length walls any logs will be discarded due to excessive bowing. However, a log considered too bowed or bent would be one with the majority of its weight not resting over the center of the wall. During the scribing process secure the log so it will not move. Finally, where curved log ends are desired, the log ends' lateral groove must be prepared as the wall is constructed. Refer to the layout and cutting procedures for arched openings in Chapter 11, Openings.

4. Scribing and cutting a rough notch.

"Rough" notching is the term used to describe the initial notching that sets the top log down close to the log below, prior to finish scribing the en-

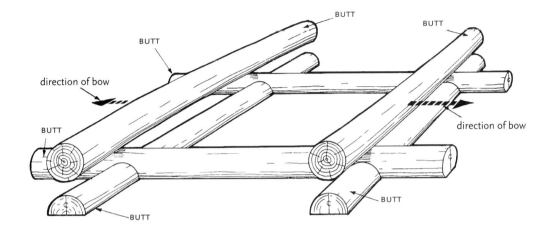

Figure 10-5
Placing wall
logs with
bows facing
outward, and
alternating
butt ends
direction on
each course.

tire log. However, it does not mean that the notch is loose and rough. On the contrary, the rough notch demands accuracy due to the large amount of wood removed initially. It must be noted that the closer the logs lie to each other after rough notching, the more accurate the finish scribe will be. Large inaccuracies near the corners of the notch cannot usually be scribed out at the finish scribe stage.

Tools: Eye and ear protection, chainsaw with chipper chain, utility knife, level, axe, indelible pencil, scriber (with bubble attachment recommended), peavey.

Procedure:
1) Align the log on the building, alternating the butts and tops.
2) Adjust the scribers to within 1"–2" (25–50 mm) of touching the log below and scribe the log on both sides of the notch, as in Figure 10-6a. Readjust the scriber and repeat this procedure for the opposite end of the log.

    Note: Do not move the log during the scribing process, and be sure to hold the scriber in a perpendicular and level position.
3) Turn the log upright and make an incision 1/8"–1/4" (3–6 mm) deep with a utility knife around the notch outline. This cut-line will help to identify the boundary of the notch when brushing down to the line with the chainsaw. It also helps to keep the notch edges from splintering and fraying. Some builders prefer to take less wood out

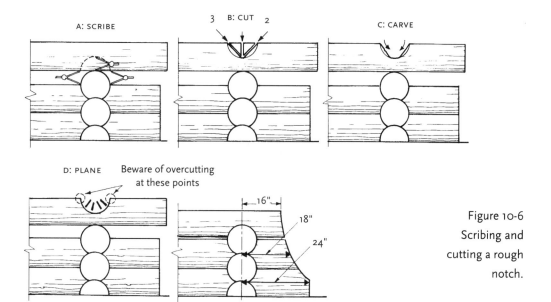

Figure 10-6
Scribing and
cutting a rough
notch.

for the rough notch and to increase the scriber distance for the finished scribe. Where this is done the utility knife cut can be omitted.

4) To cut the notch make straight cuts in the sequence 1, 2, and 3, as shown in Figure 10-6b, using the full length of the chainsaw bar. This will remove the bulk of the waste wood.

5) Carve out the side portions close to the scribe line, working the full length of the chainsaw bar from the top of the notch to the bottom (Figure 10-6c).

6) Plane the notch to the scribe line, as shown in Figure 10-6d, keeping the bar at right angles to the wood surface. Criss-crossing the planing cuts produces a smoother surface. This planing is only necessary at the top of the notch where a minimal amount of wood will be removed during the finish scribe. Be aware that there is a danger of overcutting at this point. Use the full length of the chainsaw bar when cutting the notch.

7) Repeat this cutting procedure for the opposite end of the log.

8) After the two notches of the log are cut roll the rough notched log back into position and realign it, with its weight over the wall. Trim any large knots so that the logs sit close to each other in preparation for finish scribing.

9) Prior to finish scribing the log ends must be trimmed, or curved if desired. See the view of a rough notched log in Figure 10-6e, showing the ends trimmed in preparation for finish scribing. Measure the degree of curve using the vertical centerline on the log ends as a reference.

5. Finish scribing a wall log.

The process of scribing transfers the shape and contours of one surface onto another surface, using a scriber. Here the shape of the bottom log is reproduced onto the undersurface of the log above it. During the finish scribe the whole length of the log is scribed, on both the inside and the outside of the wall. Every curve and knot must be identified so that, when the waste wood of the lateral groove and notches is removed, a self-draining, tight, chinkless fit will join the two logs together. The scriber must be held level and vertical, with the points one above the other. It becomes increasingly difficult to achieve accuracy as the scriber setting is widened (Figure 10-7).

Tools: Scribers.

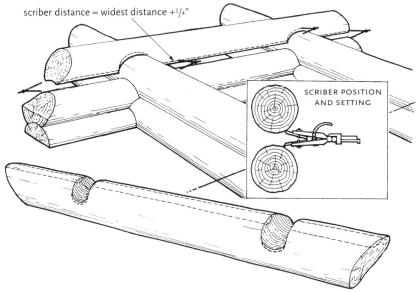

scriber distance = widest distance +$^1/_4$"

SCRIBER POSITION
AND SETTING

Figure 10-7
Finish scribing
a rough
notched log.

Procedure:

1) Determine the scriber setting by locating the widest gap between the two logs and then increase the scriber distance $1/8$" to $1/4$" (3–6 mm). The purpose of this procedure is to mate the two surfaces completely, and thus a continuous length of waste wood will have to be removed. Of course, the scriber setting will be only for the gap in the walls themselves. The log ends will be outside the living area, and so do have to keep out the weather.

2) Scribe the full length of the log, up and over the notches, around the log ends, and down the other side of the log. Make sure that:

   a) The scribers are held level and vertical with one point directly above the other.

   b) The scriber setting is not changed until the entire log is completed.

   c) A good, readable scribe line is visible. Wetting the scribe path with a fine spray of water will make an easily readable line when an indelible pencil is used.

   d) The entire log is scribed, even the log ends.

   e) The log is not moved until it has been completely scribed.

6. Cutting a round notch.

Removing the waste wood in a notch is accomplished with either an axe or a chainsaw. The steps for cutting a round notch with a chainsaw are described here. Just as important as one's cutting technique and practice is the choice of a cutting chain. I have never seen a satisfactory round notch cut with anything but a chipper chain. The rounded back of the tooth promotes the carving and brushing action necessary for cutting a round notch.

Tools: Eye and ear protection, chainsaw with chipper chain, utility knife, peavey, straightedge (level).

Procedure:

1) Wedge or log dog, with the notch upright, so the log will not move. Using the utility knife make a $1/8$"–$1/4$" (3–6 mm) incision around the notch outline. This cut-line helps to identify the boundary of the notch when planing down to the line with the chainsaw, while

also preventing the notch edges from splintering and fraying. If the wood is extremely dry and hard, a chisel and mallet will do the job. Follow the scribe line exactly during this step (Figure 10-8a).

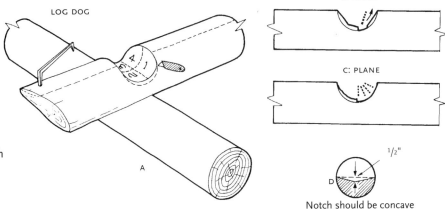

Figure 10-8
Cutting a finish round notch with a chainsaw.

Notch should be concave

2) The notch is worked in quarters, sawing half the wood out from one side of the log, then sawing the remainder out from the other side of the log.

3) Working from the bottom of the notch and on up the sides, carve out the bulk of the wood close to the scribe line (Figure 10-8b). The nose of the bar should be slightly deeper than the outer lip of the notch. To keep from overcutting the scribe line use a pivoting action, keeping the bar nose stabilized at the center of the notch, and carve with the portion of the bar that is 6" (150 mm) or so from the nose.

4) Plane down to the scribe line until the wood breaks cleanly away from the knife cut. The planing action is from the top of the notch down toward the bottom. Use the nose of the bar, keeping it perpendicular to the wood's surface. This action should resemble a sweeping motion. Criss-crossing these plane cuts with a light pressure produces a smoother outer lip surface (Figure 10-8c).

5) Complete the notches and use a straightedge (level) to check that the notch is concave. The center of the notch should be approximately 1/2" (12 mm) below the outer lips (Figure 10-8d).

Note of caution: Refer to Chainsaw Safety in Chapter 4. Use extreme caution when using the nose of the chainsaw as kickback can occur.

7. Cutting a lateral groove.

The lateral groove, if properly scribed and cut, provides a self-draining, chinkless join between the logs which, when insulated, prevents wind and weather from entering and heat from escaping the building (this groove and the notch are insulated at a later stage) (Figure 10-9).

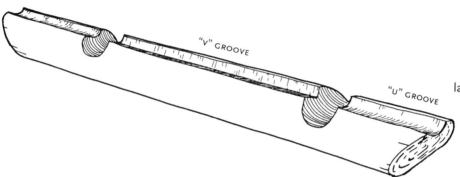

"V" GROOVE

"U" GROOVE

Figure 10-9
A log with completed notches and lateral groove.

Tools: Eye and ear protection, chainsaw, pencil, round axe, peavey.

Procedure:

1) Pencil the desired angle of cut (normal or wide scribe) on the inside of the notches, as shown. For a description of the lateral cuts see Chapter 9, section 4.

2) Position, then wedge or log dog so your saw blade enters at the proper angle and depth.

3) Keeping the blade 1/8"–1/4" (3–6 mm) inside the line, cut down the length of the log between the notches. Repeat the cut for the opposite scribe line and remove waste wood.

4) Using an axe, pare with the grain down to the scribe line. Do not remove the scribe line.

5) Round the log ends back 12" (300 mm) or so to avoid the unsightly "V" groove showing. This is easily accomplished working from the end of the log using the length of the chainsaw bar.

6) When this has been done, position the log back on the building and check for any gaps in fit.

8. Leveling the walls.

Alternating butt and top ends on each round will take care of most of the leveling work, because in a building of such small size there is little chance the wall heights will deviate very much. Nevertheless, it is important that all the walls are level, especially when approaching the last top logs. Below is the procedure for taking level readings and adjusting for any discrepancies.

Log walls can only be leveled on "even" rounds, there being an equal number of butt and top ends per corner. On a four-sided building only two logs can be leveled at one time. Since the subfloor is already level, measurements will be made/taken from this surface.

Tools: Eye and ear protection, chainsaw, tape measure, level, scriber, peavey, pencil.

Materials: Small spacer blocks for leveling.

Procedure:
1) From the level foundation or floor measure up each end of the wall to determine which of the two walls is lowest. Place the larger of the two logs on the low wall.
2) Rough notch the logs in place, then take a measurement at each corner and note heights (Figure 10-10).
3) Block the low corner of each log until it is level.
    Note: If there is a large height discrepancy it may be necessary to finish the leveling procedure on the next even round to avoid taking too much wood from one end.
4) Scribe the entire log. Do not adjust the scriber or move the log during the scribing process.
5) Continue with the construction of the walls, leveling when necessary on the even rounds.
    Special Note: For those who wish to build a long-log, notched corner house (blockwork), proceed now to Chapter 12, Roof Structures.

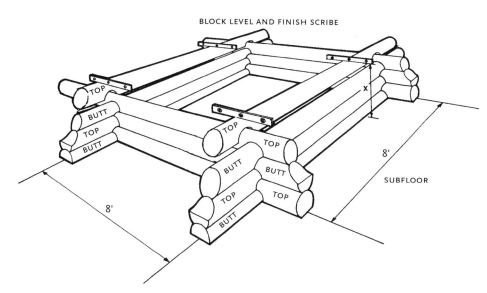

BLOCK LEVEL AND FINISH SCRIBE

Figure 10-10
Leveling the
wall height on
an even round.

9. Preparing the final round to receive the log top plate.

It is necessary to obtain an even wall height with a flat top surface to receive the final top plate (see Chapter 9, section 18). This wall height should equal the infill panel wall heights—in this case, 7'11" (2413 mm), and the size of the last round logs must be carefully chosen.

Tools: Eye and ear protection, chainsaw, scriber, tape measure, chalkline.

Procedure:

1) Upon completion, the wall height should contain an even number of logs (i.e. 8 or 10). The last two logs must cap the ones below, and the entire top surface must be flattened. So that these last two logs will not have their notches cut off during the flat-surfacing process, the log below must also be notched (Figure 10-11). Since these two sidewall logs must be notched to accept the last two gable wall logs and still provide a 6"–8" (150–200 mm) flat top surface, they must be of a substantial size. If you are working with 12" (300 mm) size logs, these two logs would be 14"–15" (355–380 mm) in diameter. Scribe and fit these two large sidewall logs in place.

2) Measure an equal distance from the floor—in this case, 7'11" (2413 mm) to match the infill wall height—chalk a horizontal line, then

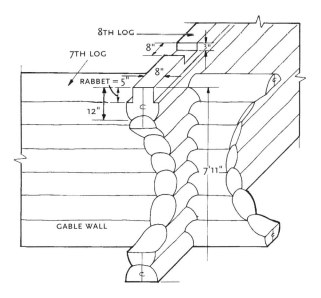

Figure 10-11
Preparing the
final sidewall
log.

cut a flat surface along the length of each log. (See the flat-surfacing procedures described in Chapter 5.)

3) Working from chalked centerlines lay out and cut the half lap notch 3" (75 mm) deep by 8" (200 mm) wide, as shown in Figure 10-11.

4) In final preparation, cut 5" (125 mm) deep rabbets down the length of each log, inside and outside. These rabbet grooves will be required for the application of skirting boards after the top plate is in place.

5) Obtain a 10"–12" (250–300 mm) diameter log and flat-surface two sides to an even 8" (200 mm) thick (Figure 10-12). Place this log into the square notches on the building and scribe it in place.

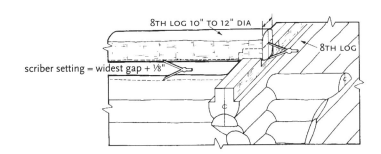

Figure 10-12
Scribing and
fitting the
gable wall
log.

6) Flat-surface these last wall logs to produce a flat, even surface for the log top plate (Figure 10-13).

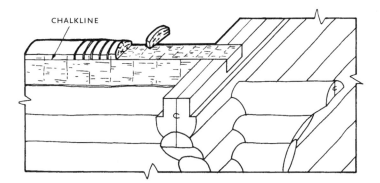

CHALKLINE

Figure 10-13
Flat-surfacing
the gable wall
in preparation
for the top
plate.

10. How to plumb-cut and spline-groove the notch corners.

After flat-surfacing the top log members to receive the top plate the walls can be cut into four equal segments. These segments will form the corners of your building. The procedure for plumb-cutting is identical to the one described in Chapter 9, section 6, or using a mini mill like the one described in Chapter 5. Spline-grooving the plumb-cut ends is identical to the procedure outlined in Chapter 9.

Tools: Eye and ear protection, chainsaw, router with 3/4 (19 mm) straight bit, level, tape measure, hammer.

Materials: Plumb-cutting jig, 1" × 4" (19 × 89 mm) straightedge, nails, pencil.

Procedure:
1) Using the plumb-cutting jig, set up and then cut the notched building into four equal corner segments (Figure 10-14).
2) Number the corner pieces, dismantle, and assemble one of the notched corners on the building subfloor corner nearest a door opening.

   Note: Cut the spline groove of the first bottom log prior to assembly, since when it is placed it will be difficult to cut the groove without accidentally cutting the floor.

Figure 10-14
Plumb-cutting
and spline-
grooving the
notched
corners.

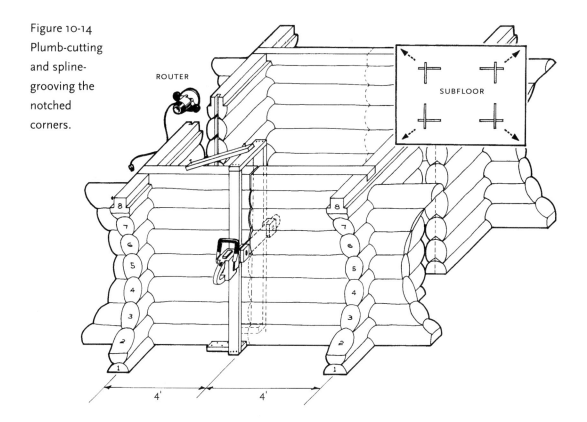

3) After the notched corner is in place, rout the spline groove, attach a post, and continue assembly of infill wall panels and posts as described in section 11, below.

11. Assembling the notched corners and placing the top plate.

Assembling the notched corners on the building subfloor is done by following the procedure for placing, insulating, pinning, and drilling for electrical wiring outlined in Chapter 9 and Chapter 15. In this case, however, the top plate should be log in order to withstand the cantilevered stresses of the roof weight.

Tools: Electric drill with $1/2$" (12 mm) and $5/8$" (16 mm) auger bits, chalk-line, 4' (1220 mm) level, sledge hammer, hammer, knife.

Materials: Numbered notched corners, wall panels and posts, 1" × 8"
(19 × 200 mm) skirting boards (rough cedar), insulation, 3/4" × 3" × 8'
(19 × 75 × 2440 mm) marine plywood strips, nails, foam roll, 2" × 6"
(38 × 140 mm) bracing.

Procedure:

1) Chalk a 4" (100 mm) inset centerline around the perimeter of the
   subfloor as shown in Figure 10-15. The centerline of the wall logs
   will be positioned on this line.
2) Place the bottom, flat-surfaced corner logs on the subfloor with a
   layer of foam roll between the two surfaces. Secure these first logs
   as described in Chapter 9.
3) Assemble the notched corners, insulating, pinning, and drilling
   for electrical wiring as you go (see Chapter 9, Chapter 15). Make
   sure the plumb-cut ends are flush. Cut the spline groove after the
   corners are completed (if they are not already done).
4) Position a post and assemble the wall panel as previously outlined.
   The procedure of starting at one corner nearest a doorway and

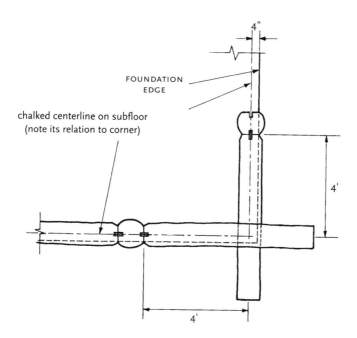

FOUNDATION
EDGE

4"

chalked centerline on subfloor
(note its relation to corner)

4'

4'

Figure 10-15
Top view of
notched corner
assembly.

working simultaneously toward the doorway and around the building is identical to the procedure described in Chapter 9.

5) After all the walls are in place, position the top plate as shown in Figure 10-16, then insulate and nail the skirting boards to the plate.

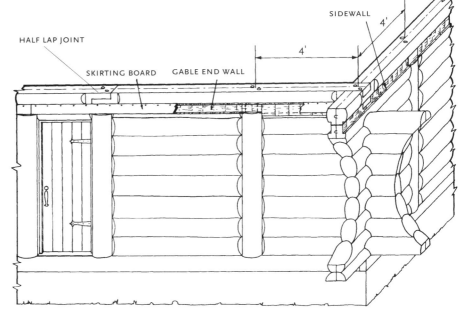

Figure 10-16 Assembly of notched corners, wall panels, and log top plate on the subfloor.

Note: Prior to placing the roof system tie beams may be needed or desired to tie the walls together or provide support for second storey floor joists. Tie beams are placed in the same manner as girder beams, following the procedures described in Chapter 13.

CHAPTER ELEVEN

Openings

"Moulding clay into a vessel,
we find the utility in its
hollowness;
Cutting doors and windows
for a house, we find the utility
in its empty space. Therefore
the being of things is
profitable, the non-being of
things is serviceable."

——LAO-TZU

DOOR AND WINDOW OPENINGS

The ancient Chinese Taoist philosopher Lao-tzu eloquently described the usefulness of empty space (void). With this statement he suggests that the most useful is often likely to be overlooked. Openings are needed to gain access into the building or between rooms, as well as to provide ventilation, illumination, and a view of the outdoor environment. Aesthetic considerations relating to the symmetry or asymmetry of positioning these openings in the structure affect appearance.

Exterior openings will always, however, be weak links in terms of heat loss because they have less insulative capacity than do solid walls. Doors and windows are responsible for approximately 30 percent of a building's heat loss through thermal conduction, and another 10 percent due to air infiltration. It is, therefore, well worth taking time to plan and install doors and windows to maximize the benefits and minimize the drawbacks. Post and beam buildings present no special difficulties in installing doors and windows, but the work may take longer in some cases than it would in a conventional frame building. A list of guidelines for planning openings, doors, and windows follows (Figure 11-1).

Figure 11-1
Standard
window
heights.

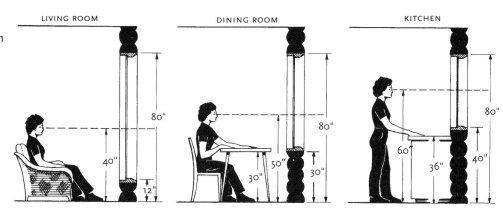

Door and window design factors

- In case of fire there should be at least two door exits.
- At least one exit door should be 36" (914 mm) wide for furniture movement in and out of the house.
- Windows to be used for ventilation should be on the windward side of prevailing summer winds, and smaller windows should be situated on the leeward side to maximize air flow.
- In the northern hemisphere south-oriented windows will maximize solar heat gain. Large, north-oriented windows would be a major source of heat loss during the winter.
- Glass area should be between 7 and 15 percent of the floor area in the room. If the house is oriented to maximize solar heat gain this will affect the percentage.
- Single large windows provide more illumination than a series of small ones.

- Doors and large windows should be placed between vertical posts in solid wood infill post and beam buildings.
- Outside doors should be insulated and, in cold climates, should incorporate a cold porch to block winter winds.
- Glass is a poor insulator. In double or triple glazed windows the dead air space between the panes serves as insulation. Insulated shutters or curtains which close at night are cheaper and afford better protection.
- Windows are manufactured in standard sizes for round figure openings; non-standard sizes cost more.
- Actual manufactured window dimensions are $1/2$" (12 mm) undersize to facilitate $1/4$" (6 mm) shim clearance within the rough opening.
- Window/door sizes are listed width first, height second.

Rough openings for doors and windows

A rough opening is an opening in a wall into which a window or door unit will be placed. A door unit consists of the actual door plus its $1^{1}/4$" (34 mm) frame. In order to place the unit within the rough opening and maintain a "shim clearance" for leveling, the opening should be $3/4$" (18 mm) larger than the entire window or door unit. Standard door heights are usually 80" (2032 mm) high. Standard door widths vary depending on their location (Figure 11-2).

Standard door sizes

Exterior front	36" × 80" (914 × 2032 mm)
Exterior rear	34" × 80" (864 × 2032 mm)
Interior service	32" × 80" (813 × 2032 mm)
Interior doors	30" × 80" (762 × 2032 mm)

1. Installing doors between posts.

When placing a door between two posts it is important that the post spacing be equal to the rough opening width. The space above the door to the top plate can be either framed or of the same infill as the rest of the walls. The door need not contain a structural header as the roof will exert no weight upon it.

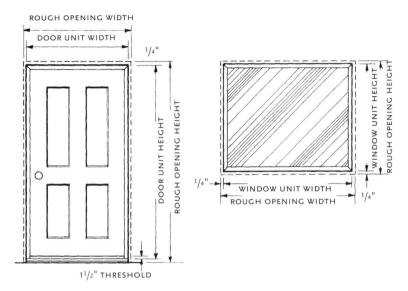

Figure 11-2
Rough openings
for doors and
windows.

Tools: 48" (1220 mm) level, tape measure, chalkline, handsaw, square, hammer, nail set, pencil, eye and ear protection, chainsaw, 1¹/₂" (38 mm) chisel, mallet.

Materials: Door unit, cedar shim wedges, insulation, caulking compound, molding trim, nails.

Procedure:
1) Insert the door frame between the posts.
2) Plumb and level the frame as shown in Figure 11-3. Shim the frame in the rough opening with the wedges, then nail through the frame and wedges into the post.
3) Insert the door and make any adjustments to ensure proper swing and closure.
4) The space above the door can either be framed or built up with whatever wall infill material (i.e. log, half-timber, frame) you are using (Figure 11-4).
5) Provide adequate drip edge or flashing protection above the door.
6) Insulate the spaces around the door, then caulk to prevent any air leaks, and apply molding strip. (See section 4, below, for additional molding trim methods.)

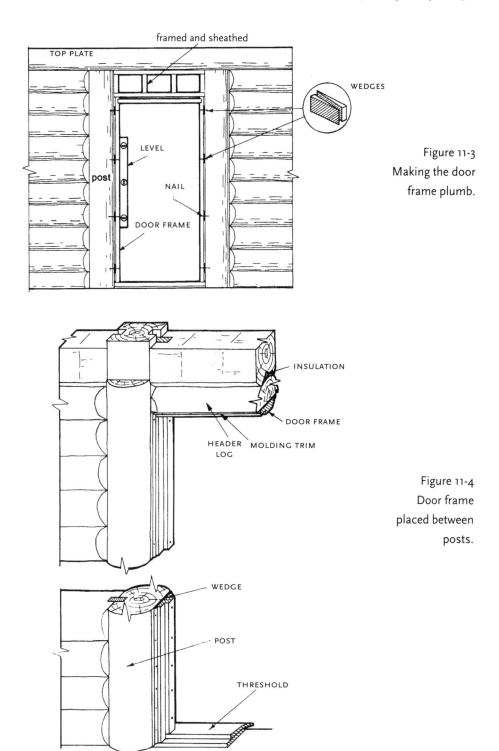

framed and sheathed

TOP PLATE

WEDGES

LEVEL

post

NAIL

DOOR FRAME

Figure 11-3
Making the door
frame plumb.

INSULATION

DOOR FRAME

HEADER
LOG

MOLDING TRIM

Figure 11-4
Door frame
placed between
posts.

WEDGE

POST

THRESHOLD

2. Installing windows between posts.

Placing windows between posts rather than within a solid log or half-timber infill wall saves on chainsaw work and eliminates the need for a settling space above the unit. Basically, installing a window between posts follows the same procedure as for installing a door—the post spacing will be equal to the rough opening width of the window unit. It will be necessary to either frame or build up wall infill to the level of the window sill and from the header to the top plate. As with the door, it is not necessary to provide a structural header, because the roof weight will not bear on the header (Figure 11-5).

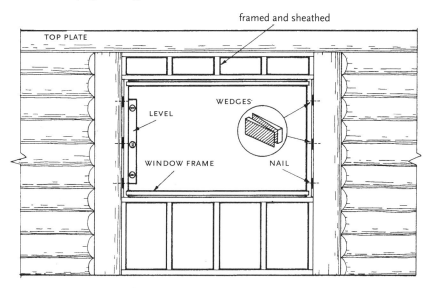

Figure 11-5
Making the
window frame
plumb.

Tools: Level, tape measure, chalkline, handsaw, hammer, square, nail set, pencil, eye and ear protection, chainsaw, 1¹/₂" (38 mm) chisel, mallet.

Materials: Window unit, cedar shim wedges, insulation, caulking compound, molding trim, nails, wall infill material, window unit.

Procedure:
1) Either frame or build up the wall infill (i.e. log, half-timber, frame) to the height of the window sill. If log or half-timber infill is used the window sill and header can be fabricated by cutting one of the infill pieces in half.

2) Insert the window unit on the sill between the posts.

3) Where log or half-timber infill is used the sill must be flat-surfaced inside and out to the thickness of the window frame to allow for the molding trim boards (Figure 11-6).

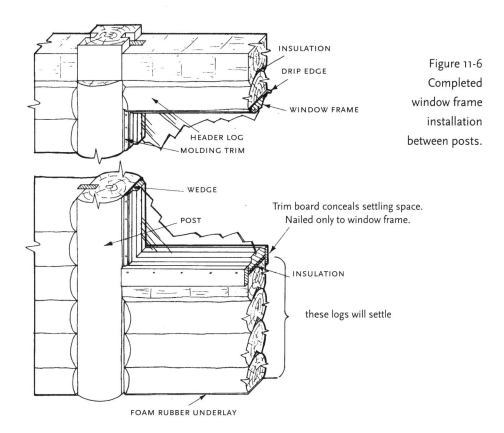

INSULATION

DRIP EDGE

WINDOW FRAME

HEADER LOG

MOLDING TRIM

WEDGE

POST

Trim board conceals settling space. Nailed only to window frame.

INSULATION

these logs will settle

FOAM RUBBER UNDERLAY

Figure 11-6 Completed window frame installation between posts.

4) Plumb and level the window, then wedge and nail it to the posts as shown in Figure 11-5.

5) Frame or place wall infill over the space above the window. Provide adequate drip edge or flashing protection above the window.

6) Insulate the spaces around the window caulk to prevent any air leaks, and apply molding strip. (See section 4, below, for additional molding trim methods.) Note that the trim boards are nailed only to the bottom of the window frame when log or half-timber infill is used. These trim boards will conceal any settling space caused by shrinkage of the infill pieces.

3. Installing windows in a solid wood infill wall.

Placing a window within a solid wood wall requires cutting a rough opening. The width of the rough opening will be equal to the window unit plus a $3/4$" (18 mm) shim clearance. The height of the rough opening, however, will be equal to the window unit's height plus the expected amount of settling of the logs or half-timbers. For green wood the amount of settling is $1/2$" (12 mm) for every 12" (300 mm) of vertical wood. For example, a window height of 48" (1200 mm) will require a settling space of 2" (50 mm).

After the rough opening is cut out, a wood spline is recessed into each side of the opening. These splines will prevent the infill pieces from being jarred out of alignment, and also serve as backing onto which to nail the window. The spline material should be 2" × 2" (38 × 38 mm) fir and can be installed using a router and $3/4$" (19 mm) straight carbide bit to cut the groove. There should also be a settling space allowance above the spline.

Plumbing and leveling the window uses the same procedure as that described in section 2, above. Trimming the window can be done in a number of ways; four methods are outlined in section 4, below.

Tools: Eye and ear protection, chainsaw, router with $3/4$" (19 mm) straight bit, tape measure, chalkline, level, hammer.

Materials: 1" × 4" (19 × 89 mm) straightedge material, 2" × 2" (38 × 38 mm) fir splines, nails, window unit.

Procedure:
1) Lay out the rough opening width by plumbing and nailing 1" × 4" (19 × 89 mm) straight boards to the wall where the window will be placed. The inside distance between the parallel boards will be equal to the window's opening width, plus shim clearance.
2) Measure the window header height (80", or 2032 mm) up from the floor, and add the calculated settling space (Figure 11-7). Chalk a level line between the boards at this height to obtain the header height.

    Note: The header and sill log (or half-timber) should have a portion of wood remaining after the rough opening is cut. This may necessitate moving the window unit up or down a couple of inches/centimeters. This is done to provide wide bearing surfaces at the header and sill. It will also ensure that the spline effectively locks the header to the sill (Figure 11-7).

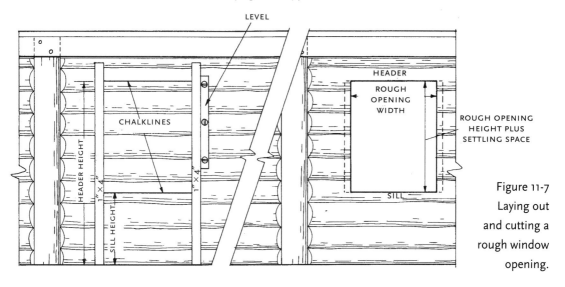

Figure 11-7
Laying out and cutting a rough window opening.

3) From the header measure down the height of the window unit plus the settling space allowance and chalk a level line between the boards, to obtain the sill height.

4) Cut out the rough opening with a chainsaw. Make the vertical cuts first, using the boards as guides. Remove the waste wood pieces.

5) Remove the sill waste wood by either making bread-slice cuts to the line and cleaning, or by plunging the saw bar horizontally through the wall and cutting along the line.

6) Remove the header waste wood by plunging the chainsaw bar horizontally through the wall and cutting along the line. Alternatively, if the top plate is not in position, the header can be removed from the wall and cut.

7) To cut the spline groove use a straight 1" × 4" (19 × 89 mm) as a guide, and rout the groove as shown in Figure 11-8.

8) Install and trim the window using one of the methods described in section 4, below.

4. Installing and trimming windows.

The following procedures are only for the installation and trimming of windows. Doors are usually placed between posts and so do not require a settling space. However, if a situation arises where a door is to be placed

Figure 11-8
Routing the
spline groove.

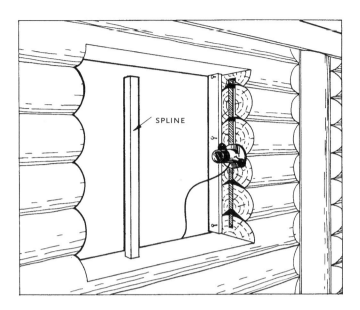

SPLINE

within a log of half-timber infill wall, it will have to be installed and trimmed in the same manner as a window.

There are a variety of methods for installing and trimming windows. The procedures, and advantages and disadvantages of each, are discussed below. Trim styles may be varied according to the builder's preference. Flashing or a drip cap should be provided in each case.

Tools: Eye and ear protection, chainsaw, tape measure, chalkline, axe, level, adze, handsaw, square, hammer, nail set.

Materials: Windows, trim boards, insulation, caulking compound, finishing nails.

Trim method A

This method sandwiches the opening between trim boards. It necessitates sawing or axing the logs back 5" (125 mm) from around the opening, on both the inside and outside, to produce a flat surface for the trim boards. Because of the thickness of the wall, the width of the window frame will have to be increased either by adding to the existing frame or by building a box frame around it. The window frame is then placed into the rough opening and nailed to the splines. The settling space above it is

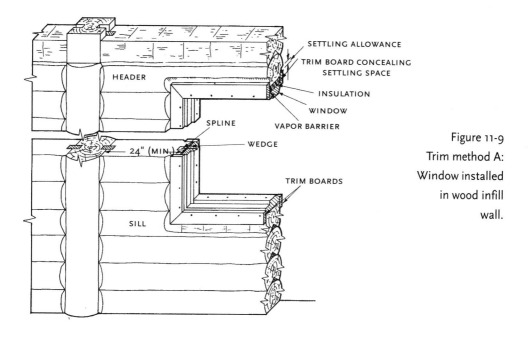

SETTLING ALLOWANCE

TRIM BOARD CONCEALING
SETTLING SPACE

HEADER

INSULATION

WINDOW

SPLINE

VAPOR BARRIER

WEDGE

24" (MIN.)

TRIM BOARDS

SILL

Figure 11-9
Trim method A:
Window installed
in wood infill
wall.

insulated and trim boards are nailed to the frame so as to overlap the axed-back logs. This method of installation is very good for preventing air infiltration and will not require further maintenance.

Procedure:

1) Insert the widened frame into the rough opening and trace around its inside and outside edges.

2) Remove the frame, then chainsaw or axe the wood, using the outside of the trace lines, back 5" (125 mm) around the rough opening to accommodate the trim boards. A contoured curve can be made to the header with the header in place. This is done by making successive bread-slice cuts, holding the chainsaw bar in a vertical position, so that the rounded bar nose produces the curve. Next remove the bulk of the waste wood with an adze, then feather to a smooth curve with a chainsaw. This method is less difficult than it sounds. *Use caution, especially when using the nose of the chainsaw.*

3) Replace the frame and nail it only to the splines and sill. Insulate the settling space and caulk any gaps between the logs and frame (Figure 11-9).

4) Finish nail the trim boards to the window frame so that they overlap the logs.

Note: If the logs are small in diameter it may not be necessary to increase the width of the window frame.

Trim method B

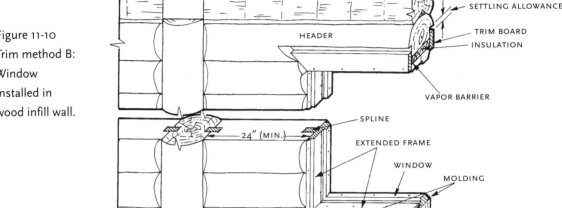

Figure 11-10
Trim method B:
Window
installed in
wood infill wall.

Tools and materials are the same as in Method A. The procedure here is similar to the one used in Method A and can be employed where very large logs are used. The header is traced out and cut back, using the method described in A. The difference here is that instead of trim boards on the sides or bottom, a molding strip is nailed to the window frame. There is little room for error in this method, especially on the sides and bottom where air might penetrate.

Procedure:

1) Insert the widened frame into the rough opening and trace its top inside and outside edge.

2) Remove the frame and cut the header log back to accommodate the trim boards. For a better appearance, also bevel back the sides of the logs.

3) Replace the frame and nail it only to the splines and sill. Insulate the settling space, and caulk any gaps between the logs and frame.

4) Finish nail the molding strips to the sides and bottom of the window (Figure 11-10).

Trim method C

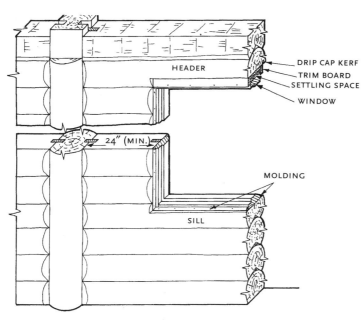

DRIP CAP KERF
TRIM BOARD
SETTLING SPACE
WINDOW
HEADER
24" (MIN.)
MOLDING
SILL

Figure 11-11
Trim method C:
Window
installed in
wood infill wall.

The tools and materials are the same as in Method A. Though this method of installation may seem easier, the greater possibility of air leaks leaves less room for error, and more time must be spent cutting and sealing. Here, the trim boards covering the settling space at the top are nailed or screwed directly into the header log. Unlike the previous methods, they then slide down on either side of the window casing during settling. Any overcutting at either the header or rough opening sides will necessitate filling with caulking. The header must be cut perfectly straight and sanded to receive the straight trim board. This requires precutting the header or scribing the trim board to fit any curves. Any place where two surfaces only butt against each other instead of overlapping will be difficult to seal against air leaks. This method also involves follow-up maintenance, for as the trim boards settle down over the window (or door) casing they must be removed and planed.

Procedure:

1) Ensure that the rough opening has been cut straight and is properly sanded.
2) Bevel back the logs on either side of the window.
3) Position the window and nail it to the splines and sill.
4) Insulate the settling space and caulk any gaps between logs and frame.
5) Nail molding strips to the bottom and sides of the window. The side strips should be the length of the window.
6) Cut a rabbet at each end of the settling space trim board, then nail or screw the board into the header on both the inside and outside. During settling the trim board will slide down over the vertical molding strips (Figure 11-11).
7) Caulk any gaps between the window trim and log work.

Trim method D

Arched windows add a touch of grace and elegance unmatched by rectangular windows or doors. The procedures for cutting an arched opening are described in section 5, below. Note that the arched window is attached firmly to the header, and the settling space is left at the sill. It is important that the calculated amount of settling space be left at the base of the nailer spline, as shown in the diagram. Tools and materials are the same as in Method A.

Procedure:

1) Lay out and cut the rough opening according to the methods described in section 5, below. In this case it would be simplest to merely trace out the window.
2) Insert the window frame into the opening and trace its width onto the log work.
3) Remove the frame, then cut back the log work to accommodate the molding and trim boards.
4) Replace the frame and nail it to the splines and header. Make sure

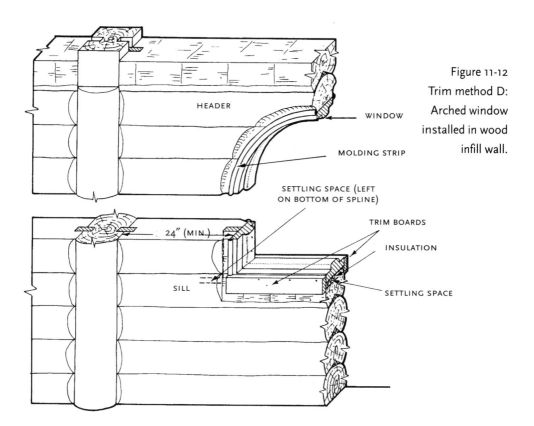

HEADER

WINDOW

MOLDING STRIP

Figure 11-12
Trim method D:
Arched window
installed in wood
infill wall.

SETTLING SPACE (LEFT
ON BOTTOM OF SPLINE)

TRIM BOARDS

INSULATION

24" (MIN.)

SILL

SETTLING SPACE

the splines have a settling space allowance at their base. Insulate and caulk any gaps between logs and frame.

5) Finish nail the molding strips and the trim boards as shown in Figure 11-12.

5. How to lay out and cut an arched opening.

Sweeping archways dividing living areas inside a home add elegance and individuality to the entire structure. If you can make, recycle, or afford to buy arched windows and doors, it is well worth the extra time and money for the resulting visual effect.

This section explains the steps for cutting arched openings in log or half-timber infill walls. The main preparation is the lateral groove which, when cut, should expose a flat or cupped face rather than an unsightly "V" groove. To cut a curved arch with the chainsaw will require the round-backed cutting tooth of a chipper chain. (A chisel chain with a straight-backed cutting edge cannot initiate a curved cut.)

Figure 11-13
Flattening
between top and
bottom scribe
lines will give flat,
mated surfaces
for arched
openings.

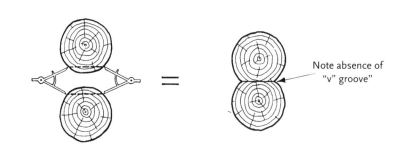

Note absence of "v" groove

Tools: Eye and ear protection, chainsaw with chipper chain, disc sander, tape measure, chalkline, level, hammer, axe, pencil or crayon.

Materials: Length of single strand wire, nails.

Procedure:

1) After an archway is cut its log or half-timber face surfaces will be exposed. Unsightly "V" grooves between the scribed pieces will look unfinished. Instead, as the infill walls are being constructed, prepare the lateral grooves where the opening will be cut out (usually 3"–4", or 75–100 mm, on either side of the cutline), to reveal either a cupped or flat mated surface.

However, cupping the lateral groove is a hit-or-miss procedure as it is difficult to remove just the right amount of wood: too much and there is a gap, too little and the scribed logs or half-timbers will not fit together exactly. The cutting procedure requires the rounded nose of the chainsaw bar. An easier, more exact method of preparing the lateral groove is to flatten the area between the scribe lines, as shown in Figure 11-13.

2) In order to prepare the lateral grooves it is necessary to know the parameters of the arched opening. Figure 11-14 shows how to lay out the archway using a wire and pencil in a modified compass arrangement. A wire is used rather than a string, because the latter will stretch. Note that lowering the focal point reduces the amount of curvature. These diagrams indicate with a broken line where the lateral grooves will have to be cupped or flattened.

3) Lay out the archway on both sides of the wall using the illustrated method.

4) Cutting the sides of the opening is quite straightforward; the use of guide boards is recommended. After the sides are completed cut the curved header or using one of the following methods:

    a) Remove the header from the wall and cut the curve.

    b) Cut the entire arch within the wall.

The second method requires a chainsaw with a sharp chipper chain. The arch is cut from the top downwards, completing half the archway before moving to the opposite side of the wall to complete the other half.

Start by penetrating the bar nose into the wood a couple of inches/centimeters and tracing the arch line. Continue doing this until about half the thickness of wall has been cut. The cut is then completed by plunging the chainsaw bar through at the top of the

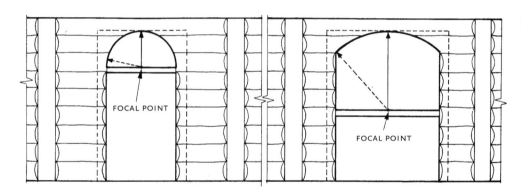

Figure 11-14
Laying out
arched
openings.

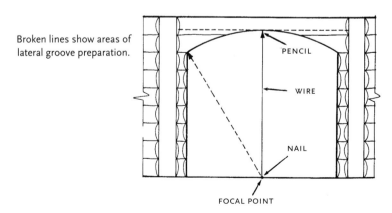

arch and, using the back of the bar, cutting downward with the initial cut as a guide. Do the same for the other half of the arch, working from the opposite side of the wall. Then disc sand the archway smooth.

Note: Some builders keep a modified chain on hand for cutting arches. Removing every second cutting tooth on one side of the chipper chain will result in a curved cut.

Roof Structures

Roof structures vary considerably in terms of style: gable, hip, dutch, mansard, etc. However, fundamental to all roofs is the necessity of keeping the weather out and ensuring structural soundness. Climate and geography are prime factors determining the design of the roof. For example, a house built in the desert with minimal rainfall would be better suited to a flat roof to provide for rain catchment, and little or no eave protection due to strong windstorms. A mountainous geography with high rain/snowfall would require a pitched roof to shed the rain and snow, with extended eaves to provide protection to the sides of the building.

Since nature dictates the basics of roof design, it stands to reason that an effective way to perpetuate regional design is to relate the roof structure back to nature. For example, mountainous geography necessitates pitched roofs, which mirror the pyramid shapes of the surrounding mountains and conifer trees. The pitched gable roof lines of the dwelling relate the building design back to nature's dominant features.

Underlying the visual roof shape is the structural roof system, which supports the tons of dead weight (roofing materials) and live weight (snow, wind loading). Strict adherence to the structural beam sizes (see Appendix III) must be observed for all component pieces. As well, the strength of the roof structure depends upon the execution of the joinery. These stress joints must be tight fitting in order to be effective. Understandably, local building authorities may require that an engineer review the plan and structure as a safety precaution.

This chapter examines various methods of constructing gable roof structures. We begin with generic terms and the geometry of the roof layout and progress through timber and log exposed beam joinery. The confusion often associated with joinery layout procedures is minimized with graphic planning, template use, and step-by-step instruction. Heavy roof members are laid out and shaped into their component parts on the ground or on the building subfloor prior to final placement. Using this approach, the builder will have the information to construct a number of roof systems and the understanding with which to create variations. Any type of roof covering can be applied in the same manner as for conventional stud frame, timber, or log structures. Moreover, as an addendum to the strength of a timbered or log roof structure, I include for the purist, instructions on how to build an insulated sod roof—the modern way. Popular in Scandinavia and Northern Europe centuries ago, it is a very durable and attractive roof covering complimentary to timber and log homes.

ROOF STRUCTURES

Conventional trussed roof systems

This type of roof framing uses either factory or site manufactured 2" × 4" (38 × 89 mm) or 2" × 6" (38 × 140 mm) frame trusses. Such a style of roof framing is common in stud frame construction today. It is included here to show that such a common method of roof framing is also possible for post and beam buildings.

Figure 12-1 shows a roof framed with conventional trusses. The building's top plate is also of the dimensional type (as described in Chapter 9) to simplify truss placement and soffit framing. The ceiling in this house is closed and no structural beams are exposed. Such a closed ceiling is often employed for kitchens, and in many cases houses will have a combination of closed and open beam ceiling combinations.

Conventional raftered roof systems

Another option with conventional framing material is to use 2" × 10" (38 × 235 mm) rafters. The air space between the plywood roof sheathing and the insulation is needed to ventilate the roof and keep it cold, to prevent accumulated snow from melting. If snow melts during freezing temper-

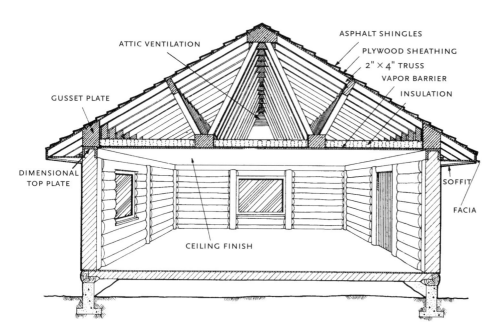

Figure 12-1
Conventional
trussed roof
for closed
ceilings.

atures, water will run down to the cold eaves where it will freeze, causing ice damming, water backup, and possible inside leaks. Roof ventilation also prevents water vapor from saturating the insulation and rendering it useless.

The open ceiling shown in Figure 12-2 has the finish material attached to the underside of the rafters. The top plate is again of the dimensional type to simplify rafter placement and soffit framing. Although Figure 12-2 shows a ridge beam, the corresponding procedures are for a rafter layout using both a ridge beam and ridge board. A ridge board is sandwiched between the rafters at the peak with the compression of the opposing rafters creating a self-supporting roof. In such a method the rafters thrust outwards, pushing at the walls, requiring countermeasures. With the ridge beam shown, the rafters "hang" from the beam and produce no outward thrust to the side walls. A supporting beam, however, must comply in size to the required span and loading. Refer to Span Tables in Appendix III.

Timber raftered roof systems (with collar-tie truss)

By relying on the size and strength of timbers one can replace the many smaller conventional frame rafter components with fewer but larger tim-

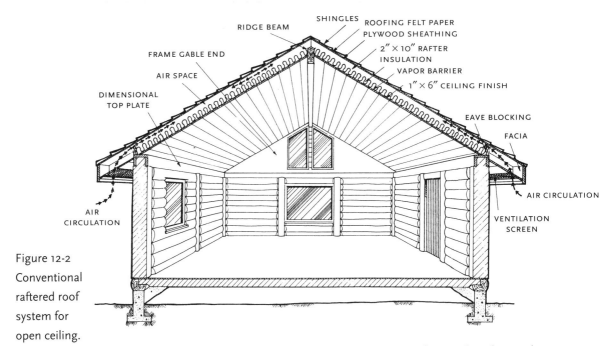

SHINGLES
ROOFING FELT PAPER
RIDGE BEAM
PLYWOOD SHEATHING
FRAME GABLE END
2″ × 10″ RAFTER
INSULATION
AIR SPACE
VAPOR BARRIER
1″ × 6″ CEILING FINISH
DIMENSIONAL
TOP PLATE
EAVE BLOCKING
FACIA
AIR CIRCULATION
AIR
CIRCULATION
VENTILATION
SCREEN

Figure 12-2
Conventional
raftered roof
system for
open ceiling.

ber principal rafters, and can then join these together with ridge and purlin beams. Incorporating a collar-tie beam half-way up the principal rafter, as shown in Figure 12-3, will keep the rafter legs from spreading or sagging due to roof loading. The roof covering illustrated here is insulated sod, common in northern Europe. As sod is heavier than the more conventional coverings, the roof structure should include a tie-beam to further arrest any spreading forces. (See section 13, below, for sod roof construction.) Open beam timber framing gives an impression of both strength and lightness unattainable by conventional framing methods. The steps in sections 4 and 5, below, which correspond to Figure 12-3, describe two methods of principal rafter joinery as well as a method for collar-tie truss construction. The top plate must be a solid wood log or timber to allow for wood removal joinery. The gable end incorporates a king post truss with struts (see section 6, below, for details.)

Timber trussed roof systems (with log ridge pole and purlins)

Figure 12-4 shows a king post with strut roof midspan truss supporting log (or timber) ridge and purlin beams. An understanding of this truss

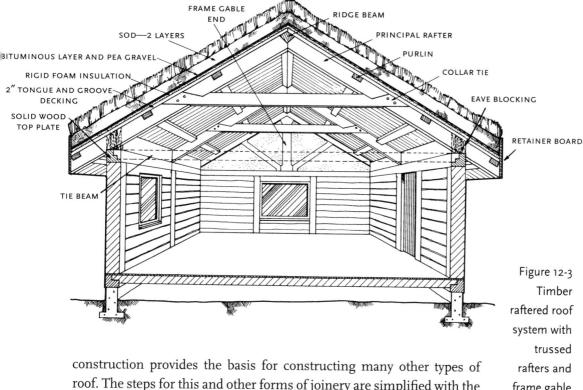

FRAME GABLE END

RIDGE BEAM

SOD—2 LAYERS

PRINCIPAL RAFTER

BITUMINOUS LAYER AND PEA GRAVEL

PURLIN

RIGID FOAM INSULATION

COLLAR TIE

2" TONGUE AND GROOVE DECKING

EAVE BLOCKING

SOLID WOOD TOP PLATE

RETAINER BOARD

TIE BEAM

Figure 12-3 Timber raftered roof system with trussed rafters and frame gable ends for open ceiling.

construction provides the basis for constructing many other types of roof. The steps for this and other forms of joinery are simplified with the use of hardboard templates. As long as the support beams conform to the tables in Appendix III, a roof structure such as this is very strong. Included in the procedural instructions are three methods of frame gable end construction which will accommodate the ridge and purlin beams.

Log ridge pole and purlin roof systems (with log gable ends)

This type of open beam ceiling is common to many log homes. Figure 12-5 shows a log ridge pole and purlins supported by log gable ends. The corresponding procedures beginning in section 9, below, give two methods for log gable end construction, and for ridge pole and purlin placement. The size of these beams are proportional to the clear span and loading. Refer to the Span Tables in Appendix III.

This building also shows a log tie beam, which serves to counteract the spreading forces exerted by the roof on the walls. To function correctly the intersecting joint at the top plate should be a locking dovetail or else be securely pinned. Note also that the rafters do not touch at the

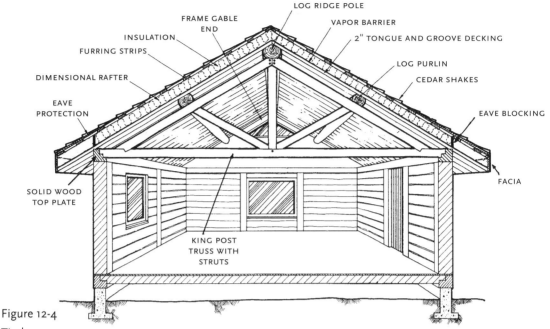

LOG RIDGE POLE

FRAME GABLE END

VAPOR BARRIER

INSULATION

2" TONGUE AND GROOVE DECKING

FURRING STRIPS

LOG PURLIN

DIMENSIONAL RAFTER

CEDAR SHAKES

EAVE PROTECTION

EAVE BLOCKING

FACIA

SOLID WOOD TOP PLATE

KING POST TRUSS WITH STRUTS

Figure 12-4 Timber trussed roof system with log ridge pole and purlins.

ridge. A 2" (50 mm) space provision has been made to prevent binding at the peak after settling of the log gable ends. A 7' (2 m) high gable end constructed of green logs will settle an anticipated 3 1/2" (90 mm) causing a slight change in the roof slope. The peak gap is incorporated for this reason.

The log materials for gable ends should be thoroughly seasoned because in addition to the settling factor, there is a natural accumulation of heat near the roof peak, as heat rises. This heat will cause rapid drying of green, short log lengths, resulting in excessive checking.

The handling of short log pieces unsupported on the ends, at breakneck heights, is awkward and sometimes dangerous. For this reason, the log gable end construction methods outlined in this book involve building them on the ground. Afterwards the finished gable end can be dismantled and reassembled on the building's top plate.

Forces at play

Apart from seismic and wind influences the roof is also subjected to two loading forces while the rest of the house frame is subject only to one. Vertical posts and horizontal beams in the house frame support vertical

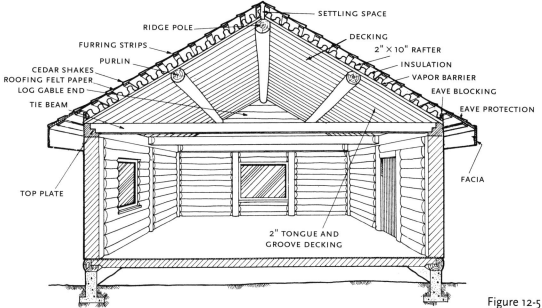

SETTLING SPACE
RIDGE POLE
FURRING STRIPS
PURLIN
CEDAR SHAKES
ROOFING FELT PAPER
LOG GABLE END
TIE BEAM
TOP PLATE
DECKING
2" × 10" RAFTER
INSULATION
VAPOR BARRIER
EAVE BLOCKING
EAVE PROTECTION
FACIA
2" TONGUE AND GROOVE DECKING

Figure 12-5 Log ridge pole and purlin roof system with log gable ends.

loads. Roofs, because of their sloping rafters, change this vertical loading into a second force which tries to spread the frame apart. It is important to visualize these forces in order to contend with them. The amount of external loading applied to a sloped roof varies with the degree of slope. The chart in Appendix III, Defining Loads, shows that as the roof increases in slope, the snow load becomes correspondingly less.

Moreover, massive structural members alone will not guarantee that the building is structurally sound. If the crucial joinery points are not tight fitting the entire framework becomes weak, in the same way that a chain is only as strong as its weakest link. Without sufficient internal structural bracing the frame will rack (distort) (see Chapter 2, Design).

Figure 12-6 illustrates how vertical forces create horizontal spreading forces on a sloped roof. These forces can be dealt with by using various ways of tying the rafters together or redirecting the force.

In A, a gable roof is shown with lone rafters. The forces created are forcing the walls apart, with no method for arresting these forces.

In B, the spreading forces are arrested by tying the walls together with the addition of joists or tie-beams. However, if the rafters are excessively long, they could sag under snow loads.

Figure 12-6
Loading forces
in relation to
structural
framing.

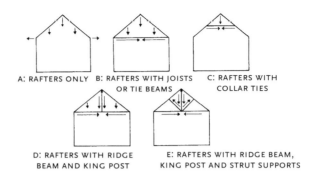

A: RAFTERS ONLY   B: RAFTERS WITH JOISTS   C: RAFTERS WITH
                   OR TIE BEAMS   COLLAR TIES

D: RAFTERS WITH RIDGE   E: RAFTERS WITH RIDGE BEAM,
BEAM AND KING POST   KING POST AND STRUT SUPPORTS

C shows a collar-tie arresting both the spreading forces and the vertical load forces which cause rafter sag.

In D, the spreading forces are redirected vertically. Here the ridge beam is supported by a kingpost, and the rafters virtually hang from the ridge beam. The rafters therefore exert no spreading force, but if they are excessively long they will sag due to vertical load force.

E shows the same arrangement as D, but with strut supports. These struts redirect some of the vertical force back upwards to support the rafter and prevent sagging.

Basic roofing principles and terms

Before one can begin construction of the roof frame the basic roofing principles and terms must be understood. Though Figure 12-7 shows a gable roof with two sloping sides, all other roof types use the same principles and terms. A roof is a combination of right-angle triangles, and the gable roof shown here employs two triangles joined back-to-back. In roofing, the altitude of the triangle is called the "rise." It is measured from the building's top plate to its peak or "ridge." The base of the triangle is called the "run." It is half the "span" or width of the building. To increase a roof slope the rise is increased while the run stays constant, rather like raising the roof of a tent. The triangle's hypotenuse is called the "line length." It is equal to the rafter length, less any overhang projection. In order to frame a roof you must know what the run and rise distances are, and these are easily taken from the building's blueprints. You must also know the line length distance of the rafter plus the overhang allowance in order to purchase the materials with which to frame the roof.

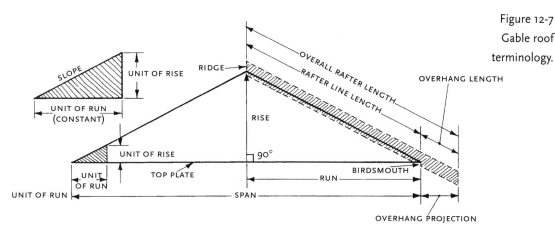

Figure 12-7
Gable roof
terminology.

Roofing terms

Span: The horizontal distance between the outer edges of the top plates; the width of the building.

Run: Half the span distance.

Rise: The vertical distance measuring from the building's top plate to the peak. The roof's steepness increases as the rise is increased.

Line length: The hypotenuse of the triangle, equal to the length of the rafter less the overhang length.

Rafter: One of a series of roof members which supports roof loads.

Overhang: The portion of the rafter and roof which projects past the building walls (approximately 3", or 1 m) to protect the walls from weather.

Ridge: Highest part of the roof formed by the joining of the opposing rafters.

Birdsmouth: A notch resembling a bird's open beak, which is cut in the rafter for joinery to the top plate.

Slope: Refers to the roof's angle of steepness; it is expressed as "pitch" in standard imperial roof terminology, and "cut of the roof" in metric terminology.

Pitch: Roof slope expressed as a variable "unit of rise" over the constant "unit of run." For example, 8/12, an 8" rise for every 12" run.

Cut of the roof: Pitch expressed in metric units. For example, 150/250, a 150 mm rise for every 250 mm run.

Unit of rise: A small triangle representing the roof

Unit of run: Slope scaled down for use on a rafter square

1. Methods for determining rafter length.

Pythagoras' theorem for determining rafter length

This theorem is useful for finding the hypotenuse (line length) of a right angle triangle, but it will not lay out the rafter ridge and birdsmouth cuts. As explained in Chapter 14, section 1, in determining the diagonals for a building's foundation layout, the following mathematical formula is used:

$$a^2 + b^2 = c^2.$$

Figure 12-8 Determining the rafter line length with Pythagoras' theorem.

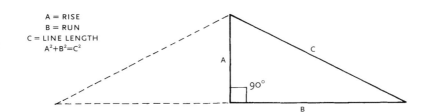

A = RISE
B = RUN
C = LINE LENGTH
$A^2+B^2=C^2$

A

C

90°

B

Examples below are for both standard and metric measurements (Figure 12-8).

Example A: $a = 10'$ $10^2 + 15^2 = c^2$
             $b = 15'$ $\sqrt{10^2 + 15^2} = c$
             c = rafter length $18'$ = rafter line length less overhang

Example B: $a = 3000$ mm $3000^2 + 4500^2 = c^2$
             $b = 4500$ mm $\sqrt{3000^2 + 4500^2} = c$
             c = rafter length 5408 mm = rafter line length less overhang

Lofting method for determining rafter length

This method involves drawing the roof shape full scale on the building's subfloor, after which the rafter dimensions and joinery details can be measured directly from the lofting plan. It is a particularly useful method for heavy log and timber truss construction, or for log ridge pole and purlin layout, where the framed gable ends must accommodate the ridge pole and purlins. For example, in section 7, below, the lofting method is used for framing the gable ends. In fact, if there is a machine on site capable of lifting the entire framework, the gable ends can be framed,

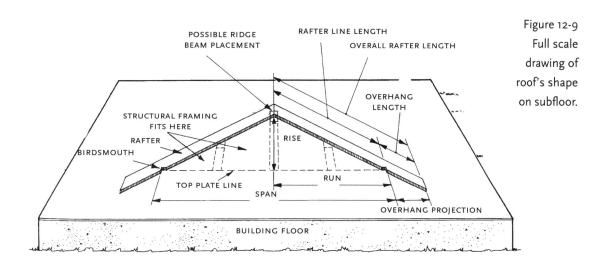

Figure 12-9
Full scale
drawing of
roof's shape
on subfloor.

sheathed, and finished—including windows—using the loft lines as guides, and then the whole gable end can be lifted into place on the building. In heavy member roof framing, lofting guarantees that the finished structure will be exactly according to plan. As well, templates can be confirmed prior to use. See Figure 12-9 for a lofting roof plan.

Stepping-off method for determining rafter length

This method uses a carpenter's metal rafter square to duplicate the roof slope. Whether you are using standard imperial building measurements or metric, the same fundamental principles apply. Figure 12-10 shows standard and metric framing squares. In each the unit of run remains constant while the unit of rise varies according to the desired steepness of the roof slope. A representation of the roof slope is noted as a small triangle and usually appears on the roof drawings of a house blueprint.

The rafter square is used in the step-off method to lay out the rafter length, as well as the ridge and birdsmouth cuts. Though a more portable method than lofting, it is not as fool-proof. It will help to try to visualize the completed rafter as it will appear in its final position on the building. Once one rafter is laid out and cut it can be used as a pattern to lay out the others.

The following two examples give standard and metric roof rafter layouts respectively.

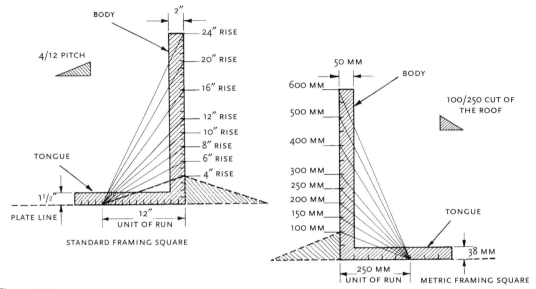

Figure 12-10
Rafter
framing
square
simulating
roof slope.

Example A: standard measurement

Procedure:

1) Determine the number of units of run from the total run of the building.

    Total run 15' = 15 units of 12" run.

2) Determine the overall length of the rafter material needed. If the roof rise height is known, the line length of the rafter can be found using Pythagoras' theorem, $a^2 + b^2 = c^2$. If not, the hypotenuse can be measured directly from the square, as shown in Figure 12-11 (i.e. $13^1/2$"), and the rafter length can be found by multiplying the hypotenuse by the number of units of run.

    Rafter line length = 15 units × $13^1/2$" = $202^1/2$"

    The length of rafter overhang can be found by multiplying the overhang projection (expressed in units of run) by the hypotenuse.

    Rafter overhang length = 3 units × $13^1/2$" = $40^1/2$"

    Adding together the rafter line length, the overhang length, and a

Figure 12-11
Measuring the
hypotenuse off a
standard rafter
square.

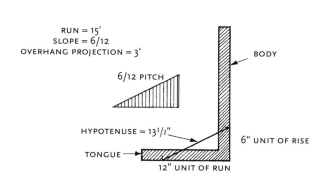

RUN = 15'
SLOPE = 6/12
OVERHANG PROJECTION = 3'

BODY

6/12 PITCH

HYPOTENUSE = 13^1/$_2$"

6" UNIT OF RISE

TONGUE

12" UNIT OF RUN

wastage allowance of 6" will give the overall length of the rafter material needed.

rafter line length = 202^1/$_2$"
overhang length = 40^1/$_2$"
wastage = 6"
overall length of rafter = 249"

3) Select a straight length of rafter material and chalk a line offset 2" parallel with the bottom edge, as shown in Figure 12-12a. In post and beam construction the roof rafters are often large timbers with dimensions that are not strictly uniform. This offset chalked line will serve as an exact line of reference, while also setting the depth of the rafter birdsmouth.

4) Begin stepping-off by aligning the units of rise and run of the square on the chalked line, and marking the ridge cut line as shown in Figure 12-12a. Continue stepping-off the square 15 times down the rafter until the birdsmouth is reached, then mark the birdsmouth as shown in the illustration.

5) To step-off the overhang turn the square over as shown in Figure 12-12b, and step-off an additional three 12" units for the desired 36" projection. Complete the tail cut as shown in the illustration.

6) If a ridge board is used it will be necessary to shorten the rafter half the thickness as illustrated in Figure 12-12c.

7) Make the necessary cuts on this pattern rafter and use it to lay out the other rafters.

Figure 12-12
Standard
measurement
roof rafter
layout.

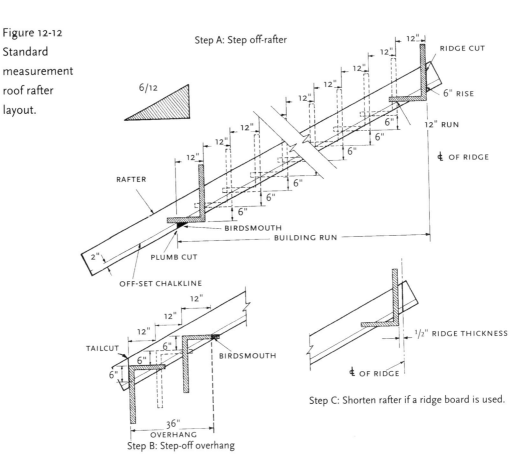

Step A: Step off-rafter

RIDGE CUT

6" RISE

12" RUN

¢ OF RIDGE

6/12

RAFTER

BIRDSMOUTH

BUILDING RUN

2"

PLUMB CUT

OFF-SET CHALKLINE

TAILCUT

BIRDSMOUTH

36"
OVERHANG
Step B: Step-off overhang

½" RIDGE THICKNESS

¢ OF RIDGE

Step C: Shorten rafter if a ridge board is used.

Example B: metric measurement

Procedure:

1) Determine the number of units of run from the total run of the building.

Building run 4572 ÷ 250 = 18.28 units of 250 mm run.

2) Determine the overall length of the rafter material needed. If the roof rise height is known, the line length of the rafter can be found using Pythagoras' theorem, $a^2 + b^2 = c^2$. If not, the hypotenuse can be measured directly from the square, as shown in Figure 12-13 (i.e. 280 mm), and the rafter length can be found by multiplying the hypotenuse by the number of units of run.

Rafter line length = 18.28 units × 280 mm = 5118 mm.

The length of rafter overhang can be found by multiplying the overhang projection (expressed in units of run) by the hypotenuse.

Rafter overhang length = 4 units × 280 mm = 1120 mm.

Adding together the rafter line length, the overhang length, and a waste allowance of 150 mm will give the overall length of the rafter material needed.

rafter line length = 5118 mm
overhang length = 1120 mm
wastage = 150 mm
overall length of rafter = 6388 mm

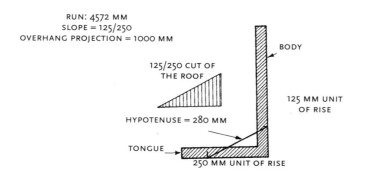

RUN: 4572 MM
SLOPE = 125/250
OVERHANG PROJECTION = 1000 MM

BODY

125/250 CUT OF
THE ROOF

125 MM UNIT
OF RISE

HYPOTENUSE = 280 MM

TONGUE

250 MM UNIT OF RISE

Figure 12-13

Measuring the hypotenuse off a metric rafter square.

3) Select a straight length of rafter material and chalk a line offset 500 mm parallel with the bottom edge, as shown in Figure 12-14a. In post and beam construction, the roof rafters are often large timbers with dimensions that are not always uniform. The offset chalked line serves as an exact line of reference, while also setting the depth of the rafter birdsmouth.

4) In order to step-off the rafter square 18.28 times it will be necessary to obtain the .28 portion of the run. When you multiply .28 × 250 (unit of run) the result is 70 mm, and is referred to as the "odd unit." To begin stepping-off, align the unit of rise and run of the square on the chalked line, as shown in Figure 12-14a inset, and mark the ridge cut line. Next, slide the square up the ridge cut line until 70 mm on the tongue of the square intersects the chalked line, as shown in Figure 12-14a. Mark this odd unit, then continue

stepping-off the square 18 times down the rafter, using the regular rise and run units, until the birdsmouth is reached. Then mark the birdsmouth as shown.

5) To step-off the overhang turn the square over, as shown in Figure 12-14b, and step-off an additional four 250 mm units for the desired 1000 mm projection. Complete the tail cut as shown.

6) If a ridge board is used it will be necessary to shorten the rafter to half the thickness as illustrated in Figure 12-14c.

7) Make the necessary cuts on this pattern rafter and use it to lay out the other rafters.

Figure 12-14
Metric
measurement
roof rafter
layout.

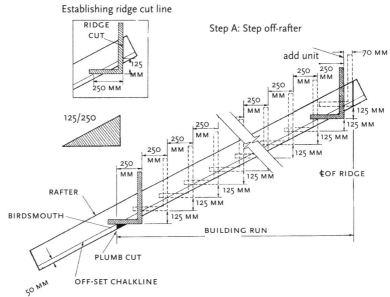

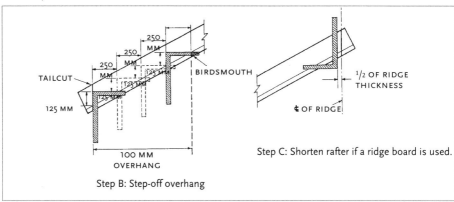

PART 1: TRANSVERSE FRAMING

In the following methods of roof framing, rafter and truss construction are explained. This type of roof construction is called transverse framing (where structural members run at right angles to the ridge line). The structural members provide the strength of the roof while their form gives the roof its slope. See Part 2 of this chapter for methods of longitudinal roof framing.

2. Placing conventional framed trusses with a closed ceiling.

Where an open, vaulted ceiling is not desired, conventional framed trusses allow for a roof system that is simple and quick to construct. The structural members comprising these trusses are either 2" × 4" (38 × 89 mm) or 2" × 6" (38 × 140 mm), depending on the span and roof slope of the house. Either plywood or metal gussets sandwich all butt-joined locations and are essential to the strength of the truss. See Appendix V for specifications for constructing a "W" truss. The following procedure describes how the trusses are placed on the building. The top plate of the building will be a dimensional one. As there is no joinery involving wood removal a log or timber top plate is unnecessary. There is, however, no gable end roof projection allowance with this dimensional top plate (Figure 12-15). This necessitates a "ladder" framework to support the roof covering, should the house design call for one. For two methods of ladder and gable end construction, see section 3, below. Figure 12-1 shows another view of this type of roof.

Tools: Tape measure, level, hammer, handsaw, pencil.

Materials: Trusses, 1" × 4" (19 × 89 mm) bracing, nails, 6 ml. vapor barrier.

Procedure:
1) Ensure that the building's top plate is level and square. Place a strip of vapor barrier around the top plate perimeter so it overhangs 12" on either side.
2) Beginning from the outside edge of the top plate at one gable end, lay out the first truss so that its position will be flush with this out-

Figure 12-15
Conventional
framed truss
for a closed
ceiling.

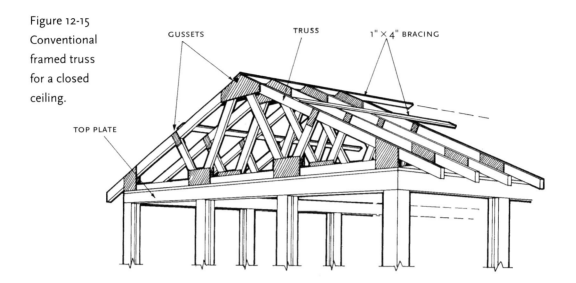

side edge. Lay out all the other trusses on 24" (600 mm) spacings, as shown in Figure 12-16. The opposite gable end truss will be set flush with the outside top plate edge, regardless of the spacing outcome.

3) Position and plumb the trusses on the layout marks, as shown in Figure 12-16. Nail the trusses to the top plate, and provide bracing to the structure.

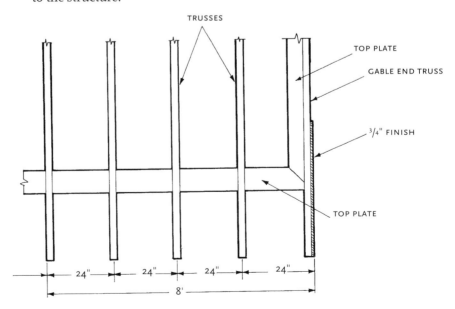

Figure 12-16
Conventional
truss spacing.

4) Apply roof sheathing and covering.

5) The ceiling's finishing material is applied to the under surface of the trusses' bottom cords, ensuring a vapor barrier and insulation are put in place. Refer to Figure 12-1 for another view of a conventional trussed roof.

3. Constructing a conventional frame rafter roof: two open ceiling methods.

Another roof construction method using conventional framing materials is the rafted roof. Unlike the previous method, this roof allows for an open ceiling. The cavity between the rafters contains the insulation and for the previously mentioned reasons, it must be ventilated.

The rafted roof may employ a ridge board or beam (Figure 12-17). As well as the difference in their appearance, there is a difference in direction of the roof loading forces. With a ridge board the vertical load forces exert a spreading force on the rafters, which in turn transmit these forces horizontally to the side walls. With a ridge beam, however, the rafters virtually hang from the timber, and the load forces are exerted vertically through the gable support posts, under the beam, and along the rafter's

Figure 12-17 Constructing a raftered roof: ridge board method.

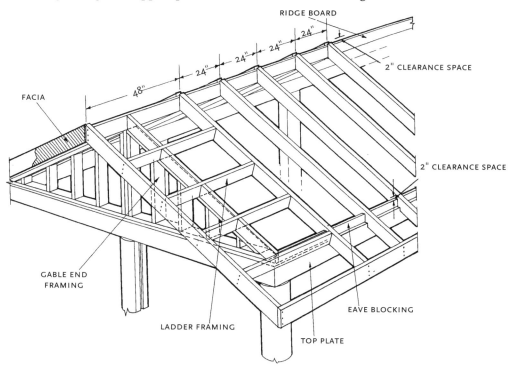

length. Unlike a ridge board, the ridge beam now serves as a structural support, and its size will be dependent upon the loading and span factors, just as for a floor girder. Appendix III contains information on roof beam sizes.

The dimensional top plate described here does not allow for a gable roof projection. If an overhang is desired, as is usually the case, a ladder must be constructed. This ladder can be made in two ways, just as the gable end itself can be built in two ways, depending on whether a ridge board or ridge beam is used. Two methods of rafter frame construction are explained below. Figure 12-2 provides a useful reference for these procedures.

Tools: Rafter square, tape measure, chalkline, level, circular saw, hand-saw, hammer, pencil.

Materials: 2" × 10" (38 × 235 mm) rafters, 2" × 6" (38 × 140 mm) gable end material, 2" × 8" (38 × 184 mm) ridge board or ridge beam (see Appendix III), nails.

Procedure: Ridge board method.
1) Ensure that the building's top plate is level and square.
2) Lay out the rafter spacing according to Figure 12-18 on both the top plate and ridge board.

Figure 12-18
Rafter layout for the ridge board method.

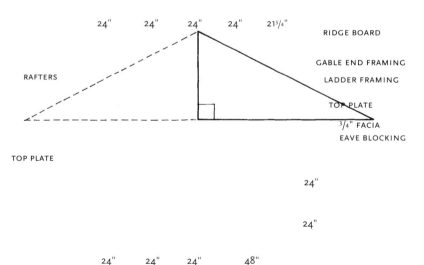

3) Lay out and cut the rafters (see the stepping-off method above).

4) Construct the gable ends according to Figure 12-19 and position them on the building. Gable end layout and construction can be simplified by being lofted on to the subfloor.

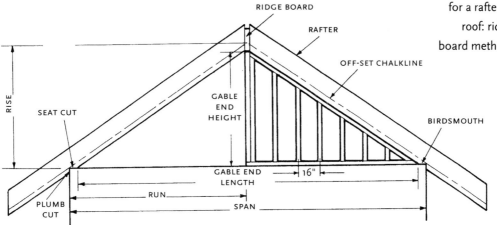

Figure 12-19
Determining
gable end
dimensions
for a raftered
roof: ridge
board method.

5) Position the ridge board, making sure it is straight and level.

6) Nail the rafters to the ridge board, maintaining a gap at the ridge for air circulation (Figure 12-17). Construct the gable end ladder at this time also.

7) Apply roof sheathing and covering. The ceiling's finishing material is applied to the undersurface of the rafters.

Procedure: Ridge beam method.

1) Erect and brace the ridge beam on gable support posts, as shown in Figure 12-20. The height of the ridge beam can be determined from Figure 12-19.

2) Lay out the rafter spacings, as shown in Figure 12-21.

3) Lay out, cut, and place the rafters. To lay out the ridge beam notch refer to the Figure 12-20 inset.

4) Construct the gable end ladder, and fill in the gable end framing as shown in Figure 12-20. The length of the ladder may vary depending on the amount of overhang desired.

5) Apply roof sheathing, covering, and interior finish.

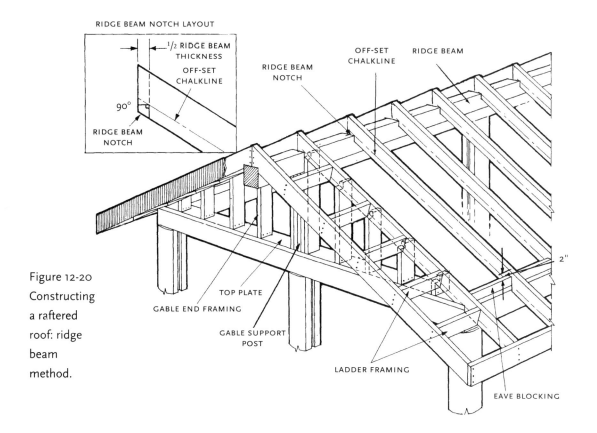

Figure 12-20
Constructing
a raftered
roof: ridge
beam
method.

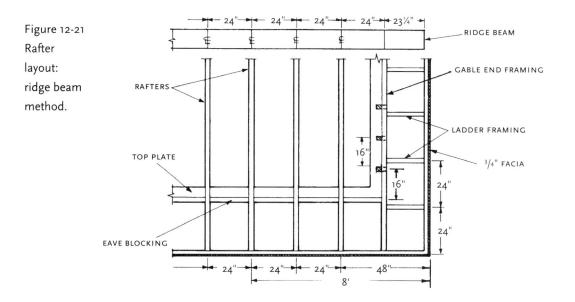

Figure 12-21
Rafter
layout:
ridge beam
method.

4. Constructing a timber frame rafter roof: two open ceiling methods.

The two joinery methods described below both involve principal rafter construction. Each of the rafters is joined together by either a continuous or segmented ridge beam and purlins, to form the roof frame on which the roof covering will be placed. Usually timber principal rafters are spaced 6' to 10' (2 to 3 m) apart where ridge and purlin beams are used. The closer the rafter spacing, the smaller the beam sizes required. Except where snow loads are excessive, rafters spaced at 3' (1 m) require only 2" × 6" (38 × 140 mm) decking to tie them together, instead of ridge beams and purlins (see Appendix III).

The first method of principal rafter construction employs simple lap joinery at the ridge and plate. The second method employs a variation of the mortise and tenon joint, called a fork and tongue, at the ridge and a tenoned birdsmouth at the plate. The latter method is stronger, especially at the plate location, since the rafter is tenoned into the top plate. In the former, pinning is very important since the rafter birdsmouth is merely lapped on the top plate, and roof thrust could cause it to slip. Steel pins are used as fasteners at the joinery locations. The top plate for both of these methods must be either log or timber to allow for wood removal and pinning. Metal anchor fasteners are often used in this instance because they won't be visible. Refer to Fasteners and Anchors, Chapter 6.

Since neither of these principal rafters relies on a mechanism of restraint (i.e. collar tie, truss), excessive roof loading could cause an outward thrust of the rafters and possible spreading of the side walls. Where such loading could occur a tie-beam should be included, with locking dovetail joinery described in Chapter 13, section 6. To simplify joinery layout, hardboard templates are used. The same templates will also be used for more complicated joinery layouts. This type of roof is shown in Figure 12-3.

Tools: Eye protection, circular saw, crosscut handsaw, electric drill with 5/8" (16 mm) or 1" (25 mm) auger bit, rafter square, chalkline, 3 lb (1.5 kg) sledge hammer, tape measure, slick or 1 1/2" (38 mm) chisel, pencil.

Materials: 1/8" (3 mm) hardboard, rafter material, 5/8" (16 mm) steel pins.

Figure 12-22
Constructing
a timber
raftered roof:
method A.

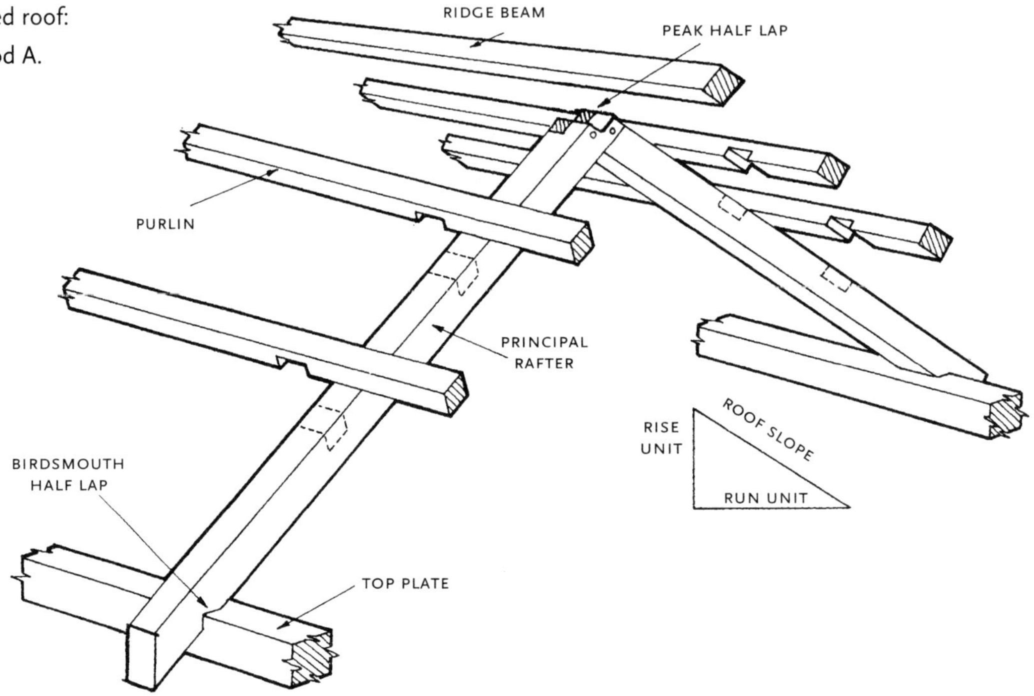

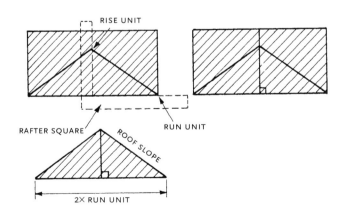

Figure 12-23
Constructing
a ridge
template.

Procedure: Method A.

1) Lay out and cut the ridge template out of a piece of ⅛" (3 mm) hardboard, as shown in Figure 12-23.

2) To lay out the rafter a rafter square is used to "step-off" the number of run units down its length. Figure 12-24 shows the method of layout, beginning at the ridge. It is important to make use of the offset chalked line during this procedure. Make sure that both the ridge plumb line and the plate birdsmouth are marked out. Note the additional material allowance at the ridge; this extra material is for the joinery.

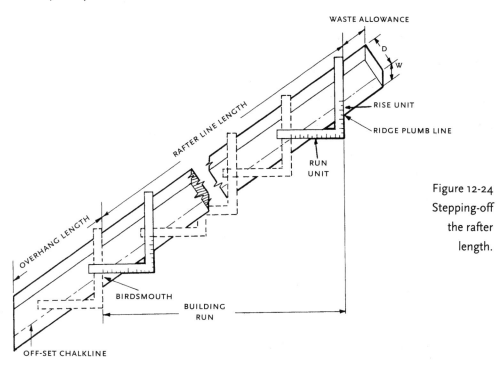

WASTE ALLOWANCE

D

W

RAFTER LINE LENGTH

RISE UNIT

RIDGE PLUMB LINE

RUN UNIT

OVERHANG LENGTH

BIRDSMOUTH

BUILDING RUN

OFF-SET CHALKLINE

Figure 12-24
Stepping-off
the rafter
length.

3) Figure 12-25 shows the layout of the ridge half lap using the ridge template. Begin by aligning the slope of the template to the top surface of the rafter, and align the center "rise" line of the template with the ridge plumb line. Mark line *a*.

Next, slide the template down the distance of the rafter depth, *d,* and mark line *b*. The resulting parallel lines identify the half lap portion.

4) Remove the waste wood and lay out the half lap, as shown in Figure 12-25.

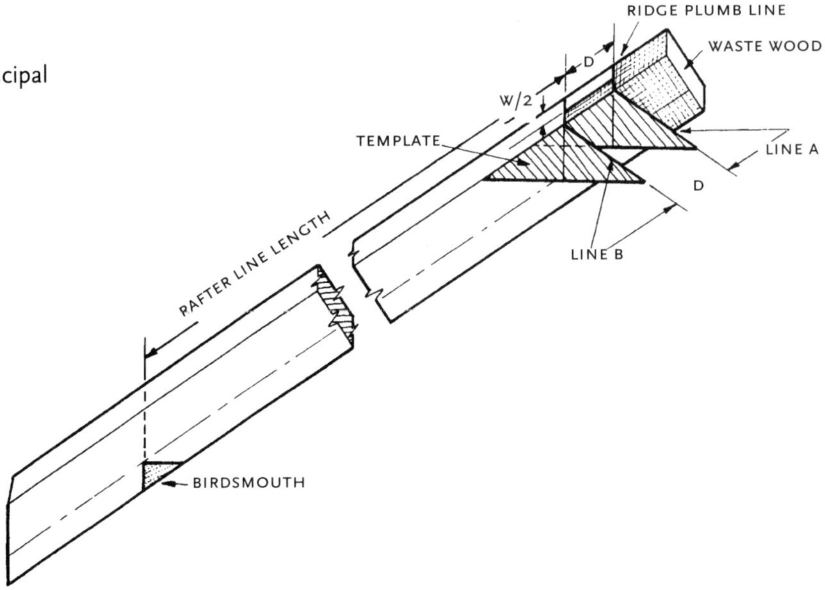

Figure 12-25
Layout of the principal
rafter: method A.

5) Figure 12-26 shows the completed birdsmouth and ridge half lap joints. Repeat these procedures for all rafters, pin them, and position on the building.

6) After all the principal rafters are in place, brace firmly, then install ridge beam and purlins, as shown in Figure 12-22. Pin these beams to the rafters.

Procedure: Method B.

1) Lay out and cut the tenoned birdsmouth template out of a piece of ⅛" (3 mm) hardboard, as shown in Figure 12-28.

2) If the rafter timber has been milled fairly accurately, the stepping-off procedure can be omitted and the rafter can be laid out using only the templates. To do so, begin by aligning the ridge template so its sloped surface matches with the top face edge of the rafter, mark, then remove the waste wood (Figure 12-29).

3) Next, lay out the tongue depth by sliding the template down the distance of the rafter depth, *d*, and mark. Lay out the fork on the opposing rafter leg in the same manner (Figure 12-29).

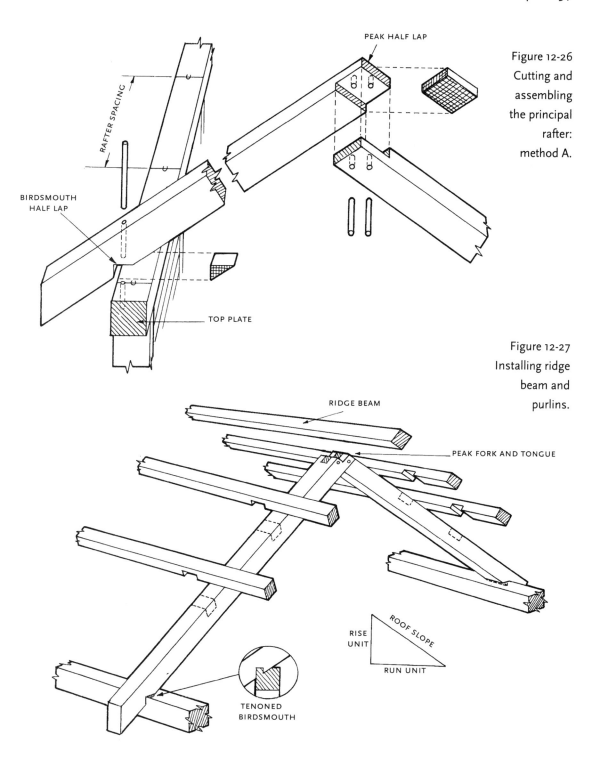

PEAK HALF LAP

RAFTER SPACING

Figure 12-26
Cutting and
assembling
the principal
rafter:
method A.

BIRDSMOUTH
HALF LAP

TOP PLATE

Figure 12-27
Installing ridge
beam and
purlins.

RIDGE BEAM

PEAK FORK AND TONGUE

RISE
UNIT

ROOF SLOPE

RUN UNIT

TENONED
BIRDSMOUTH

Figure 12-28
Laying out and
cutting the
birdsmouth
template.

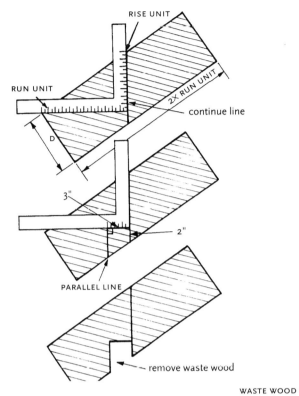

Figure 12-29
Laying out the
fork and tongue
with the
birdsmouth
template on the
rafter.

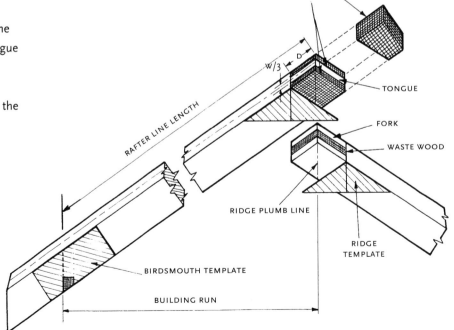

4) Remove the waste wood of the fork and tongue on the two rafter legs.

5) To lay out the tenoned birdsmouth, measure down the line length of the rafter and position the template as shown in Figure 12-29. Mark and remove the waste wood.

6) To lay out the birdsmouth mortises on the building, align the template at each end of the top plate, as shown in Figure 12-30, and chalk layout lines.

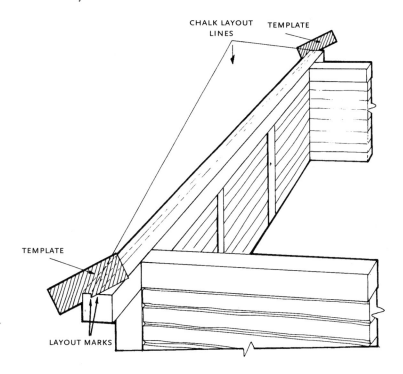

CHALK LAYOUT LINES   TEMPLATE

TEMPLATE

LAYOUT MARKS

Figure 12-30
Laying out the birdsmouth mortises on the building's top plate.

7) Remove the mortise waste wood to a depth and angle equaling the birdsmouth tenon.

8) Assemble and brace the rafters to position on the building (Figure 12-31). Install ridge beam and purlins, as shown in Figure 12-27.

5. Constructing a collar-tie trussed rafter.

Installing a collar-tie half way up the principal rafter will prevent sagging from excessive loads, while at the same time the locking nature of the half lap dovetail will arrest the spreading forces. This binding of the prin-

Figure 12-31
Assembling
rafters on the
building.

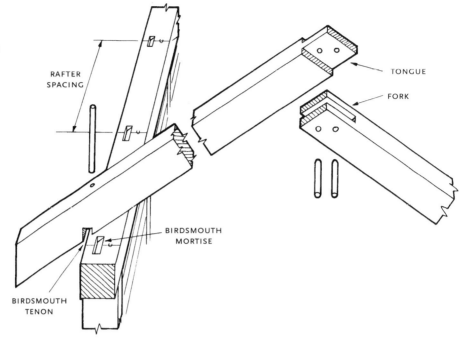

RAFTER
SPACING

TONGUE

FORK

BIRDSMOUTH
MORTISE

BIRDSMOUTH
TENON

cipal rafter is the reason for the term "trussed" rafter. The joinery at the ridge and plate is the same as in Method B, above. The dovetail joinery of the collar-tie must create a tight fit in order for it to properly do its job. The best way to ensure a tight joint is to use a template or trace the tenon dimensions of the collar-tie to produce the rafter mortise. Figure 12-3 shows this kind of roof.

Tools: Eye protection, circular saw, crosscut handsaw, electric drill with $5/8$" (16 mm) or 1" (25 mm) auger bit, rafter square, tape measure, slick, $1^1/2$" (38 mm) chisel, pencil.

Materials: Collar-tie material, $5/8$" (16 mm) steel pins.

Procedure:

1) Construct the principal rafters following the directions for Method B in section 4, above. Make sure the distances between the rafter birdsmouths are equal to the span of the building (Figure 12-32).

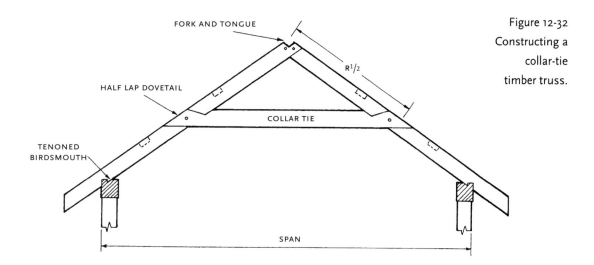

Figure 12-32
Constructing a
collar-tie
timber truss.

2) Lay the collar-tie timber on the principal rafter, so it is half way down the rafter's line length.

3) Lay out the collar-tie dovetail tenon by tracing the rafter sides onto the collar-tie to produce two parallel lines (Figure 12-33a). Next drop a distance of 2" (50 mm) on the inside line and join the two parallel lines with this third sloping line.

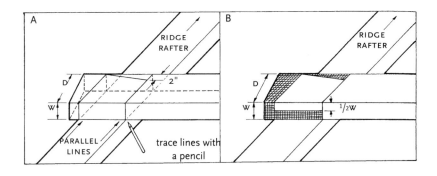

Figure 12-33
Laying out and
cutting the half
lap dovetail
tenon.

4) Lay out the dovetail half lap by dividing the width of the collar-tie tenon in half (Figure 12-33b).

5) Remove the waste wood of the tenon.

6) Reposition the collar-tie, and trace around the tenon to produce the female mortise (Figure 12-34a).

Figure 12-34
Laying out
and cutting
the half lap
dovetail
mortise.

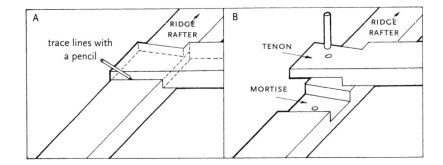

7) Remove the waste wood of the mortise, and pin the collar-tie to the rafter (Figure 12-34b).

Note: In a severe seismic disturbance this half lap joint has the potential to uncouple. To prevent this, through-bolting the joint is recommended, or use a fully housed and pegged mortise and tenon joint in place of a half lap. Refer to Fasteners and Anchors, Chapter 6.

6. Constructing a king post truss.

A. Lofting and preparing the template

A king post truss allows the rafters to hang rather than to exert a spreading force upon the side walls of the building. The struts of the truss redirect this vertical weight force back upward to give support to the rafter and prevent its sagging. The configuration of this support truss makes it ideal for roofs where loading is most excessive, as with sod roofs, for example.

In this section the king post truss is shown as a mid-support truss. Although it is possible to ascertain the individual length of each truss component by using the methods described, the use of a lofting plan is recommended. This full-sized plan, drawn on the building's subfloor, will graphically illustrate all of the member lengths and angles of joinery. It also allows the testing of the two templates that will be used for the joinery layout. The ridge and birdsmouth templates described above in section 4, Method B, will be used here. However, since the rafter legs of the truss are tenoned into the tie-beam and do not form an overhang, a slight adaptation to the birdsmouth template will be necessary. The tie-beam forms an integral part of the king post truss, and is often used in coordination with principal rafters. Its function is to tie or lock the side walls of the building and prevent any spreading forces created by the principal rafters. To serve this function the tie-beam should be joined to the top plate with a housed dovetail in order to provide a locking action while still retaining its strength. The execution of the housed dovetail template and joint are described in Chapter 13, section 6, and again in Chapter 6 (Figure 12-4 shows this kind of roof).

Tools: Tape measure, rafter square, chalkline, handsaw, pencil.

Materials: Tenoned birdsmouth template (see section 4, Method B, above).

Procedure:

1) Loft the roof plan on the subfloor using chalked lines, as shown in Figure 12-35.

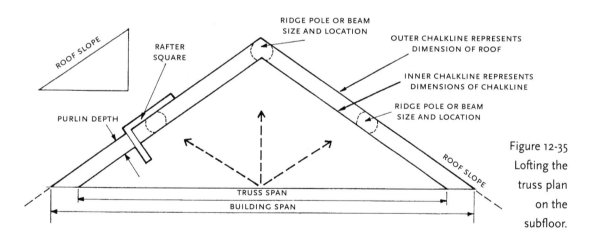

Figure 12-35 Lofting the truss plan on the subfloor.

2) Continue the lofting plan to include the size of the truss members, as shown in Figure 12-36. From this completed loft plan the individual member lengths can be measured (include tenon and waste allowance). Check also the accuracy of the templates.

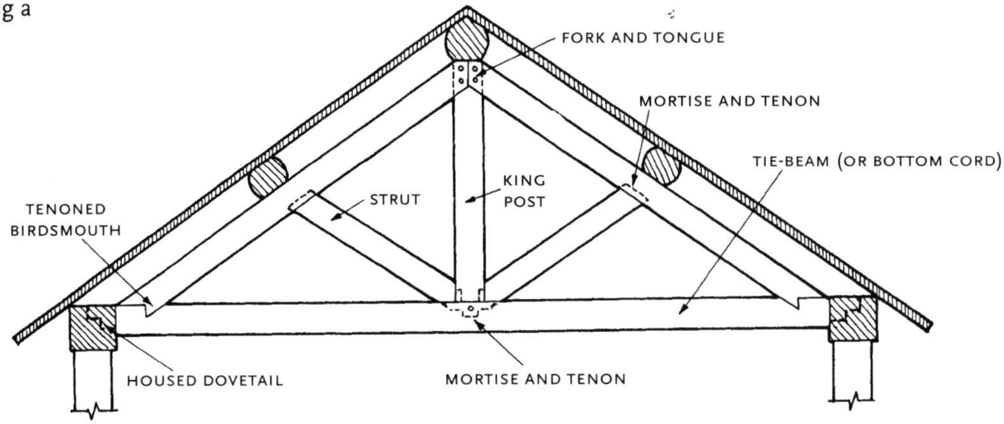

Figure 12-36
Constructing a
king post
truss with
struts.

FORK AND TONGUE

MORTISE AND TENON

TIE-BEAM (OR BOTTOM CORD)

KING
POST

STRUT

TENONED
BIRDSMOUTH

HOUSED DOVETAIL

MORTISE AND TENON

3) Follow Figure 12-37 for the adaptation of the tenoned birdsmouth
template.

Figure 12-37
Adaptation of
tenoned
birdsmouth
template.

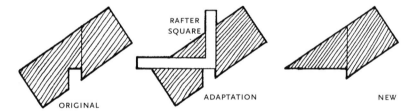

ORIGINAL

RAFTER
SQUARE

ADAPTATION

NEW

B. Laying out and cutting the truss

The layout of the truss joinery is accomplished with the aid of the ridge,
birdsmouth, and housed dovetail templates. These templates rely on the
"squareness" of the rectangular beams. If the accuracy of these milled
beams is poor it will be necessary to chalk reference lines on the beams to
"represent" accurate beam dimensions. In such a case the template
would be aligned with the accurate chalkline. Tenon and mortise layout
also must always originate from a chalked centerline (refer to Joinery
Layout, Chapter 6).

If you are constructing log instead of squared timber trusses, you need only square enough of the log surface to facilitate joinery. The use of chalked centerlines for log truss layout is imperative.

Tools: Eye protection, circular saw, crosscut handsaw, electric drill with ⅝" (16 mm) or 1" (25 mm) auger bit, rafter square, chalkline, 3 lb (1.5 kg) sledge hammer, tape measure, slick, 1½" (38 mm) chisel, mallet, pencil.

Materials: Ridge, birdsmouth, and housed dovetail templates, truss materials, ⅝" (16 mm) steel pins.

Procedure:

1) Begin by laying out the rafter ridge plumb line (step A, Figure 12-38). Align the ridge template so that its slope matches the rafter's top edge, as shown. The center rise line of the template is used to identify the rafter ridge plumb line. Remove the waste wood. Repeat this procedure for the opposite rafter.

2) Continue with the ridge fork layout by sliding the template down

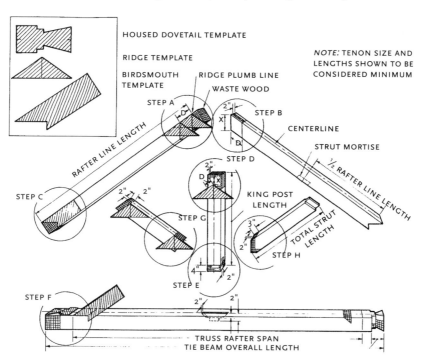

Figure 12-38
Layout of king post truss joinery.

HOUSED DOVETAIL TEMPLATE

RIDGE TEMPLATE

BIRDSMOUTH TEMPLATE

NOTE: TENON SIZE AND LENGTHS SHOWN TO BE CONSIDERED MINIMUM

RIDGE PLUMB LINE

WASTE WOOD

STEP A

STEP B

CENTERLINE

STRUT MORTISE

RAFTER LINE LENGTH

½ RAFTER LINE LENGTH

STEP D

STEP C

KING POST LENGTH

STEP G

TOTAL STRUT LENGTH

STEP H

STEP E

STEP F

TRUSS RAFTER SPAN

TIE BEAM OVERALL LENGTH

the distance of *d*. (Refer to its position on the king post or measure directly from the lofting plan.) Using the center rise line of the template, mark the depth *d* of the fork joint. Continue these layout lines around the rafter. From the chalked centerline on the rafter lay out the 2" (50 mm) width of the fork mortise. (The 2" (50 mm) body of the rafter square works well for such mortise or tenon layout.) Remove waste wood as shown in Figure 12-38, step B. Repeat this procedure for the opposite rafter.

3) Measure down the rafter's line length and lay out the birdsmouth, using the tenoned birdsmouth template as shown in Figure 12-38, step C. Remove waste wood, and repeat this procedure for the opposite rafter.

4) Next lay out the king post tongue by aligning the peak template on the centerline at a distance marked *x*, equal to the face of the rafter. Mark the layout lines, then lay out the tongue tenon using the 2" (50 mm) body of the square as a template (step D). Remove waste wood.

5) Measure down the king post's total length, including the 2" (50 mm) tenon, and cut off any waste allowance. Lay out and cut the 4" (100 mm) long by 2" (50 mm) wide tenon (step E).

6) Next, measure and cut the tie-beam to its overall length (Figure 12-35). Then measure and mark onto the tie-beam the truss rafter span, as shown in Figure 12-38. Lay out the tenoned birdsmouth mortise on the tie-beam by aligning the template, as shown (step F). Chalk a centerline on the top of the beam and lay out the housed dovetail tenons on either end, using the template. Remove the waste wood.

7) To lay out the strut joinery, begin at the foot of the member where it joins the king post. Align the ridge template so its sloped edge aligns with the edge of the strut face. The resulting right angle created by the rise and run of the template is then marked onto the strut foot. Remove the waste wood from the strut foot (step G).

8) Measure the overall length of the strut to include the 3" (75 mm) long tenons at either end, and cut off any waste allowance. Lay out the 2" (50 mm) wide tenons at either end, using the body of a square as a template. Remove waste wood and repeat the procedure for the opposite strut (step H).

9) After all the truss member tenons have been cut, double check their dimensions, then lay out and cut their respective mortises. Always lay out from a chalked centerline.

10) The completed king post truss joinery is shown in Figure 12-39. Assemble all the component pieces, then pin them together. Place the truss on the building.

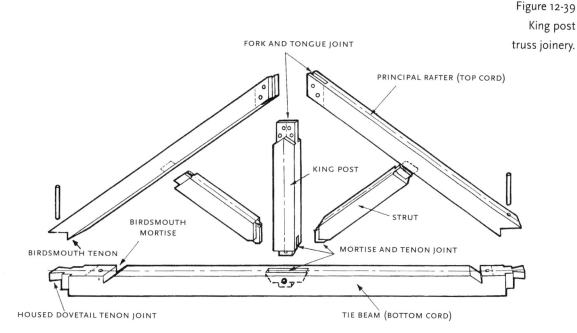

Figure 12-39
King post
truss joinery.

FORK AND TONGUE JOINT

PRINCIPAL RAFTER (TOP CORD)

KING POST

STRUT

BIRDSMOUTH MORTISE

BIRDSMOUTH TENON

MORTISE AND TENON JOINT

HOUSED DOVETAIL TENON JOINT

TIE BEAM (BOTTOM CORD)

PART 2: LONGITUDINAL FRAMING

The methods that follow come under another type of roof construction, called longitudinal framing. Here the structural members run parallel with the ridge line. In this type of construction the roof obtains its sloping form from the shape of the gable end frame. After the gable ends are framed and in place the longitudinal ridge and purlin beams are installed, locking the two gable ends together, giving the roof its strength and a surface on which to apply the covering. These structural beams (log or timber) must be of sufficient size for the roof weight and span. See Appendix III for the necessary specifications with examples for determining the size of structural beams in a given application.

7. Constructing frame gable ends with log ridge pole and purlins for an open ceiling.

Although it is possible to frame up the gable ends in place on the building, it is easier to construct them by lofting and building them on the subfloor. The frame may be built in two halves, and then manually placed on the top plate. However, if a suitable lifting machine is available on site, the entire gable end can be built to include windows and finish, and then be lifted into place. Lofting the plan will also give the precise size and slope cut of the ridge pole. (Figure 12-40 shows this kind of roof.)

Tools: Rafter square, adjustable T-level, chalkline, tape measure, pencil, hammer, handsaw, circular saw (optional).

Materials: Framing materials, sheathing materials, nails, windows (optional).

Procedure:
1) On the subfloor lay out the building's span, run, rise, and roof slope lines (Figure 12-40a).
2) Aligning the body of a framing square on the roof slope line, measure down the tongue the specified thickness for the purlins (i.e. 10", or 250 mm). Mark in several locations and chalk these lines (Figure 12-40b).
3) Locate ridge pole and purlins between these two lines.
4) Frame the entire gable end on the subfloor, using these lines as guides, as shown in Figure 12-40c.
5) Flat-surface the ridge pole to the angle given on the lofting plan. (Use an adjustable T-bevel.) The purlins need only be flat-surfaced and squared where they must pass through the gable end pockets (see Figure 12-40c inset).

8. Installing support posts in a frame gable end.

Posts incorporated within a frame gable end create an interesting design variation, as well as providing structural support. If a lifting machine is available on site no more work is involved in adding posts than there is in straight framing. The lofting method of layout on a subfloor is employed here as well.

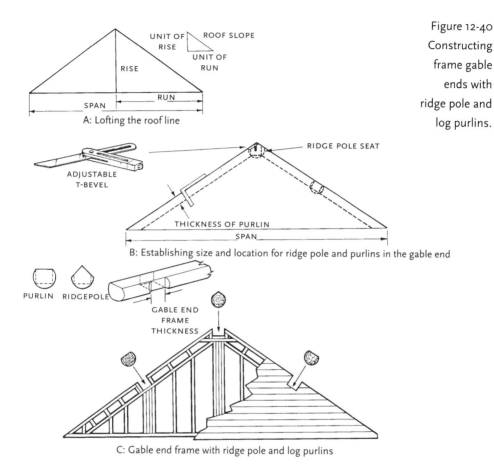

Figure 12-40
Constructing
frame gable
ends with
ridge pole and
log purlins.

UNIT OF RISE

ROOF SLOPE

UNIT OF RUN

RISE

RUN

SPAN

A: Lofting the roof line

ADJUSTABLE T-BEVEL

RIDGE POLE SEAT

THICKNESS OF PURLIN

SPAN

B: Establishing size and location for ridge pole and purlins in the gable end

PURLIN   RIDGEPOLE

GABLE END FRAME THICKNESS

C: Gable end frame with ridge pole and log purlins

Tools: Rafter square, adjustable T-bevel, tape measure, chalkline, circular saw, chainsaw, electric drill with $1/2$" (12 mm) auger bit, handsaw, hammer, pencil, eye and ear protection, 3 lb (1.5 kg) sledge hammer.

Materials: Posts, framing materials, sheathing materials, caulking compound, nails, $1/2$" (12 mm) steel pins.

Procedure:
1) Flat-side two sides of the posts for a uniform thickness (refer to Chapter 5).
2) Loft the gable end on the building subfloor as described in section 7, above.

3) Place posts in their respective places, within the chalked guide lines.

4) Frame the sections between the posts (Figure 12-41).

Figure 12-41
Frame gable end
with support
posts.

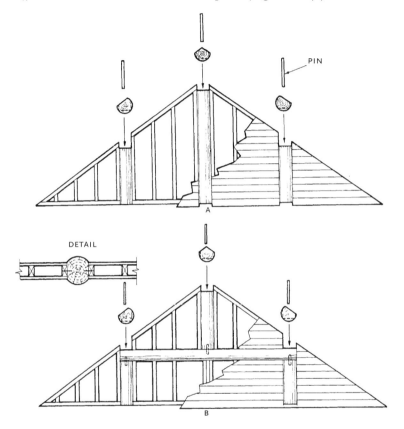

5) Sheath and apply siding, leaving pockets clear for the ridge pole and purlins.

6) Cross-brace and position the gable ends on the building, using an adequate lifting device such as a crane or skyline rig.

7) Flat-side and square the ridge pole and purlins where they cross the gable ends. Obtain the angles from the floor layout.

9. Constructing log gable ends with log ridge pole and purlins for an open ceiling.

Although many people like the appearance of log gable ends, it is difficult and dangerous to construct them high up on the building's top plate. It is also difficult to achieve an air-tight seal between the gables and the roof covering. What follows is a method for prefabricating log gable ends on the ground where quality can be better controlled and danger avoided. (Figure 12-5 shows this type of roof.)

Tools: Builder's level, tape measure, eye and ear protection, chainsaw, level, chalkline, hammer, shovel, pencil scribers.

Materials: Dry gable end logs, 3' (1 m) post lengths (6), nails.

Procedure:
1) Lay out and square the building dimensions on the ground (Figure 12-42).
2) At each gable end dig holes and place posts as shown. Level all these posts to an equal height using the builder's level, and cut to height with a chainsaw.
3) Chalk a line on the top surface of these posts to represent the outside edge of the top plate.
4) Flat-surface the bottom logs, and place one at either gable end with

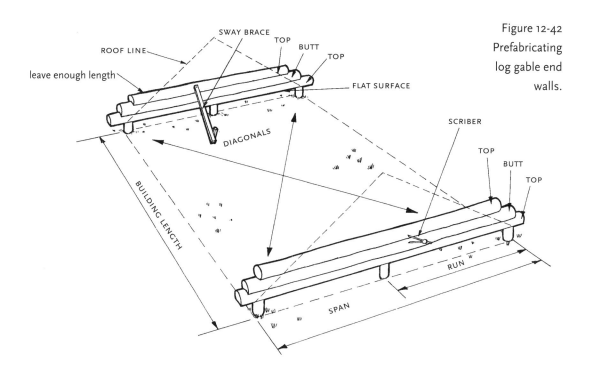

Figure 12-42
Prefabricating
log gable end
walls.

Figure 12-43
Placement of
purlins and
ridge pole.

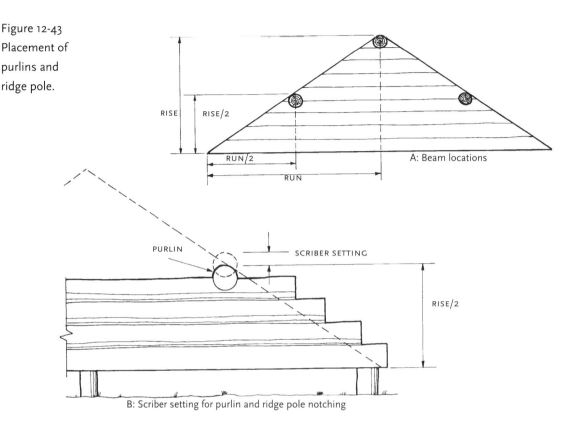

RISE

RISE/2

RUN/2

RUN

A: Beam locations

PURLIN

SCRIBER SETTING

RISE/2

B: Scriber setting for purlin and ridge pole notching

the butts aligned in the same direction. Toe-nail these first logs so they will not move.

5) Construct the gable wall, alternating butts and tops on each course. Make sure that the logs are long enough to accommodate the roof slope cut (Figure 12-42). Sway bracing the gable ends is required for they will be unstable until the beams are in place, locking the two ends together.

6) Build up each wall to the height of the purlin placement, making sure that each wall is progressing equally. Take level heights and adjust on "even" rounds.

The purlins and ridge pole can be notched in the gable ends, or inserted after the gable end walls are built. (For instructions, see section 10 or 13, below.) In either case, they are positioned in the same way in relation to the rise and run of the roof slope. Figures 12-43a and b show beam location and placement.

10. Laying out and cutting a double-scribed square notch for log gable ridge pole and purlin placement.

A double-scribed square notch has special applications for places where the log's structural strength must be maintained. This is the case with cantilevered timbers, and in places where the ridge pole and purlins notch into a log gable end. Due to its squared, flat internal surfaces, this notch not only retains the log's strength but also prevents it from twisting. (This would also make it useful for the final top plate logs in long log buildings.)

The "double" in the term "double-scribe" refers to two scribe lines, one outlining the notch on the top log and the other identical one outlining the notch on the bottom log. "Square notch" refers to the internal squared mating surfaces of the notch. The scribing procedures described below are best accomplished using the Starrett No. 85 – 9" (228 mm) scriber, with bubble attachment. It is recommended because it accommodates two pencils, which allows one to mark the scribe lines on top and bottom logs simultaneously. If the scriber does not have to be turned upside down to mark the bottom log, inaccuracy is avoided.

Tools: Eye and ear protection, chainsaw, scriber (preferably with 2 indelible pencils), ruler or straightedge, tape measure, gouge with mallet, slick, pencil, peavey.

Procedure:
1) Place the purlin in position on the gable ends and block so that both ends are level.
2) Set scriber as shown in Figure 12-43b and level the bubble attachment. (If there is no bubble attachment you must rely on your own skill.) Do not readjust scribers until both ends of the log are completed.
3) Mark out the "double scribe" by scribing around both beam and gable wall logs. If double pencils are not available, turn scribers upside down and repeat the process (Figure 12-44a). Check to see that the scribe line is legible. A fine spray of water on the scribe's path, together with indelible pencils, will produce a clear line.
4) Mark out the "square notch" portion by positioning the scriber approximately half way down the notch on the top log (Figure 12-

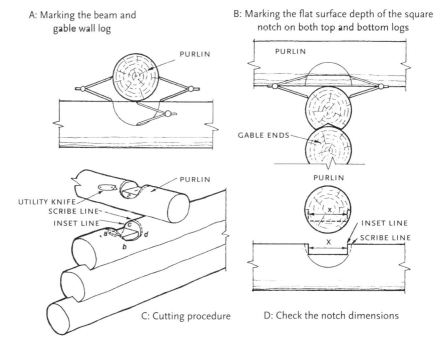

A: Marking the beam and gable wall log

B: Marking the flat surface depth of the square notch on both top and bottom logs

C: Cutting procedure

D: Check the notch dimensions

Figure 12-44
Scribing and cutting a square notch.

44b). Where the two points of the scriber touch each scribe line, mark with a dot. Repeat this process in the four locations on both sides of the log. Then, join these dots together with a straight line on both the top and bottom of each log. These lines will indicate the flat, squared portions inside the notch. There is no need to worry if these lines are not exactly level, as each cut surface will still correspond with its opposite surface. However, a slight slope toward the outside of the notch will ensure drainage of any accumulated moisture.

5) Repeat this entire scribing process for the opposite end of the log before moving the log or adjusting the scribers.

6) Roll the beam toward the inside of the gable end, and finish laying out the notch by joining points a–b and c–d with straight, inset lines (Figure 12-44c). Do this on both log ends. This establishes the square portion's layout.

7) With a utility knife, make an incision $1/8"–1/4"$ (3–6 mm) deep around the notch outline. This cut-line helps to identify the boundary of the notch when "planing" down to the line with the chainsaw. It will also prevent the notch's edges from splintering and fraying.

8) Cut the notch by first removing the waste wood off the top, flat-surface portion. This is easily done by making multiple bread-slice cuts to the line, then removing the debris with a slick.

The curved portion of the notch can be cut to the line using a gouge and mallet.

9) Measure between the finished notch faces for accuracy, as it is difficult to lift and roll the beam once it is positioned (Figure 12-44d).

10) Repeat the entire process for the opposite end of the log.

11. Cutting the roof slope for log gable ends using a jig.

Cutting the gable end roof slope is quick and accurate using the same type of guide rail mill jig as the one described in Chapter 5. For this application it will be necessary to piece the guide rails between the ridge pole and purlins.

Tools: Eye and ear protection, chainsaw, hammer.

Materials: $1/2$" (12 mm) carriage bolts, $3/4$" (19 mm) plywood pads, guide rails, nails.

Procedure:
1) Attach plywood pads to the chainsaw bar, as shown in Figure 12-45. The spacing may vary according to the size of the gable end logs.
2) Space and nail the guide rails parallel to each other on either side of the gable end as shown. The guide rail spacing will be the same as the chainsaw bar pad spacing.
3) Starting at the peak, cut the gable ends down to the plate. When doing this, have someone else apply moderate pressure to the pads, using two sticks.

12. Inserting the nailing spline for log gable ends.

The nailing spline is an essential part of a log gable end. The roof decking should be nailed into this spline when it passes over the gable ends, so as not to inhibit any possible settling of the gable end.

Tools: Eye and ear protection, chainsaw, chalkline, hammer, tape measure, handsaw.

Figure 12-45
Cutting the
gable end roof
slope using a
guide rail jig.

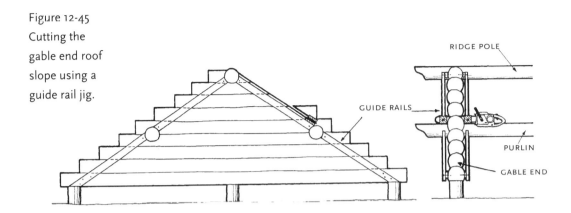

Materials: Nails, 2" × 4" (38 × 89 mm) splines.

Procedure:

Figure 12-46 shows a 2" × 4" (38 × 89 mm) spline. Chalk guide lines down the center of the sloped surface equal to the spline width, and cut a groove so that the spline will come flush with the surface. Repeated chainsaw cuts to the correct depth followed by honing of the groove with the bar nose works well here. Alternatively, use a router with a ³/₄" straight bit to remove waste wood. Remember to always use a straight-edge guide for the router to follow.

Figure 12-46
Cutting and
inserting a gable
end nailing spine.

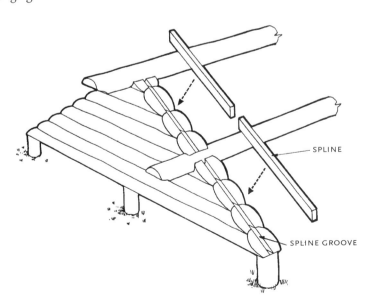

13. Placing ridge pole and purlin inserts for log gable ends.

Instead of notching the purlins and ridge pole into the gable ends as they are being constructed, build the gable ends, then cut the roof slope and insert the purlins and ridge pole into their pockets. With this method the purlins and ridge pole can be flat-sided before placing them in the gable ends. It is important to have sufficient sway bracing as the gable ends are very unstable until the purlins and ridge pole are in place.

Tools: Eye and ear protection, chainsaw, tape measure, chalkline, scribers, level, hammer, drill with $5/8$" (16 mm) auger bit.

Materials: $5/8$" (16 mm) lag screws, insulation, foam roll, bracing, $1/2$" (12 mm) steel pins, roof slope cutting jig.

Procedure:
1) Build up the gable ends, sway bracing as you proceed.
2) Flat-side and square the purlins and ridge pole where they cross the gable ends (Figure 12-47).
3) Cut the roof slope and insert the nailing splines.
4) Cut pockets in the gable ends so the purlins and ridge pole will fit flush with the roof slope surface, as shown.
5) Number the gable end logs and replace them on the building. Add a layer of foam roll and lag screw the first gable end log to the top plate. Put the gable logs in place, insulating and pinning where necessary.

14. Constructing a sod roof.

The visual impact of a solid wood post and beam house built on a foundation of rock and crowned with the greens and golds of a sod roof is unrivaled. Such a house looks and feels like a true embodiment of the environment. The positive psychological effects of living within the protective walls of such a dwelling are little understood by a society that insists on segregating man from nature.

Not so long ago, sod roofs were one of a few primitive protective roof coverings. Then, if it rained for two days outside it rained for a week inside! But the problems and complexities associated with these primitive sod roofs are solved by the modern materials at our disposal today. We now have the means for constructing a warm, weatherproof sod roof with

Figure 12-47
Log gable
ends with
ridge pole
and purlin
inserts.

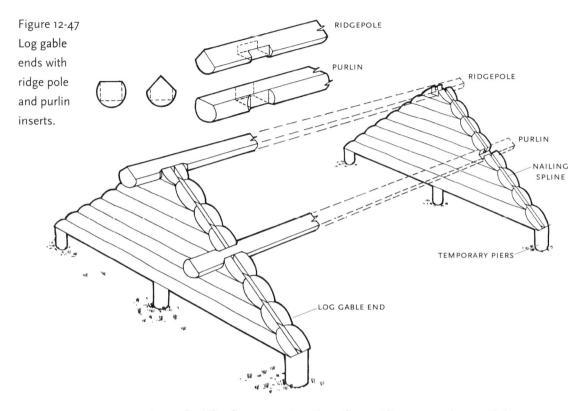

RIDGEPOLE

PURLIN

RIDGEPOLE

PURLIN

NAILING
SPLINE

TEMPORARY PIERS

LOG GABLE END

many times the life of a conventional roof, providing we understand the materials' properties and limitations.

A roof covering composed of two layers of sod is heavier than a conventional covering due both to its physical properties and the increased snow load retained. The average (dead) weight of a conventional roof system is 20 lbs per sq. ft. (100 kg/m²), compared with the 51 lbs per sq. ft. (250 kg/m²) of a sod roof system. Part of this weight increase is due to the increased size and number of roof frame components required to support the extra weight.

Sod, like many other roof coverings, has an optimum slope to which it can be applied. The ideal grade for sod is between 20°–25°. Any grade below 18° inhibits rapid water runoff, while a roof grade greater than 25° creates the risk that the sod will slip. Where grades are slightly steeper than 25°, chicken wire can be laid across the ridge and down the roof to prevent this problem. As well, a strong retaining board anchored directly to the rafters will be needed to hold the sod covering while permitting unobstructed water runoff (refer to Figure 12-48).

Without additions, the grass and root system of sod is not waterproof. The traditional method was to use birch bark as an underlay between the sod and roof decking. The bark, with its high creosote content, resisted rot and formed a somewhat waterproof membrane. Today its use is impractical in comparison to the various waterproof materials available. A waterproof, rootproof 2-ply granulated S.B.S. (styrene, butatine, styrene) modified bitumen sheet membrane covering is recommended. This material is commonly used on flat sloped roofs as well as underneath indoor gardens and may be obtained through a quality roofing supply source. "Modified" refers to the chemical conditioning which gives this material flexibility even at hot temperatures and also prevents root damage. How to apply this roofing membrane is explained below.

There is some question concerning the insulative value of sod since there is as yet very little recorded data available. Testimony from individuals living under sod roofs in northern Europe and Scandinavia, however, gives sod a very favorable rating. Apparently, the older sod with its established network of roots offers the most loft, and therefore the most

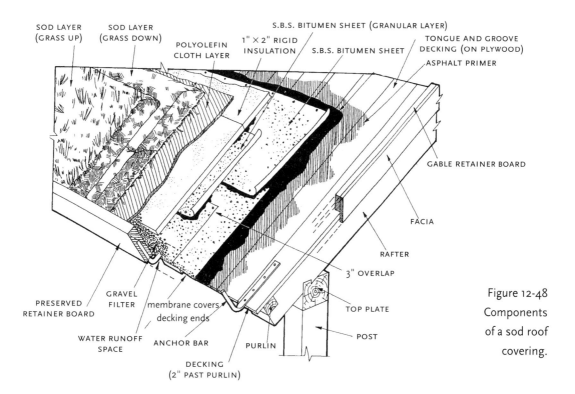

Figure 12-48
Components of a sod roof covering.

dead air space as compared to younger, denser sod. During the winter the added snow layer contributes to both the overall thermal resistivity and the thermal mass potential. During the summer, the shade of the growing bunch grass together with the substantial root system allows for slow, steady moisture evaporation cooling. Shown graphically, there would be a gradual heat-loss curve much like the one for a solid timber or log wall, due to the time delay factor of thermal mass. However, because of today's stringent building regulations, the sod roof will include a 2" (50 mm) layer of extruded polystyrene rigid foam insulation to be sandwiched between roof membrane and sod. As well, to allow moisture transference while preventing organic matter from touching the insulation, a polyolefin woven cloth layer is used to separate the sod from the insulation. This cloth material is widely used in landscaping.

Materials: Preserved retainer boards, anchor bars (galvanized), asphalt primer, asphalt, 2-ply bitumen sheet membrane (described above), rigid foam insulation, polyolefin cloth, 5"–6" (125–150 mm) thick sod (2 layers), mop, roofing nails, gravel, lead (chimney flashing).

Tools: Hammer, knife, tape measure, torch, gloves.

Procedure:

1) Construct the roof frame to accommodate the extra roof weight. Refer to Structural Tables, Appendix III, based on 51 lbs per sq. ft. dead weight.

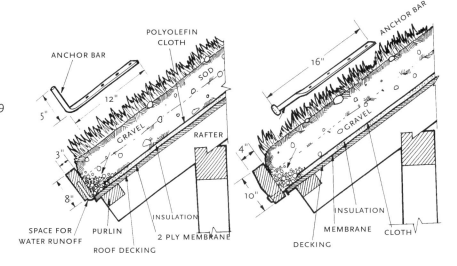

Figure 12-49
Retainer
board.

2) Deck or sheath the roof. Where tongue and groove decking is used and the seams are not tight there is a possibility the hot tar will seep through. In such a case, apply a plywood sheathing over the decking.

3) Fasten the anchor bars to the rafters as shown in Figure 12-48. See Figure 12-49 for retainer boards and anchor bars.

4) Apply an asphalt primer to the roof deck.

5) Once the first layer is in place, nail the top edge to the roof deck. Restrict the nailing area to the upper 3" (75 mm) edge of the sheet (Figure 12-48).

   Note: A single ply, slightly thicker bitumen sheet with an asphalt-coated undersurface is available. To apply the roof membrane start at the bottom and simply heat the undersurface with a torch until it is soft, then lay it in place on the roof deck.

6) Working your way up the roof, lay the next bitumen sheet so its bottom edge overlaps the top edge of the first layer by 3" (75 mm). Torch this sheet into place (Figure 12-48). Continue this process until the entire roof is covered with this membrane.

7) Position the retainer boards, gravel filter, and insulation as shown in Figure 12-49. Do not nail the insulation to the deck.

8) Place the polyolefin cloth over the insulation, then cover it with two layers of sod, preferably with older, well-established roots. The first sod layer should be placed grass side down with the second layer placed grass side up, staggering all joints.

9) Figure 12-50 is a diagram of the chimney flashing. The flashing material must be lead, as zinc will deteriorate with a chemical reaction to humus water.

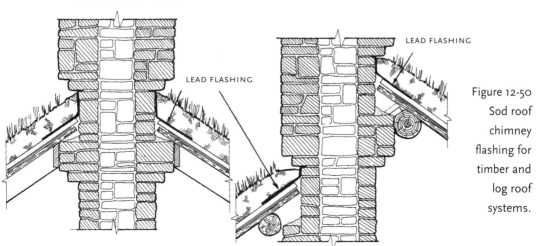

LEAD FLASHING

LEAD FLASHING

Figure 12-50
Sod roof
chimney
flashing for
timber and
log roof
systems.

CHAPTER THIRTEEN

Floor Systems

The floor system is really a flat roof system, its structural components of sills, girders, and joists doing effectively the same work as the top plates, beams, and rafters of the roof. Care must be taken to ensure that the foundation is level and square to accept the floor system. The quality and sizing of the floor members must conform to Code—that is, to be without structural defects and adequate for the loading and spans (refer to Structural Beam Loading and Sizing in Appendix III).

Whether the foundation will be continuous or piers, it is most important that it be strong and level. Any large deviations of the floor's level surface will impair wall tightness between the posts and solid wood infill panels, especially if the panels are prefabricated.

The structural support components of a floor consist of sills, girders, and floor joists. Figures 13-1 to 13-5 show examples of floor types. The log floor components shown in these figures can also be applied to entirely squared timbers. The subsequent drawings show log joinery details with just enough flat surface and dimensional squaring to illustrate the work. However, the layout and cutting procedures for squared timber are identical.

1. The various floor systems, with sill anchorage.

Procedures:

Figure 13-1 shows two types of frame subflooring constructed on a continuous concrete foundation. For information on post anchorage, refer to Chapter 6. The anchorage of the sill is either a bolt type or none at all, as in the stepped foundation. The advantages of a frame lumber floor are its relative ease and speed of construction, and the level surface obtained. This type of floor does not make an attractive exposed ceiling in the basement or second storey. Note the additional support blocking under the posts, which is necessary because the weight of the roof is transmitted to the foundation via the posts. This is shown as an alternative to the preferred method of resting the post directly on supportive concrete. Ensure proper flashing and a moisture break (foam roll) to prevent moisture damage.

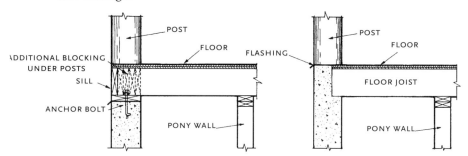

Figure 13-1 Frame floor system on continuous foundation.

Figure 13-2 shows a frame floor placed on a pier foundation. Here the built-up sill and girder are anchored to the piers with anchor bars. A built-up sill of this type will not need additional blocking under the posts.

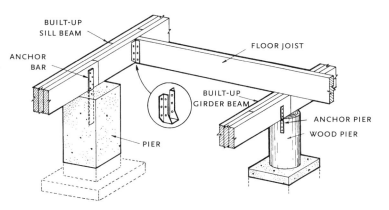

Figure 13-2 Frame floor system on a pier foundation.

Figure 13-3 shows a log or timber floor placed on a continuous preserved wood foundation. Here the midspan support girder is positioned below the floor joists with the joists spiked or lag bolted into it. This type of floor, when decked with 2" × 6" (38 × 140 mm) tongue and groove flooring, makes an attractive exposed ceiling for a basement. Ensure solid support to ground under weight-bearing posts.

Figure 13-3
Log or timber
floor system on
continuous
preserved wood
foundation.

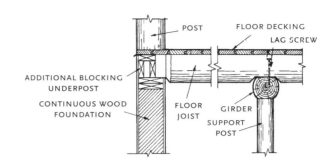

Figure 13-4 shows a log or timber sill anchored to the foundation with a bolt embedded in the concrete. Here the girder and floor joists are at the same level as the sills, and no headroom is lost as in the previous method. In this case, however, strength is taken from the girder, and intermittent support posts should be placed. Further instructions for this type of sill, girder, and joist joinery follow later in this chapter. When decked with 2" × 6" (38 × 140 mm) tongue and groove this floor makes an attractive open ceiling for a basement or second storey.

Figure 13-4
Log or timber
floor system on
a continuous
concrete
foundation.

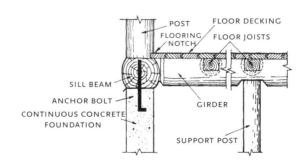

Figure 13-5 shows a floor system for use on a pier foundation when an insulated floor is necessary. It is a method quite similar to the one in Figure 13-2, except that the laminated sill and girder have now been replaced by a log or timber sill and frame ponywall. A ponywall is a short structurally supportive frame wall which, in this case, is substituted for the girder beam. If the foundation piers were made of preserved wood, the sill could be either spiked or lag bolted.

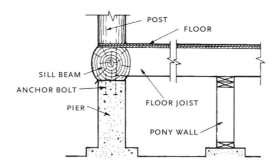

Figure 13-5
Combination log
or timber and
frame floor
system on a pier
foundation.

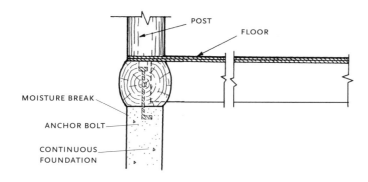

Figure 13-6
Combination log
or timber and
frame floor
system on a
continuous
foundation.

2. Stress forces.

A floor system is comprised of horizontal beams called sills, girders, and joists. These are structural members and as such must conform in size to the amount of load they will carry over the distance (span) between supports. When a loading force is applied to a beam (by furniture, people, etc.) it creates stress forces within the wood. Figure 13-7 illustrates the internal forces created as a result of the loading force applied.

When a beam is expected to carry too much load or to span a distance too great for its size, limiting factors such as fiber failure and/or excess bending come into play. Figure 13-8 illustrates how proportionally less load can be carried by a beam as the span increases. The limiting factors are apparent in these diagrams as well.

In the majority of cases excessive bending will be the main limiting factor in relation to the floor beam size and span. Excessive bending of

Figure 13-7
Forces at play on a
horizontal beam.

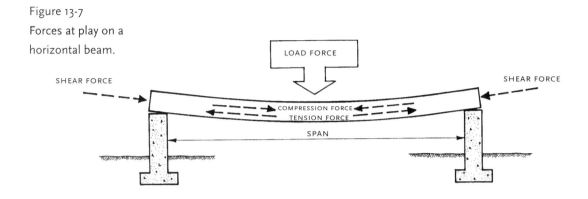

Figure 13-8
Limiting
factors
created by
variable
loading
and span.

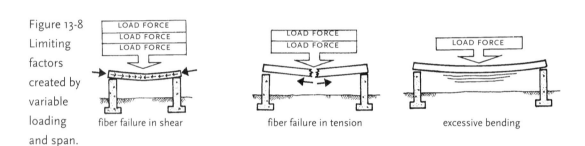

fiber failure in shear   fiber failure in tension   excessive bending

the beams creates a "springy" floor—not in itself unsafe but bothersome
nevertheless. The National Building Codes specify that main floors bend
or deflect no more than 1" in 360" (1 mm in 360 mm) of span. Roofs are
to deflect no more than 1" in 240" (1 mm in 240 mm) of span, using drywall (gypsum board) as a finish. When using wood as a finish material
greater deflection is allowed.

See Appendix III to determine structural beam sizes for a given load
and span.

3. Determining girder sizes and spacing.

Girders are considered the "backbone" of a floor system, since they carry
most of the floor weight. To determine the size of the girder beam needed
for a given span refer to Appendix III.

Girder spacing between supports is usually no more than 16" (5 m).
Thus, a building with a span of 30" (9 m) between foundation walls
would have one mid-support girder, while a 40" (12 m) span would have

Figure 13-9
Girder
spacing.

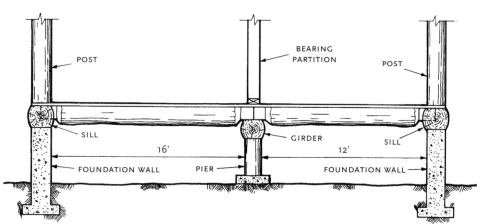

two. Girders should be placed directly below bearing partitions. This may call for a slight adjustment in the girder spacing (Figure 13-9). Note that in a pier foundation there must be a pier located directly below every log or timber post to provide extra support, and wherever there is a weight-bearing joinery intersection.

4. Sill corner joinery: How to lay out and cut a half lap corner joint.

Once the foundation is in place the next job is to flat-side the sill logs to sit on the foundation, and to join these together at the corners of the building. One way to produce a level sill plate is to join together the logs at the corners with a half lap joint.

Tools: Eye and ear protection, chainsaw, tape measure, chalkline, carpenter's square, slick, level, pencil.

Procedure:
  1) Flat-surface the sill logs to a uniform thickness (8"–10", or 200–250 mm).
  2) Place the first two opposing sill logs on the building. If flashing is not being used place them slightly overhanging the foundation

edge to provide a drip cap. A kerf cut with a circular saw to the underside edge of the log sill aids in preventing rain from penetrating between the foundation and sill beam: this is called a drip cap, or drip edge specifically.

3) Square the sides of these sill logs where they cross the corner of the foundation (Figure 13-10a). Always work from a chalked centerline.

4) Place the next two sill logs in position on the foundation so the ends rest on the sill logs below.

Figure 13-10
Layout and
cutting
procedures for
a half lap joint.

5) Trace the sides of each timber at the joints and lay out the depth of each half lap by extending vertical lines at the corners (Figure 13-10b). The depth of the notches are to equal half the sill depth (D/2).

6) Roll the sidewall sill logs back and remove the waste wood in all notches (Figure 13-10c).

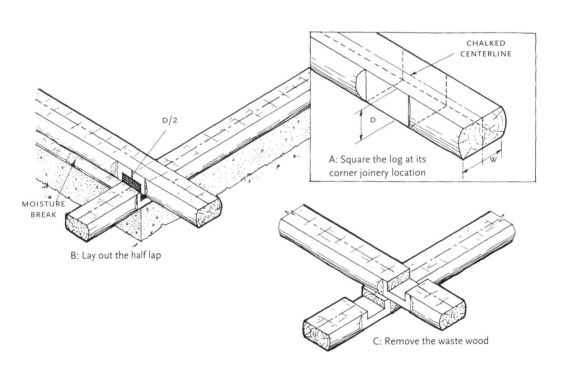

CHALKED CENTERLINE

D/2

D

W

A: Square the log at its corner joinery location

MOISTURE BREAK

B: Lay out the half lap

C: Remove the waste wood

7) Join the sill logs together, providing the necessary moisture break between the sills and foundation. The moisture break can be either an asphalt shingle or a layer of closed-cell foam roll. It prevents moisture siphoning from the concrete foundation into the sill members, a process which can eventually lead to rot.

5. Sill corner joinery: How to lay out and cut a dovetail corner joint.

Another way of joining sill logs at the corners is by using a dovetail mortise and tenon joint. This method, like the last, produces a level sill plate. Mating the timbers and tracing the joint is not possible here, so a dovetail template is employed to save time and simplify the layout for this and other occasions. The dovetail joint has a locking capacity and is preferred over the half lap joint. Refer to Chapter 6 for more information on joinery.

Tools: Eye and ear protection, chainsaw, pencil, tape measure, level, hand crosscut and ripsaw, electric drill with 3/4" (19 mm) bit.

Materials: 1/8" (3 mm) hardboard template, 3/4" (19 mm) hardwood pegs.

Procedure:

1) Flat-side the sills to a uniform thickness (8"–10", or 200–250 mm).
2) Cut the sill logs to the exact length of the foundation. Allow for a drip cap overhang if flashing is not used.
3) Square the side of the sills back from each end so that all sills are of equal width (Figure 13-11a). Always work from a chalked centerline.
4) Make a template, such as the one shown in Figure 13-11 inset, out of 1/8" (3 mm) hardboard.
5) Trace out the mortise and tenon as shown in Figure 13-11a.
6) Cut out the mortise and tenon as shown in Figure 13-11b. Test the mortise with the template, and if the joint is too tight shave the tenon slightly.
7) Repeat for all corners, then drill and peg, as shown in Figure 13-11c.
   Note: If a post peg tenon is used to lock the dovetail mortise and tenon together, then pegging is not required.

6. Joining girders to sills: How to lay out a housed dovetail tenon and mortise.

The housed dovetail accomplishes the job of locking a girder between two support sills (Figure 13-11). The dovetail portion locks the joint while the housed portion retains the timber's strength. To simplify and dupli-

Figure 13-11
Layout and
cutting
procedures
for a dovetail
corner joint.

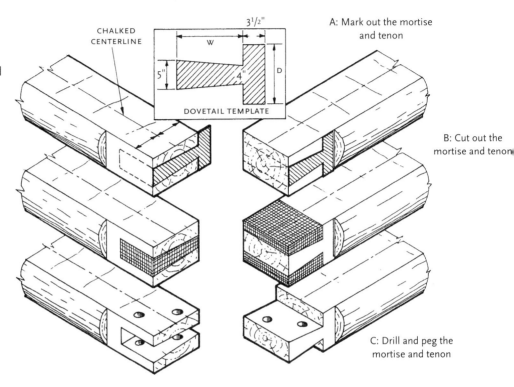

A: Mark out the mortise and tenon

B: Cut out the mortise and tenon

C: Drill and peg the mortise and tenon

cate layout procedures a template is used for the joint. For cutting procedures see sections 7a and 7b, below.

Tools: Pencil, tape measure, chalkline, level.

Materials: ¹/₈" (3 mm) hardboard template.

Procedure:

1) Cut the girder to final length. Squaring the two ends makes tenon layout and cutting easier but is not necessary. The final girder length is measured from between the sill plate centerlines. Refer to section 4, above, for squaring procedures.

2) Make a template, such as the one shown, out of ¹/₈" (3 mm) hardboard. The width and length dimensions may vary according to the

size of the logs used. It is wise to have several different-sized templates on hand (see Figure 13-12 inset).

3) Mark out the housed dovetail tenon as shown in Figure 13-12a, aligning the template with the chalked centerline on the beam. If all tenons can be of equal dimensions layout procedure will be simplified.

Figure 13-12
Layout
procedures for
a housed
dovetail joint.

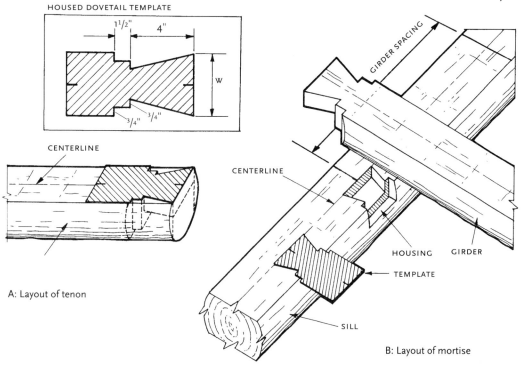

HOUSED DOVETAIL TEMPLATE

GIRDER SPACING

CENTERLINE

CENTERLINE

HOUSING   GIRDER

TEMPLATE

A: Layout of tenon

SILL

B: Layout of mortise

4) Cut the tenons. (See section 7a, below. Refer to Chapter 6 for more information.)
5) Mark out the girder spacing by measuring down the sill centerline.
6) Using the template lay out the housed mortises. For the housed portion drop the lines down using a level (see section 7b, below).
7) Cut the mortises (see section 7b, below).
8) Position the girder between the sills.

7a. Joining girders to sills: How to cut a housed dovetail tenon.

This procedure for wood removal of a housed dovetail tenon is applicable to various other joints. Try to visualize the completed tenon before cutting.

Tools: Eye and ear protection, chainsaw, slick, handsaw, pencil, carpenter's square.

Procedure:

Figure 13-13
Cutting a
housed dovetail
tenon joint.

1) Drop layout lines down vertically, using a carpenter's square or level (Figure 13-11a).
2) Make vertical cuts and remove waste wood sections 1, 2, and 3. Remember to barely leave the layout line (Figure 13-13a).

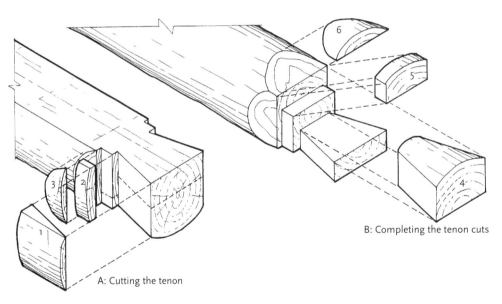

A: Cutting the tenon

B: Completing the tenon cuts

3) Roll timber upside down and remove waste wood sections 4, 5, and 6. Clean up with a slick (Figure 13-13b).
   Note: Horizontal cuts are difficult to execute with a chainsaw. An alternative method is to make a series of vertical kerfs to the line and remove the waste wood with a slick or a handsaw.
4) Repeat procedures for the opposite end of the timber.

7b. Joining girders to sills: How to cut a housed dovetail mortise.

This procedure for the wood removal of a housed dovetail mortise is applicable to various other joints. Again, try to visualize the completed mortise before cutting.

Tools: Eye and ear protection, chainsaw with safety chain, 1" (25 mm) forstner bit and electric drill or hand brace, tape measure, slick, 1" (25 mm) chisel, level.

Procedure:
1) Drop layout lines down vertically using a level (Figure 13-12b).
2) Drill holes along the back side of the dovetail to a depth of its male counterpart (Figure 13-14a). These holes allow for easier wood removal.

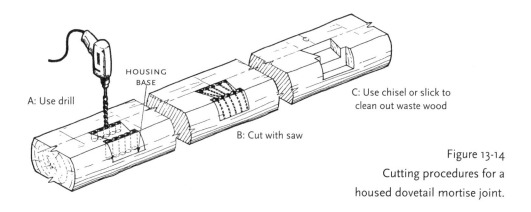

HOUSING BASE

A: Use drill

B: Cut with saw

C: Use chisel or slick to clean out waste wood

Figure 13-14
Cutting procedures for a housed dovetail mortise joint.

3) Drill holes along the back side of the housing shoulder to the depth of its base (Figure 13-14a).
4) Make a series of kerf cuts using a chainsaw as in Figure 13-14b.
5) Remove waste wood and clean the mortise using a slick or chisel, as in Figure 13-14c.
6) Fit the girder beam in place between the sills.

8. Joining floor joists: How to lay out, cut, and place a joist using a squared tenon and mortise joint.

This is the easiest method for constructing and installing a log floor joist. It requires squaring the ends of the joists, then cutting pocket mortises in the sill and girder so that the joists can sit level. Once this has been done the floor decking can be installed.

Refer to the floor joist size tables in Appendix VI for joist sizes for a given span. Appendix VI consists of two tables: a log to frame conversion table and a joist size table. From these two tables one can obtain the correct joist size for a given span and spacing, whether for log, timber, or common lumber.

Tools: Eye and ear protection, chainsaw, chalkline, tape measure, carpenter's square, slick, pencil.

Procedure:
1) Flat-surface a 2"–4" (50–100 mm) nailing surface on all the floor joists.
2) Chalk a centerline onto the flat surface. This will ensure that the squared tenons will be in alignment during layout.
3) Cut the joists to length. There should be 2"–3" (50–75 mm) minimum portion of uncut wood remaining between inline joists on a girder. This uncut wood retains the strength of the girder.
4) Lay out and cut squared tenons on each end of the joists. Use the carpenter's square for layout by aligning it to the centerline. If possible make all squared tenons of equal dimensions to simplify joinery procedures (Figure 13-15a). Make the vertical cuts and remove the side waste wood. Then, lay out the depth of the tenon on the sawn flat sides, turn the timber on its side, and remove the bottom waste wood.

The best way to lay out the joist pocket mortises is to position the finished joists on the building at their correct spacings and trace around the tenons. Then drop vertical lines and cut the mortise depths so that all the joist top surfaces sit level.

Another method is to place a mark an equal distance up from the foundation or floor on each end of the sill and chalk a depth line (Figure 13-15b inset). This line establishes the bottom of the mortise seats. Next chalk a line on top of the sill log, down its full length, providing a 3" (75 mm) minimum joist bearing surface. Lay out the joist spacings. Then, measuring on either side of the spacing's centerline, lay out the joist width and drop vertical lines down to the mortise seat chalkline.

5) Remove the mortise waste wood by making a plunge cut at the

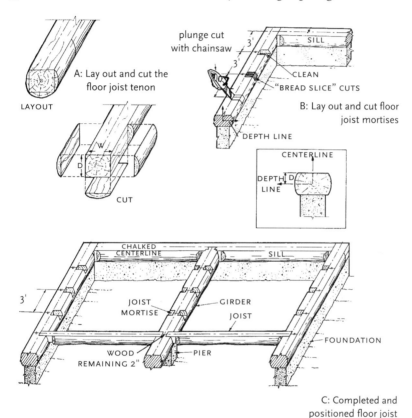

A: Lay out and cut the floor joist tenon

LAYOUT

CUT

plunge cut with chainsaw

SILL

CLEAN

"BREAD SLICE" CUTS

B: Lay out and cut floor joist mortises

DEPTH LINE

CENTERLINE

DEPTH LINE

CHALKED CENTERLINE

SILL

JOIST MORTISE

GIRDER

JOIST

FOUNDATION

WOOD REMAINING 2"

PIER

Figure 13-15 Constructing and placing a floor joist.

C: Completed and positioned floor joist

back to the depth of the mortise. Make the vertical side cuts next to the depth of the mortise. Cut out the remaining portion by making successive "bread slice" cuts to the depth line and remove waste with a slick. WARNING: Using a chainsaw to make a plunge cut is dangerous even when using an anti-kick safety chain. Alternatively drill relief holes at the back of the mortise pocket and finish with a chisel or stick.

6) Position the floor joist as in Figure 13-16c.

Figure 13-16
Layout and
cutting
procedures
for a half lap
dovetail
joint.

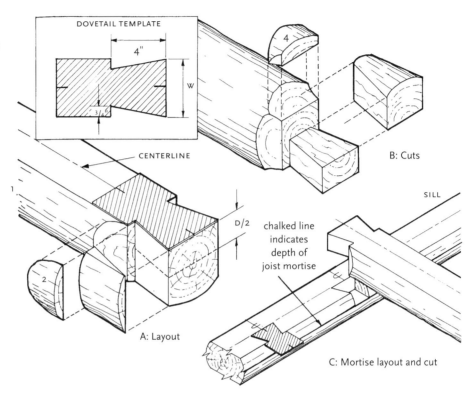

DOVETAIL TEMPLATE

4"

W

3/4"

CENTERLINE

4

B: Cuts

1

D/2

chalked line
indicates
depth of
joist mortise

SILL

2

A: Layout

C: Mortise layout and cut

9. Joining floor joists: How to lay out and cut a half lap dovetail tenon and mortise.

The dovetail is a self-locking joint—most useful when timbers are in tension, as with purlins which are set flush into trusses. Another common use is for joining joists to girders or sills.

Tools: Eye and ear protection, tape measure, chainsaw, chalkline, carpenter's square, pencil.

Materials: ⅛" (3 mm) hardboard template.

Procedure:

1) Cut the joist or purlin to final length. Squaring the two ends makes tenon layout and cutting easier, but is not necessary.

2) Out of ⅛" (3 mm) hardboard make a template like the one shown in the inset to Figure 13-16. The width and length dimensions may vary according to the size of logs used. Again, it is wise to have a couple of different size templates on hand.

3) Mark out the dovetail tenons as shown in Figure 13-16a, aligning template center marks with the chalked centerline on the timber. If it is possible to make all tenons of equal dimensions this will simplify joinery procedure.

4) Make vertical cuts and remove waste wood sections 1 and 2.

5) Roll timber upside down and remove waste wood sections 3 and 4, as in Figure 13-16b. Clean with a slick.

6) For joist spacing, chalk a centerline down the girder and sill and mark out spacings. There should be a minimum of 2"–3" (50–75 mm) uncut wood remaining between inline joists on the girder.

7) It is best to lay joists in place and trace around the tenon, especially with severely bowed timber. Or use the template to cut the mortises if manual help is not on hand to assist in lifting the joists.

8) The mortise depth is determined by the amount of tenon wood remaining. Chalk a level line, equal to the tenon thickness, onto the sill and girder face to locate the mortise seat.

9) To cut the mortise make a couple of relief cuts to the mortise depth. Chisel the base of the mortise clean, as shown in Figure 13-16c.

10. How to cut a flooring notch.

If flooring is laid after the walls are in place then a notch is needed around the inside perimeter of the building onto which the flooring can fit. Walls placed on a full subfloor do not need a flooring notch since the flooring is already laid prior to wall placement.

Tools: Eye and ear protection, chalkline, chainsaw, tape measure.

Procedure:

1) Using the level top surface of the joists as a guide, chalk a line the length of the wall. Do so on the inside of all walls.

2) Using this line as a guide, chainsaw a 2"–3" (50–75 mm) kerf horizontally into the logs.

3) Cut diagonally down at a 45° angle to meet the first cut and clear waste away (Figure 13-17).

Figure 13-17
Cutting a
flooring notch.

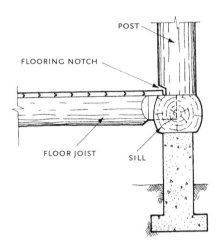

POST

FLOORING NOTCH

FLOOR JOIST

SILL

CHAPTER FOURTEEN

Foundations

The foundation is your attachment to earth; expect the unexpected and build for it.

By definition a foundation is a supportive body which serves to raise the house structure above the decay-causing earth, at the same time transferring and equally distributing the weight of the building to the ground. Historically foundations were as primitive as a rock wedged under each corner of the building. Today, it is a continuous or intermittent supportive body composed of either concrete, rock and mortar, or preserved wood. The foundation of a log post and beam house is the same as any conventional frame house, the exception being that the weight bears on the posts, and extra reinforcement under the posts and attention toward proper anchorage of the post is then required.

The installation of any foundation involves the same basic procedures:

- Site testing
- Building layout
- Grade levels and excavation
- Foundation layout construction

SITE TESTING

Testing the site prior to excavation and building is more accurately a feasibility study to determine any potential costly problems. Property lines and setbacks must be verified and clearly indicated at the site. Hydro and driveway access should also be shown on the site plan. The minimum distances between well and septic is regulated by health authorities. Keep in mind that the septic tank and field should be downhill from the house; it's costly to go against gravity. Drilling, blasting, and heavy machinery for site development are costly so don't be entirely swayed by a low selling price.

The optimum building site will have a slight grade or slope to allow for good drainage. A stable, sandy gravel is the best substrate. Stay away from low land with wet clay soil and a high water table. Many building authorities require a perculation test of the soil substrate to determine its drainage ability, and may recommend the inclusion of perimeter drainage tile and gravel around the foundation footing. Another factor which must be considered is the frost level, which is the depth that the winter frost penetrates into the ground. This level can be ascertained from the local building authority or your neighbors. The foot (called footing) of the foundation must be below this level of frost penetration to prevent frost heave damage to the foundation which will throw the building off level.

BUILDING LAYOUT

1. How to lay out the building dimensions.

Generally the outside perimeter of a building's foundation will be the same as the outside dimensions of the building itself. Therefore the foundation will be the same shape as the building you want to construct. Consider a simple 30' × 40' (9 m × 12 m) rectangular building. In order to make all the corners 90° angles you must first start with a right angle triangle. This can be done easily on site by using multiples of 3–4–5 as described below. Once this first right angle triangle is determined it is a simple matter to locate the fourth corner of the rectangle and check for its overall squareness. The procedures are as follows.

Tools: Tape measure, 3 lb (1.5 kg) hammer.

Materials: Six 2" × 2" × 18" (38 mm × 38 mm × 450 mm) stakes, string that will not stretch, nails.

Procedure:

1) Clear the vegetation from the proposed site.
2) Establish corner A by sinking a nail-topped stake into the ground (Figure 14-1).

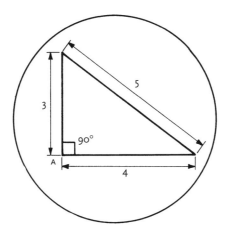

Figure 14-1
Establishing
right angle
foundation
corners.

3) Beginning from corner A lay out a right angle triangle by measuring out a distance of 3 and 4 units (feet/meters) or multiples thereof. When the hypotenuse equals 5 (or multiples thereof) the corner will be 90°.
4) To find corners B and C simply extend the legs of the triangle the length and width of the foundation.
5) From corners B and C locate corner D. Corner D will be at the intersection of the foundation length and width measurements.

Figure 14-2
Measuring
diagonals for
squareness.

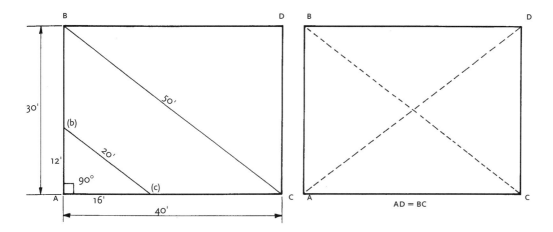

6) All corner angles should be 90°. Check for squareness by measuring the diagonals. AD should equal BC (Figure 14-2). Any adjustment can be done by moving corner D slightly. Connect the string to the nail-topped stakes to form the foundation outline.

7) Diagonals can be obtained mathematically by using the Pythagorean theorem:

$$a^2 + b^2 = c^2$$

$$302^2 + 402^2 = c^2$$

$$900 + 1600 = c^2$$

$$2500 = c^2$$

$$\sqrt{2500} = c$$

$$50 = c$$

8) Variations to a square or rectangular building (i.e. L-shaped) simply require additional right angles and can be laid out accordingly.

GRADE LEVELS AND EXCAVATION

Since the earth's surface or grade is not perfectly flat it is necessary to establish marks at each of the foundation layout corners that are level to one another so the house will not sit at an angle. A grade level can be determined by using a "builder's level" like the one described in Tools, Chapter 4 or by using a "water hose level." Procedures on the use of both these levels are explained below.

Once a level grade mark is determined the next step is to excavate or remove the required amount of earth down to an equal depth below the grade mark. In areas where there is no frost penetration, the ground need only be scraped level to remove the top soil down to undisturbed substrate. In areas of frost penetration it is necessary to excavate a minimum of 1' (300 mm) below the frost line.

Before establishing grade levels, decide whether you want a continuous or pier foundation. If a continuous foundation is desired it will be necessary to extend the foundation lines 3' (1 m) beyond the corners to allow working room around the building foundation. A building whose dimensions are 30' × 40' (9 m × 12 m) would be extended to 36' × 46' (11 m × 14 m) in this case.

In order to preserve the foundation lines and grade level for continuous foundations after the ground has been excavated, the common procedure is to erect batterboards. The builder has the option of doing this or repeating the foundation layout in the excavated cavity. The process of extending the foundation lines by erecting batterboards is not necessary for pier foundations.

2. How to establish grade levels using a builder's level.

This instrument is merely a telescope mounted on a tripod which can rotate 360°. Once set up and placed level it will give a level horizontal reading in any direction it is pointed. As the instrument is more comfortable for the operator if it is set up at eye level, it is necessary to transfer the reading closer to the ground so it can be marked directly on the foundation corner stakes. The procedure for establishing grade levels using this instrument is as follows.

Tools: Builder's level, rod marked in feet and inches or meters and centimeters, pencil.

Procedure:
1) Rent a builder's level and rod. (The rod can be substituted for a stick.)
2) Set up a level instrument (according to instructions) in the center of the building location.
3) Establish a grade level mark that is common to all corner points (Figure 14-3). Transfer this mark onto the stakes.

3. How to establish grade levels using a water hose level.

As water finds its own level, a level can be fabricated using a common garden hose and water. Because of its flexibility this type of level can accurately set grade levels even around blind corners. Outlined below is the procedure for constructing a water level and using it to establish equal grade levels. I will take this opportunity to illustrate setting equal grade

Figure 14-3
Establishing
equal grade
levels with a
builder's level.

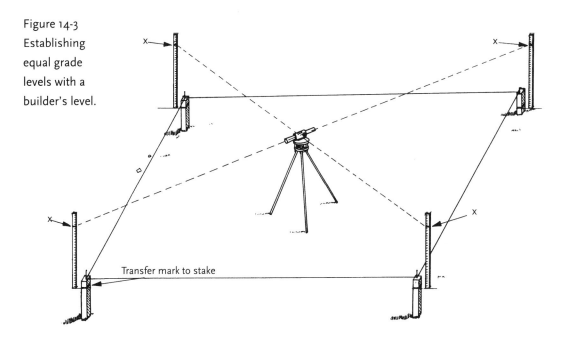

Transfer mark to stake

levels onto batterboards which will be used where a continuous foundation is desired.

Tools: Hammer, level, pencil, utility knife.

Materials: 50' (15 m) semi-clear garden hose, water, 2 corks, nails.

Procedure:

1) Lay the hose on the ground with the ends turned up, fill with water to within 6" (150 mm) or so from the other end, and cork both ends. Remove the corks, cut a groove in each one, and replace them in each end. This is to prevent the water from spilling out while at the same time preventing a vacuum being created inside the hose which will give a false reading. Make sure there are no trapped air bubbles in the hose (a clear hose is recommended).

   Note: Air bubbles displace water and give a false reading. Adding a few drops of glycerine breaks down the surface tension of the water and reduces the risk of false readings.

2) Set and level the batterboards at the high ground corner of the ex-

Figure 14-4
Establishing
equal grade
levels with a
water level.

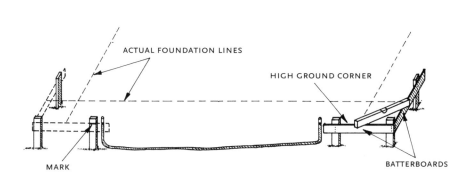

ACTUAL FOUNDATION LINES

HIGH GROUND CORNER

MARK

BATTERBOARDS

tended building foundation line. Use a common level for this procedure and refer to section 4, below, for information concerning
batterboard construction.

3) Have someone hold one end of the hose so the water line is level
with the set batterboard. Mark on the batterboard stakes where the
corresponding water level shows at the opposite end of the hose.

4) Continue this procedure and mark equal grade levels on all the batterboard stakes (Figure 14-4).

4. How to erect batterboards
(for use with continuous foundations).

After the corners of the house have been located the next step is to erect
batterboards. The batterboards preserve the outline of the house and the
grade level during the excavation (Figure 14-5).

It is important that the batterboards are solidly placed to resist movement and are of equal elevation. Error here can affect the building's dimensions and/or squareness.

Tools: 3 lb (1.5 kg) hammer, tape measure, handsaw, plumb bob, level.

Materials: 2" × 4" × 30" (38 × 89 × 750 mm) stakes, 1" × 6" (19 × 140
mm) batterboards, strong string, nails.

Procedure:
1) Drive in corner stakes a minimum of 5' (1.5 m) from foundation
lines.

Figure 14-5
Batterboard
placement.

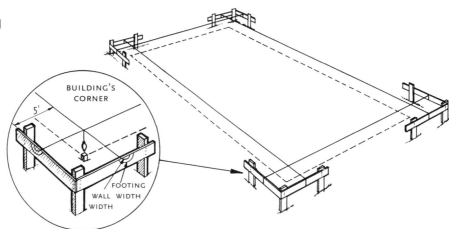

2) Nail horizontal batterboards onto the stakes so that the tops are all level at the same grade (see section 3, above, for leveling procedures).

3) Stretch a strong, taut string or wire between opposite batterboards and adjust so it is directly over the nail-topped stakes. A plumb bob is useful for setting the lines.

4) The intersecting lines will identify the building foundation's outside corner. Check squareness by taking diagonals; double check building dimensions at this time. Make saw kerfs where the string crosses the batterboards in case the string breaks later.

5) Excavate 3' (1 m) outside the building's foundation lines.

5. How to establish excavation depths.

Besides serving the function of outlining the building's perimeter, batterboards establish a level plane over uneven ground. By measuring down an equal distance from these batterboard string lines in all four corners, a level plane below the frost line is quickly established.

Tools: Tape measure, shovel, pick.

Equipment: Backhoe or tractor with front end loader.

Procedure:

1) Determine the frost line depth from the local building authorities.
2) Excavate 1'–2' (300 mm–600 mm) below the frost line and 3' (1 m) outside the building's foundation lines. It is important to place the footings on undisturbed ground.
3) Check excavation depth by measuring down from the batterboard string lines (Figure 14-6).

Figure 14-6
Checking
excavation depth.

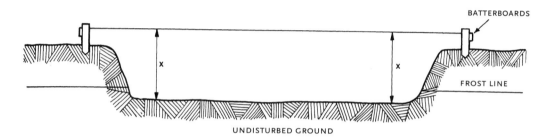

BATTERBOARDS

FROST LINE

UNDISTURBED GROUND

Excavation Math

To find the number of cubic yards (cu. yds.) of earth to excavate, multiply the length by the width by the depth of the excavation. The result will be in cubic feet (cu. ft.). To find the cubic yards, divide the cubic feet by 27.

Example: Given a 40' × 30' × 4' depth excavation:

$40 \times 30 \times 4 = 4{,}800$ cu. ft.

$4{,}800 \div 27 = 178$ cu. yds.

FOUNDATION CONSTRUCTION

Within the realm of continuous and intermittent supportive foundations there are many types. For example, continuous foundations include poured concrete, concrete block and mortar, rock and mortar, preserved wood, steel, and rigid foam block. Intermittent or pier foundations include the same supportive mediums with the exception of rigid foam block. There are less materials and labor associated with pier foundations; however, a structural sill beam is required to support the floor joists, and the space between the piers will need to be filled in later. Due to the extensive resources available about foundation construction I will touch only briefly on form work and concrete placement.

6. Building pier foundations.

Pier foundations lend themselves to post and beam buildings, for it is not essential to provide continuous support under a sill log or timber that is strong enough to need only periodic support. Besides the saving on labor and materials, there is an added advantage: the possibility of an earlier start, since the structural support piers can be placed and the work begun, leaving the spaces between the piers to be filled in at a later time. It must be noted that pier foundations are not usually used where there is a basement or for two-or-more-storey houses. For information on the types of anchor fasteners to use for the various sill types refer to Chapter 6.

Tools: Eye and ear protection, chainsaw (if using wood posts), chalkline, tape measure, handsaw, hacksaw, level, hammer, pencil, cement mixing tools if applicable (see Concrete and mortar, section 8, below).

Materials: Cement forms or wood posts, anchor fasteners, cement ingredients (if applicable), nails, 1/2" (12 mm) reinforcing bar.

Procedure:
1) Lay out foundation lines and take diagonals. Batterboards are not necessary.
2) Locate piers under all weight-bearing posts, at 8'–10' (2.5 m–3 m) spacings around the building's perimeters. The piers are to be placed inside the foundation perimeter line so as to provide a drip cap or ledge to prevent water from collecting between the sill and pier (Figure 14-7). Refer also to Layout, Chapter 6.
3) Dig holes below the frost line and place a 4" (100 mm) thick concrete footing so it fills the base of the hole. Into this wet concrete place a grid of reinforcing bars so it is suspended in the mixture.
4) Using a water level or builder's level, establish equal elevation levels on all pier formwork.
5) Construct the piers in the following manner (Figure 14-8):
   Place reinforcing bar into forms and pour concrete to level line (Figures 14-8a and b). Refer to section 8, below, for information on

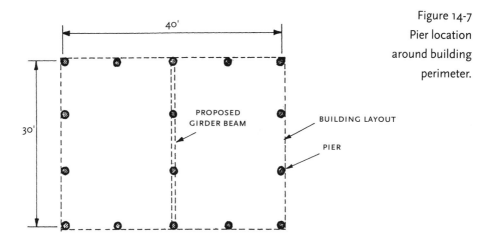

Figure 14-7
Pier location
around building
perimeter.

concrete. Insert anchor fasteners while the concrete is still wet. Ideally the anchors should be firmly connected to the reinforcing bar.

Or, using the excavated hole as the form, construct piers from rock and mortar (Figure 14-8c). Insert anchor fasteners while the mortar is still wet.

Or, place the preserved posts into the excavated holes and backfill with gravel (Figure 14-8d). Transfer the level line to the posts and cut off waste with a chainsaw.

Figure 14-8
Pier formwork
types.

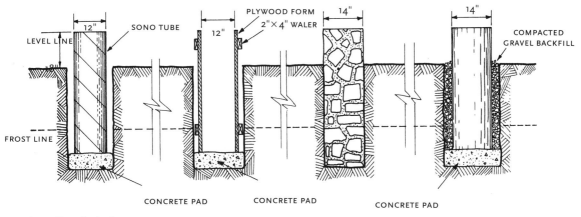

6) Place a moisture barrier, such as high density foam roll or an asphalt shingle, between the piers and floor sills. Flexible closed-cell foam strip comes in a roll and can be purchased at any hardware store just for this purpose.

7) Skirt or fill between the piers with rock and mortar to protect against weather and prevent creatures from entering the crawl space (Figure 14-9). This can be done at a later time.

8) Apply metal flashing to prevent moisture from accumulating between the foundation and sills.

Figure 14-9
View of pier
foundation.

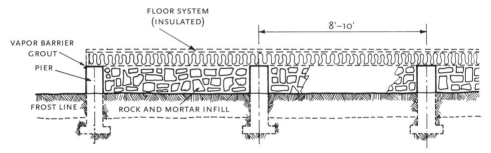

7. How to build continuous concrete foundations.

Although more expensive than pier foundations, a continuous foundation affords more structural support and better protection from the weather. In some areas building authorities don't permit pier foundations for houses with more than one storey. For information on concrete mixing and pouring see section 8, below. For information on which anchor fasteners to use for the various sill types refer to Chapter 6. Note that if the frost penetration is deep in your area (i.e. 5', or 1.5 m), adding the extra few feet of foundation wall to provide a 7'6" (2.25 m) headroom would add another floor area with only marginal costs. Check the availability and cost of form rentals. Often it is not worth constructing your own.

Tools: 4' (1220 mm) level, tape measure, hammer, handsaw, sledge hammer.

Materials: Plywood forms, 2" × 4" (38 × 89 mm) (studding, walers, stakes, bracing), 2" × 10" (38 × 235 mm) footing forms, 1/2" (12 mm) reinforcing rod, tie wire, nails, cement ingredients.

Procedure:

1) Construct footing forms and place reinforcing rod. Refer to a good carpentry book for more details (see Bibliography). Refer to section 8, Concrete and mortar, below.

2) Pour concrete footings and insert a beveled strip of oiled wood to form a keyway (to be removed after drying). This keyway will serve to lock the foundation wall to the footing.

3) Construct wall forms according to Figure 14-10. If a dropped (corbelled) floor system (i.e. where the top of the floor is level with the concrete foundation wall) is desired then add a flooring ledge as shown in the diagram. Use an additional reinforcing rod if the wall is tall, as in a full basement.

4) Brace wall forms securely.

5) Pour concrete walls to level line and insert anchor fasteners while the concrete is still wet. Ideally the fasteners are connected directly to the reinforcing rod.

6) Strip forms in 5 days but keep concrete moist for an additional 7–14 days.

7) Place moisture barrier and flashing to prevent moisture accumulation between foundation and sills. Standing moisture will rot unpreserved wood.

8) If properly proportioned and mixed, a concrete wall is waterproof. However the usual procedure is to coat the exterior wall with a bituminous (waterproof) layer.

9) A basement or crawl space will be warmer if the outside of the wall is insulated (Figure 14-11).

10) Drain tile and gravel should ring the perimeter of the foundation unless the substrate has good drainage (Figure 14-11).

8. Concrete and mortar.

A house is only as strong and durable as the foundation that supports it and the roof above. Since the majority of foundations are made of concrete it will be helpful to add some practical hints on how to work with it.

Figure 14-10
Concrete foundation
form work.

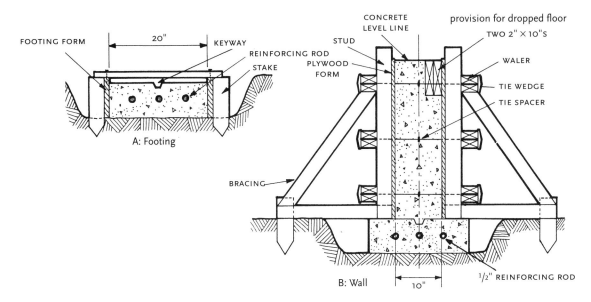

FOOTING FORM

20"

KEYWAY

REINFORCING ROD

STAKE

A: Footing

CONCRETE
LEVEL LINE

provision for dropped floor

TWO 2" × 10"S

STUD

PLYWOOD
FORM

WALER

TIE WEDGE

TIE SPACER

BRACING

B: Wall

10"

1/2" REINFORCING ROD

Figure 14-11
Continuous
concrete
foundation with
crawl space.

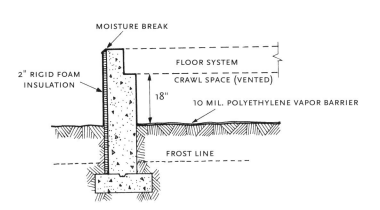

MOISTURE BREAK

2" RIGID FOAM
INSULATION

FLOOR SYSTEM

CRAWL SPACE (VENTED)

10 MIL. POLYETHYLENE VAPOR BARRIER

18"

FROST LINE

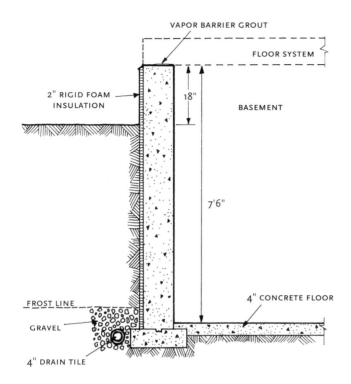

VAPOR BARRIER GROUT

FLOOR SYSTEM

2" RIGID FOAM
INSULATION

18"

BASEMENT

7'6"

FROST LINE

GRAVEL

4" CONCRETE FLOOR

4" DRAIN TILE

Figure 14-12
Continuous
concrete
foundation with
basement.

Indeed, observing various construction projects has made me aware that many contractors and tradespeople are ignorant of concrete and its material properties. I have seen ready-mixed batches of quality controlled concrete delivered on site, only to be watered down to make it flow more easily and further with less paddling, as well as excessive handling and over-vibration leading to aggregate separation, and improper follow-up procedures leading to improper hydration ("curing") process. The result is a poor foundation that lacks strength, watertightness, and durability—all of which could have been prevented. As a last note, remember that concrete is strong in compression but requires an armature of reinforcing steel rod to provide lateral shear strength. Listed below are a few tips for making good concrete.

Procedure: Refer to Figure 14-16, Concrete and mortar tools.

1) Select the proper ingredients and rent or borrow the necessary tools.

2) Correct proportioning: Formula 1–2–3 mix is one part cement, two parts sand (moist), and three parts gravel by volume.

3) Thorough mixing: Every particle of sand and gravel must be completely covered with cement paste. The strength, durability, and watertightness of concrete are controlled by the amount of water used per sack of cement. The less water the better the quality of concrete—as long as the mixture is plastic and workable. It is best to mix a small trial batch according to the table formula. If this batch is not satisfactory DO NOT ADD WATER—instead add or reduce the quantity of aggregate or change the proportion of fine and coarse aggregate.

How to mix concrete

a) Set mixer in motion.

b) Add specified amount of water.

c) Add a small quantity of both fine and coarse aggregate.

d) Add the amount of cement necessary.

e) Add the rest of the aggregate a little at a time, alternating between small amounts of sand, then gravel.

f) After all the ingredients are in the mixer, continue mixing for at least three minutes, or until all the materials are thoroughly coated and the concrete has a uniform color.

Placing the concrete into the forms should be done within 45 minutes. Transport the concrete carefully to avoid excess agitation which can cause separation of the fine and coarse aggregate.

How to place concrete

a) Place as near as possible to final resting position in the wall.

b) Begin at a corner and deposit concrete uniformly in even layers around the forms, not more than 12" (300 mm) at one time. Concrete is very heavy, and therefore overloading could cause failure of the formwork. However, care must be given to prevent a "cold joint" whereby one batch of concrete is allowed to solidify separately from the entire mix. This weakens the wall.

c) Spade or vibrate the concrete to compact it and eliminate air pockets and honeycombing. Overworking the mix causes an excess of water and fine material to be brought to the surface.

d) Further care is required to see that the concrete is worked into the corners and angles of the forms, and around reinforcing work.

e) If the mixture becomes sloppy as forms are filled, make a stiffer mix by varying the proportions of sand and gravel.

f) Trowel off to the level line indicated on forms.

How to cure concrete Proper curing increases the strength and durability of the concrete. Hydration (hardening) of the concrete continues only in the presence of water and a suitable temperature. Loss of water stops hydration and causes concrete to shrink, creating surface stresses which may result in surface cracking. Correct curing and hardening occurs if concrete is kept moist and warm. Concrete gains strength rapidly within seven days, while near maximum strength is achieved in 28 days.

- Leave forms in place to reduce surface moisture loss.
- In hot weather, sprinkle or apply wet coverings.
- Seal the surface with plastic sheets or a liquid membrane compound.
- Cover for a period of five days minimum in warm weather and seven days minimum in cool weather.

Mortar Mortar is a bonding agent designed to join together elements such as rock, brick, or concrete blocks. A mortar mix contains water, masonry cement, and sand but no coarse aggregate. A proper workable mixture will readily adhere to vertical surfaces and to the underside of horizontal surfaces. It should spread easily yet not be so fluid that it runs out of mortar joints.

Apply mortar only to DRY rocks, bricks, or blocks.

Concrete Volume

Concrete for footings and walls is estimated by the cubic yard. Volume is calculated the same way as for excavation. The length of the footing/wall in feet multiplied by the width in feet, multiplied by the depth in feet, and divided by 27 will give the amount of cubic yards in the footing/wall.

Example 1:

Given a foundation footing measuring 30' long × 2' wide × 1' deep.

$30 \times 2 \times 1 = 60$ cu. ft. $60 \div 27 = 2.2$ cu. yds.

Example 2:

Given a foundation wall measuring 30' long × 6" wide × 4' deep.

30 × .5 × 4 = 60 cu. ft.   60 ÷ 27 = 2.2 cu. yds.

9. Constructing foundations for permafrost areas.

When moisture in the ground freezes it expands in volume causing a buckling of the ground, known as frost heaving. When thawing occurs during the summer air spaces are left which collapse once weight is applied. This ground movement is disastrous for building foundations and structures, causing distortion and breakage. In areas with minimal frost depth, placing the foundation footings below this unstable frost penetration (called the "frost line") is the answer. In areas of very deep frost penetration, or where the earth stays permanently frozen below the surface, a concrete wall foundation is not the answer.

Experiences in the Arctic have shown me three proven methods of constructing foundations in permafrost locations. The first and most expensive is to drill down to stable frozen earth, insert piers, and build the structure on these supports. A less expensive method is to lay down a compacted gravel pad down and build on this stable surface leaving the frozen ground undisturbed. The third and cheapest method is to excavate a trench down to permafrost if possible, insulate and fill with compacted gravel, and use this stable surface to build on. These last two methods require that the crawl space under the house be left cold in order to minimize ground movement caused by freeze-thaw cycles. A cold crawl space necessitates an insulated floor as well as heat-taped plumbing and waterlines where they may be exposed to freezing. Illustrated below are the two methods involving the gravel pad and trench construction. The footing and piers can be of either concrete or preserved wood for both types.

Procedure:

GRAVEL PAD Ideally the gravel pad should be placed during the winter when the ground is still frozen; however, winter working conditions often prevent this.

Lay down the coarse gravel in 6" (150 mm) layers, compacting each layer. Do not try to remove any of the top soil as, once removed, the freeze-thaw penetration goes deeper. Construct the foundation on top of the pad as shown in Figure 14-13.

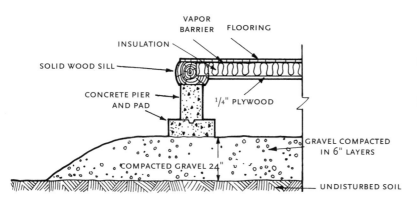

GRAVEL TRENCH The trench should be excavated during the summer, when the ground surface is not frozen. Dig a 3' (1 m) wide trench down to frozen ground along the building's perimeter line. The extruded styrofoam and compacted gravel should be placed as the excavation proceeds, to avoid additional thawing of the frozen ground. Once this ground is thawed, annual freeze-thaw cycles will continue to create unstable ground. Construct the foundation on top of the gravel berm, as shown in Figure 14-14.

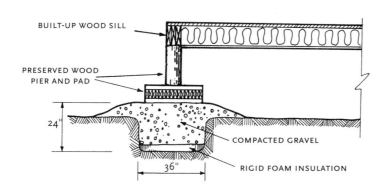

10. How to construct foundations for marshy areas.

A building foundation must rest on firm ground. The common procedure when building in marshy or loose soil conditions is to drive posts down through the loose substrate until they rest on firm ground. Next a granular soil berm is built up to provide drainage and then construction begins, using the posts as a foundation.

In areas where firm ground cannot be reached, a "raft" type of footing is placed in a shallow excavation to support the building. The courthouse public building in New Orleans is supported on bales of cotton. This is possible because organic material will not rot when deprived of oxygen. Therefore, whether cotton, straw bales, or a corduroy footing of logs are used, they will not rot if back filled with oxygenless soil. The procedure for a raft footing constructed of logs is outlined below (Figure 14-15).

Figure 14-15 Section of a raft footing for marshy areas.

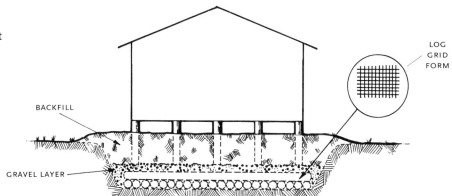

Procedure:

1) Obtain the log material—common poplar or cottonwood will do. There is no need to preserve these logs. It is best if the log lengths span the entire length and width of the excavated hole.

2) Excavate the building location to a depth of at least 3'–4' (1–1.2 m) below the ground surface. It may be necessary to pump the hole dry during excavation.

3) When the excavation is deep enough, set down the first layer of logs, side by side. Alternate butts and tops to compensate for the taper and to obtain a tighter course.

4) When the first layer is completed, lay the second layer in the same manner.

5) Apply a thick layer of gravel or sawdust over this cribbing.

6) Backfill the remainder of the cavity and berm slightly to permit runoff.

7) Build the foundation on this compacted berm. Sinking preserved posts down to the crib level to elevate the building above ground is also an option for a pier type support.

11. Concrete/Mortar Tools

Shovel: Used for measuring ingredients and placement of mixture.

Wheelbarrow: Used to transport the mixture.

Cement/Mortar mixer: A power driven mixer is easier and does a better job of mixing than working by hand.

Mortar hoe: The two holes in the blade provide for better mixing by hand.

Trowel: Used for applying and smoothing the mortar.

Jointer: Used for finishing mortar joints in brick and rockwork. A spoon can also be used.

JOINTER

TROWEL

HOE

CONCRETE MIXER

Figure 14-16 Concrete and mortar tools.

CHAPTER FIFTEEN

Utilities and Finishing

ELECTRICAL WIRING ROUGH-IN

Electrical wiring should only be undertaken by the owner/builder who is familiar with its procedures (and dangers). The information below relates to general prewiring for solid wood building construction. Persons interested in wiring their home should consult appropriate sources.

Additional information on wiring E.P.S. infill panels can be found in Chapter 7.

1. Electrical wiring layout.

It is essential to preplan the electrical work in order to avoid unsightly and dangerously exposed wiring. Such planning should be done in consultation with an electrician and must comply with the local residential Building Code.

Figure 15-1 shows a typical electrical layout for a solid wood post and beam house. The receptacle outlets, for the most part, are positioned within 18" (450 mm) of the floor. In log or timber walls, the receptacles will be in the first or second log or timber, which necessitates predrilling for the supply wires. Kitchen receptacles are located in the counter splash-boards, and rely on the cavities behind cabinets for running the electrical wires. Switches are commonly placed near doorway openings which serve as pathways for the wiring to feed the fixture. Overhead lighting or fans will require access from the ceiling cavity. The floor, ceiling, and stud partition cavities conceal the electrical wires as they snake from source to application site; there is very little predrilling through solid logs or timbers required with proper planning. See section 2, below, for predrilling receptacle outlets, and for a jig for cutting receptacle and switch box cavities.

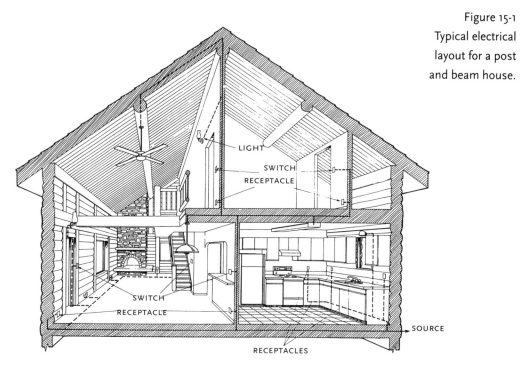

Figure 15-1
Typical electrical
layout for a post
and beam house.

2. Predrilling and cutting mortise cavities for electrical wiring using a simple jig.

The major part of the predrilling is confined to wires servicing receptacle outlets. Since these outlets are located within 18" (450 mm) of the floor, or in the first or second wall log or timber, it will be necessary to predrill as the infill wall is being placed on the subfloor. When the drilling is completed, the receptacle box cavity (and switch cavity) is cut, using the mortising jig described below. Electrical wire can then be fed through the access hole to service the box, or a "fish" wire can be threaded through, which will later be used to pull through the electrical wire.

Tools: Eye protection, electric drill (or hand auger) with 1¹/₄" (32 mm) auger bit, level, pencil.

Materials: "Fish" wire (coat hanger wire), strong cord.

Making the jig

Tools: Eye and ear protection, chainsaw, square, hammer, tape measure, brace and 1" (25 mm) bit, crosscut handsaw, saber saw, pencil, 1" (25 mm) chisel.

Materials: 1/2" × 1⁵/₈" (12 × 40 mm) long carriage bolts with nuts and washers, ³/₄" (19 mm) plywood, finishing nails, wood glue, receptacle boxes.

Procedure:

1) Place the first log on the subfloor and mark out the drilling locations. Locate wall receptacles no more than 12' (3.5 m) apart and within 6' (1.8 m) from doors or other openings. The number of fixtures per wiring circuit is controlled by the Electrical Code and the local inspector.

2) Drill down through the center of the first log to gain access to the crawl space or basement.

Figure 15-2 Predrilling for electrical receptacle outlets.

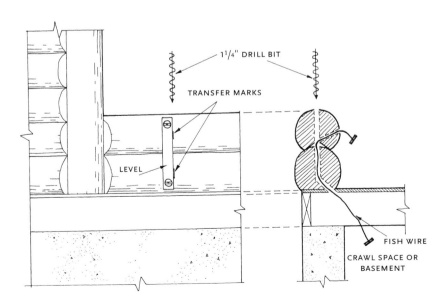

3) Using a level, mark the place where the hole is on the side of the log, then drill a diagonal hole down to meet this first hole. If there is insufficient clearance from the floor, the receptacle outlet can be placed in the second log. In this case, fit this next log in place (Figure 15-2).

4) Using a level, transfer the mark onto the second log, then drill down to meet the hole beneath. The lateral groove will cover the hole if it is drilled on the centerline of the log.

5) On the face of the second log, drill in to meet the vertical hole. The receptacle box will be placed at this junction.

Constructing the mortising jig

1) Lay out, cut, glue, and nail together a ³/₄" (19 mm) plywood box, following the dimensions in Figure 15-3. Then glue and nail the box to the plywood backing sheet.

2) Cut two ³/₄" (19 mm) plywood pads and fit them to the chainsaw

Figure 15-3
Fabrication and
use of the
mortising jig.

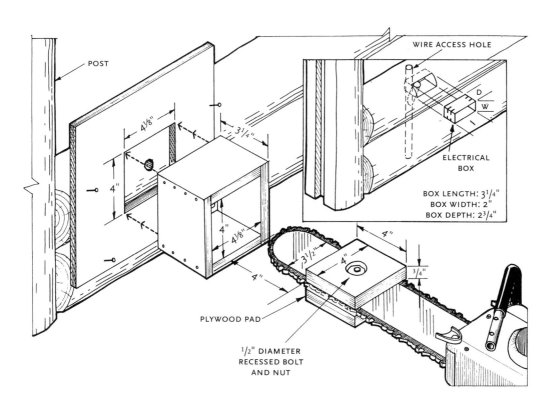

bar, using the carriage bolt, nut, and washer. The bolt and nut should be recessed.

3) The bar with pads should slide into the plywood box with minimal clearance.

4) Center the mortising jig over the predrilled electrical hole, and cut out a cavity with successive plunge cuts of the chainsaw. For duplex receptacles or switch cavities, simply move the jig box over to create the extra space.

5) Using the coathanger wire, "fish" a length of cord from under the floor out through the receptacle hole. Then tie a stick on either end so that the cord cannot pull back through (Figure 15-2). Later, the electrical wire will be taped onto the cord and pulled through to service the receptacle.

3. Plumbing and water lines.

Like the electrical work, plumbing work requires careful planning. Since it is unrealistic to try to drill a 3"–4" (75–100 mm) diameter main stack hole through solid log or timber walls, these lines are best placed within a 2" × 6" (38 × 140 mm) stud wall. It is wise to align the kitchen and bathroom back-to-back, using this stud wall and a single set of lines to service both areas. In houses with a second floor or basement, the plumbing and water services should be located above and below each other wherever possible to save on materials and labor.

Drain, vent, and water lines must comply with the local Residential Code specifications. Figures 15-4 and 15-5 show a typical layout. Because of their ease of installation, most homebuilders use P.V.C. plastic drain and vent lines, and copper water lines. Plastic drain and vent lines must be anchored between floors. This necessitates the installation of an expansion joint to absorb the plastic's thermal expansion and contraction (Figure 15-4 inset). Specifications concerning slopes, distances, fixtures, cleanouts, etc. are controlled by the Plumbing Codes.

Figures 15-6 and 15-7 show a basic drain, vent, and water line rough-in for a bathroom. The dimensions in Figure 15-6 indicate where the pipe and fixture tie together. In most cases new fixtures come with rough-in dimensions and installation instructions. Figure 15-7 shows the piping rough-in complete and ready for the fixtures. For additional information refer to the sources in the Bibliography.

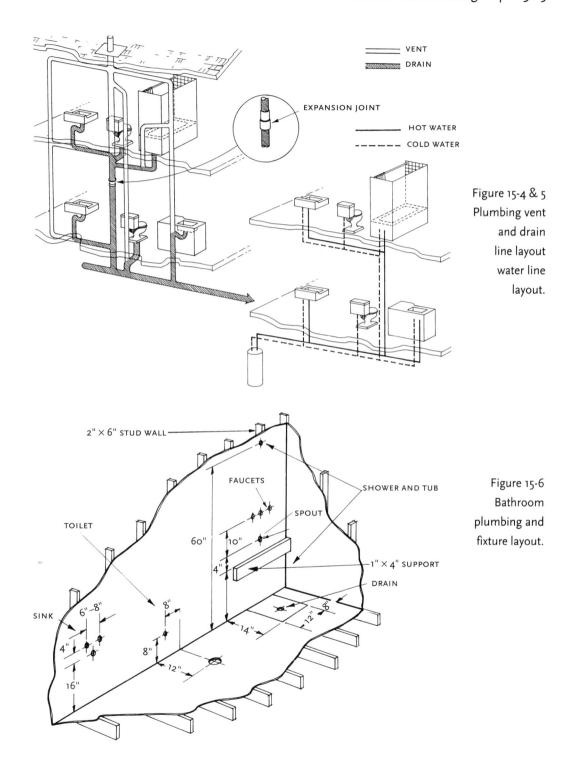

VENT
DRAIN

EXPANSION JOINT

HOT WATER
COLD WATER

Figure 15-4 & 5
Plumbing vent
and drain
line layout
water line
layout.

Figure 15-6
Bathroom
plumbing and
fixture layout.

2" × 6" STUD WALL

FAUCETS

SHOWER AND TUB

SPOUT

TOILET

60"

10"

4"

1" × 4" SUPPORT

DRAIN

SINK

6"–8"

8"

4"

8"

14"

12"

8"

16"

12"

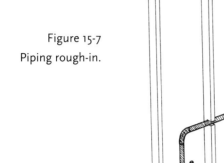

Figure 15-7
Piping rough-in.

VENT

DRAIN

4. Installing frame partitions.

Any major frame partitions, especially load-bearing ones, should be attached to the vertical posts and not to log or timber infill pieces. Attaching a frame partition to a post is a simple matter of flat-surfacing the face of the post and nailing the partition to it. Attaching a partition wall to the E.P.S. infill wall system outlined in the beginning of this book is acceptable as long as the wall is also attached firmly to the top plate and to the floor structure. Where a partition wall must tie into a log or timber infill wall, there are two methods of attachment. Bear in mind that the horizontal infill pieces must be left free to settle unimpeded by the partition. How to attach partition walls to solid log or timber infill is explained below:

Tools: Eye and ear protection, chainsaw, adze, chalkline, level, tape measure, hammer, handsaw.

Materials: 2" × 4" (38 × 89 mm), 2" × 6" (38 × 140 mm) blocking, 1" × 6" (19 × 140 mm) rough cedar, common nails, finishing nails, 6" (150 mm) spikes with washers, 1" × 4" (19 × 89 mm) straightedge.

Procedure:
1) Figure 15-8 and its inset are self-explanatory diagrams for butting and nailing a frame partition to a vertical post.

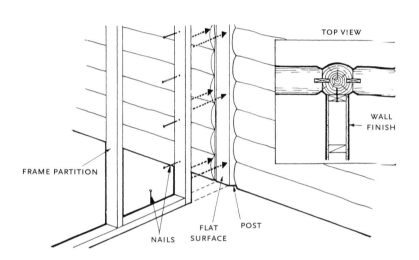

Figure 15-8
Attaching a frame
partition to a
vertical post.

TOP VIEW

WALL
FINISH

FRAME PARTITION

NAILS   FLAT   POST
         SURFACE

2) Figure 15-9 shows a method by which a slip joint is recessed into a channel which has been cut into the wall infill. The channel provides a vertical backing as well as eliminating any gaps caused by the curve of the logs. The slip joint allows the infill pieces to settle unimpeded, and provides a finished edge to which drywall or paneling can be butted. Steps 3 to 7 describe how to construct and install this type of frame partition attachment.

Attaching a partition to log or timber infill with a slip joint.
3) Construct a slip joint by nailing a 1" × 6" (19 × 140 mm) on either side of a 2" × 4" (38 × 89 mm), as shown in Figure 15-9. The length of this slip joint will be the same as the height of the partition.
4) Plumb the slip joint and nail it temporarily in place against the wall where the partition will be located. Temporarily nail in place a 1" × 4" (19 × 89 mm) straightedge on either side to be used as chainsaw guides.

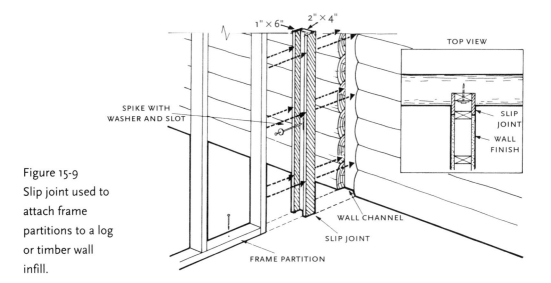

Figure 15-9
Slip joint used to
attach frame
partitions to a log
or timber wall
infill.

5) Remove the slip joint and make three or four chainsaw cuts the length of the wall channel to a depth nearing the lateral groove. Use an adze to remove the waste wood. The result should be a plumb, vertical channel.

6) Position the slip joint and nail the top and bottom to the logs, using a spike with a washer slipped through a slot in the 2" × 4" (38 × 89 mm). This will allow the log wall to settle unimpeded.

7) Figure 15-9 inset shows a top view of the slip joint, where the finish material butts to the 1" × 6" (19 × 140 mm) and nails into the 2" × 4" (38 × 89 mm) stud.

Butted and kerfed method for attaching a partition to log or timber infill.

1) Figure 15-10 shows an alternative method for attaching a frame partition to a log or timber infill wall. This method is most frequently used in closets. First, the partition is plumbed and nailed to the log wall, using a spike and washer inserted through a slot cut with the chainsaw.

2) Then, run a chainsaw kerf down either side of the partition, providing a groove into which the finish material will fit. Figure 15-10 inset shows the kerf cuts.

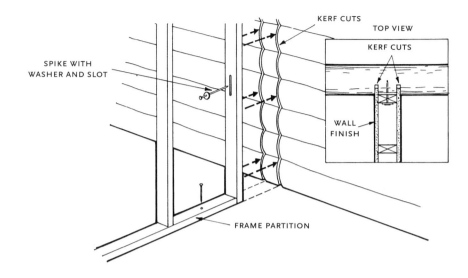

SPIKE WITH
WASHER AND SLOT

KERF CUTS

TOP VIEW

KERF CUTS

WALL
FINISH

FRAME PARTITION

Figure 15-10
Butted and kerfed
method of
attaching a frame
partition to a log
or timber wall
infill.

5. Attaching frame walls over log or timber walls.

Some builders prefer to attach a stud frame wall right over the log or timber wall in the kitchen or bathroom, to facilitate the installation of the plumbing, electrical wiring, cabinets, and counters. The easiest method for attaching a frame wall over a log or timber wall is to affix it to the vertical posts, top plate, and floor, leaving the infill pieces to settle unimpeded. The directions for such a procedure follow.

Tools: Eye and ear protection, chainsaw, adze, level, tape measure, chalkline, hammer, handsaw, chisel, pencil.

Materials: Stud wall material, 1" × 4" (19 × 89 mm) diagonal bracing, nails.

Procedure:
1) Flat-surfacing the posts to accept the frame wall can be done when the posts are being milled. If the decision to attach the frame wall is made after the walls are up, the posts can be flat-surfaced by making repeated vertical cuts with the chainsaw and then removing the waste wood with an adze to produce a surface flush with the top plate face.

2) Construct the frame wall, as shown in Figure 15-11, and nail it solidly to the posts, top plate, and floor.

3) Put in place any electrical or plumbing rough-in, and apply the finish material to the frame wall.

4) Alternatively use a stud frame or E.P.S. infill method rather than a solid log or timber infill wall.

Figure 15-11
Attaching a frame wall over a log or timber wall.

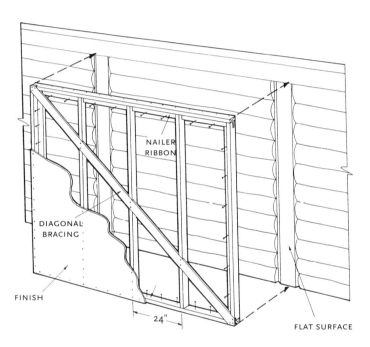

NAILER RIBBON

DIAGONAL BRACING

FINISH

24"

FLAT SURFACE

6. Installing cabinets and counters.

There are two methods for attaching cabinetry to a log or timber infill wall. The first method involves slightly recessing the cabinets and counters into the log wall. In this case, the electrical wiring and plumbing are hidden behind the counters, with the main stack contained within a stud wall located in the kitchen or bathroom.

The second method involves building a frame wall over the log wall. The cabinets and counters are attached directly to the false wall, with the wiring and plumbing hidden in its cavity.

Note: Installing cabinetry against stud frame or E.P.S. infill walls is identical to conventional construction.

Tools: Eye and ear protection, chainsaw, adze, level, handsaw, hammer, electric drill with wood bits, Robertson screwdriver (red), tape measure, chalkline, pencil.

Materials: Cabinets and counters, framing materials, drywall, common nails, drywall nails, #10 Robertson wood screws.

Procedure:

1) Figure 15-12 shows the cabinets and counters recessed into the log wall. Begin the layout on the log wall where the cabinets and counters will be situated.

2) Recess the cabinets and counters by making vertical chainsaw cuts 2"–3" (50–75 mm) deep into the log. Remove the waste wood with an adze.

3) Hang the cabinets by screwing them into one log only (Figure 15-12). The counters are screwed to the floor and wall. Allow for a settling space above the counter splash board.

Figure 15-12
Attaching
cabinets and
counters to a
log or timber
wall.

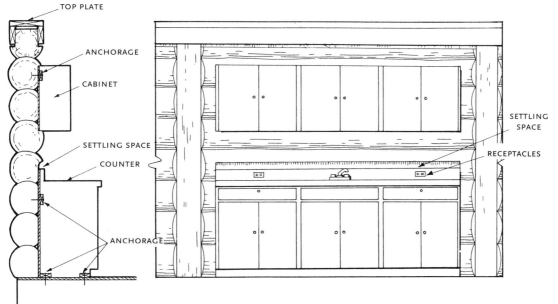

4) Locate a stud wall near the sink to contain the main plumbing stack. Attach it to the log wall using one of the methods described in section 4, above.

5) Figure 15-13 shows the cabinets and counters attached to a false frame wall. Attach this frame wall using the method described in section 5, above.

6) Sheath the frame wall with drywall, placing wiring and plumbing in the cavity.

7) Attach the cabinets and counters to the frame wall, as shown in Figure 15-13.

Figure 15-13
Attaching
cabinets and
counters to a
frame false wall.

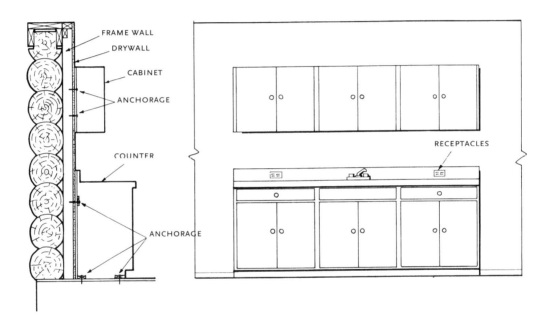

7. Stair construction.

In building a staircase several safety factors must be taken into account. In order to effect safe passage there must be no deviation in tread or riser sizes. There should be adequate headroom, and guard rails with balusters must be installed on at least one side of each run on all stairs.

The construction of a stairway is greatly affected by the nature of its attachment to the wall. Affixing stairs to a horizontally laid-up log or timber infill wall, both of which are subject to settling, will result in an altered stair angle. However, compensatory measures can be taken to deal with these settling effects. (Such measures must also be taken when installing stairs in a long-log notched corner building—blockwork.) On the other hand, the method for affixing stairs to the stable vertical posts, the top plate of a post and beam house, or to the E.P.S. infill is identical to the methods widely used with conventional frame buildings.

In planning the stair design, keep in mind that the stairway should enhance the architectural style of the house, while providing maximum utility within the space available. Figure 15-14 shows the components of a typical staircase (with landing).

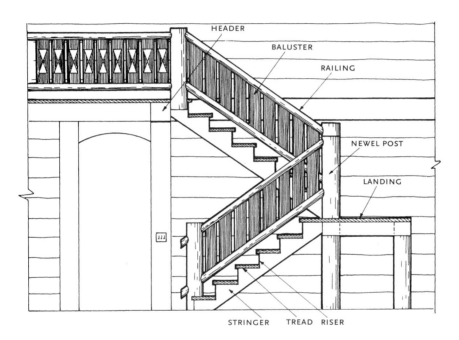

HEADER
BALUSTER
RAILING
NEWEL POST
LANDING
STRINGER   TREAD   RISER

Figure 15-14
Parts of a
staircase
stairwell.

8. Making calculations for a straight run staircase.

The optimum height for a riser is between 7"–8" (178–203 mm) and the optimum width of a tread between 9"–10" (228–254 mm). The slope of the stairs will vary with the proportion of riser height to width of the tread. If the riser height is increased, the stairs become steeper. A comfortable stair slope is achieved if the sum of the riser and tread equals 17" (432 mm). (These measurements do not include the tread nosing projection.)

There must also be adequate headroom with a minimum of 80" (2032 mm), and adequate stair width with a minimum of 36" (1 m). The stairway's approach and landings should also be a minimum of 36" (1 m). As well, there must be ample clearance around corners for the movement of people and furniture. The directions which follow are for a straight run staircase, the fundamentals of which can be applied to other stair configurations. See section 15, below, for instructions on how to construct a timber spiral staircase.

Tools: Tape measure, pencil and paper.

Procedure:

1) Establish the total rise by measuring the distance between the two finished floors (eg., 102", or 2590 mm) (Figure 15-15).

2) Calculate the number of stair risers by dividing the total rise by an optimum riser height. For example: 102" ÷ 7 = 14.57 (2590 mm ÷ 178 mm = 14.55) risers.

3) Since the number of risers must be a whole number, assume the number of risers to be 14 and redivide this number into the total rise to find the exact riser height: 102 ÷ 14 = 7.28 or 7^{1}/$_{4}$" (2590 ÷ 14 = 185 mm).

4) Calculate the tread width by subtracting 7.28" (185 mm) from 17 (432 mm) which equals 9.72 or 9^{3}/$_{4}$" (247 mm).

5) To find the total run of the stair refer to Figure 15-15. Note that the

Figure 15-15

Stair calculations.

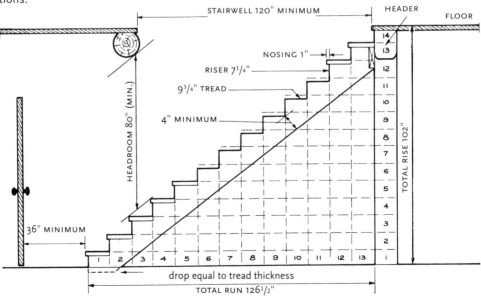

second floor landing constitutes the 14th tread. Therefore the total run is 13 treads long or 13 × 9.72 = 126.36 or 126^1/$_2$" (13 × 247 mm = 3211 mm).

6) Before proceeding further check to see if a staircase of these dimensions will fit within the space and headroom available. Adjust if necessary.

7) Calculate the length of the stair stringers by using Pythagoras' theorem: $a^2 + b^2 = c^2$, where c is the stringer.

Example with standard measures

$\sqrt{102^2 + 126.5^2} = c$

162.5" = c

(add waste allowance)

Example with metric measures

$\sqrt{2590^2 + 3211^2} = c$

4125 mm = c

(add waste allowance)

9. Laying out a log stringer.

Begin by selecting a dry, straight-grained log of substantial size and length. Mill the two opposite sides flat. Once this has been done, the log is cut lengthwise in half to produce the two stringers on which the layout work can begin.

Tools: Tape measure, sharp pencil, chalkline, steel square, circular saw with combination blade, crosscut handsaw.

Materials: Log stringer pieces.

Procedure:

1) Prepare the log for layout as explained above.

2) Chalk a guide line along the outside edge of each stringer. This line will represent a straightedge from which to work. It will also serve to prevent confusion and the production of two right or left stringers.

3) Starting at the bottom (butt) of the stringer, align the steel square so that the 9^3/$_4$" (245 mm) tread mark on the body and the 7^1/$_4$" (185 mm) riser mark on the tongue are touching the guide line (Figure 15-16).

4) Lay out the tread and riser by stepping-off 13 times along the stringer, carefully beginning each new tread at the ending of each riser mark.

Figure 15-16
Layout for a log
stringer.

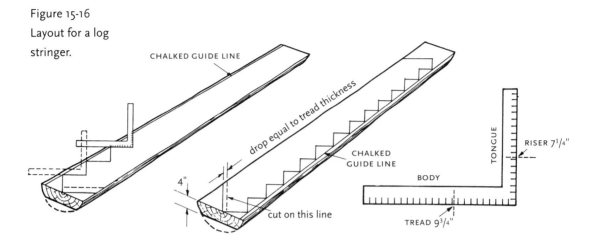

CHALKED GUIDE LINE

drop equal to tread thickness

CHALKED
GUIDE LINE

4"

BODY

TONGUE

RISER 7¹/₄"

cut on this line

TREAD 9³/₄"

5) After the desired number (13 in this example) of treads and risers are marked out, square off the ends as shown in Figure 15-16. (Note that in the example, the 14th tread and riser is the second floor.)

6) Repeat this procedure for the other stringer. When they are matched up they should be identical.

7) Whatever the thickness of the tread material, it will be necessary to cut this amount from the bottom of each stringer. This is called the "drop" allowance.

8) Using the circular saw and a sharp blade, carefully cut out the stringers. If housed treads are desired then it is unnecessary to cut the stringers.

9) Level them, and attach the stringers solidly to the header.

10. Fastening dimensional or log treads to the stringers.

With the stringers securely fastened in place, the placing of the treads can begin. If housed treads are desired it will be necessary to rout the dado grooves with the stringers detached from the heads (Figure 15-17). Otherwise cut the stringers as mentioned above and attach the treads as explained in the following procedures.

Whether you are using dimensional or log slab treads the material should be dry and relatively defect-free. For easy passage of both people and furniture, the minimum stair width is 36" (1 m) clear of the handrail.

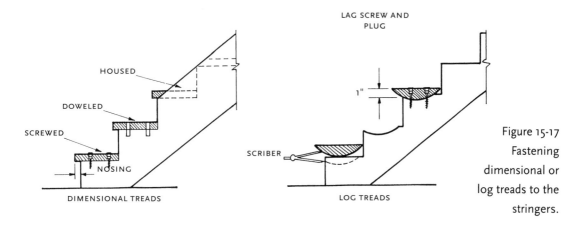

Figure 15-17
Fastening
dimensional or
log treads to the
stringers.

Tools: Eye and ear protection, chainsaw, scriber, 1¹/₄" (32 mm) gouge chisel, mallet, electric drill with ⁵/₈" (16 mm) bit and ³/₄" (19 mm) countersink, crosscut handsaw, socket wrench.

Materials: Tread material, ³/₄" (19 mm) hardwood dowels and wedges, lag screws, wood glue.

Procedure:

1) Cut all pieces of the tread material to equal lengths. (For example: 36" + 2" (1 m + 50 mm) overhang on either end = 40" treads.)

2) Stretch a taut string line down the length of one of the stringers. The string line should extend 2" (50 mm) past the outer edge of the stringer. Lay the treads in place so that each touches the string. This will bring them all into alignment.

3) Mark out and drill countersink and pilot holes for screws, or dowel holes, depending on which is to be used to fasten the treads to the stringers.

4) If using log slab treads, level the treads in both directions, then scribe them into place. The depth of scribe will be the tread thickness minus the 1" (25 mm) tread exposure (Figure 15-17).

5) When the positioning and drilling are completed, glue should be applied to the joining surfaces, and the tread securely screwed or dowelled in place. The countersunk screwheads can be concealed with wood plugs.

11. Fastening the log newel posts.

The newel posts are primary structural elements in the balustrade. For this reason it is very important that they are fastened securely in position. They will, however, only acquire their full structural potential when the railings and balusters are in place.

There are a multitude of design and joinery options for newel posts. The example described below has the newel post attached directly to the staircase.

Tools: Eye and ear protection, chainsaw, tape measure, scribers, level, 1¹/₂" (38 mm) chisel or slick, electric drill with ³/₄" (19 mm) and ¹/₂" (12 mm) bits, pencil, socket wrench.

Materials: Lag screws, newel posts, ³/₄" (19 mm) wood plugs, wood glue.

Procedure:
1) Position the newel post to sit on the corner of the staircase. Then block and plumb it (Figure 15-18).
2) Trace the corner of the staircase onto the underside of the post, then extend vertical lines up at the corners to equal the depth of the riser and tread.
3) Remove the newel post and cut out the waste wood. In this example the post rests firmly on the floor.
4) Reposition the post and scribe to the contours of the log stringer. Remove the post to cut waste wood.
5) Reposition the post, lay out the lag screw holes, then countersink and drill the holes. Apply a generous amount of glue to the joining surfaces and screw the post firmly in place.
6) Plug the countersink holes.
7) Repeat the above procedure for all newel posts.

12. Fastening the railings to the newel posts.

The material used for railings should be dry. The tree species jack pine, or banksian pine (*Pinus banksiana*), makes excellent stair railings, as it is quite common to find poles which hold to a uniform thickness of 4" (100 mm) or so.

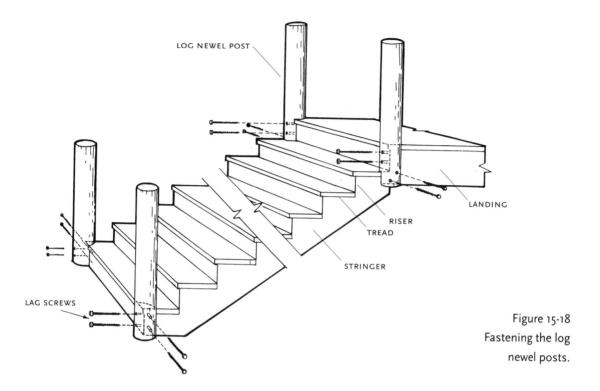

LOG NEWEL POST

LANDING

RISER

TREAD

STRINGER

LAG SCREWS

Figure 15-18
Fastening the log
newel posts.

There are many possible ways of joining the railings to the newel posts. Two common methods are described below. The important criteria are the height at which the top handrail is placed (dictated by the Building Code), and the secure fastening of the railings.

Tools: Eye and ear protection, chainsaw, tape measure, chalkline, string-line, electric drill with ³/₄" (19 mm) and ¹/₂" (12 mm) bits, 1¹/₂" (38 mm) chisel or slick, socket wrench, pencil, router with ³/₄" (19 mm) straight bit (optional).

Materials: Lag screws, railings, ³/₄" (19 mm) wood plugs, wood glue, hardwood wedges.

Procedure:

1) Prepare the railings to receive the balusters. (See section 13, below, then sand to remove rough edges and splinters.) Figure 15-19 shows the two methods of railing attachment.

2) Stretch a taut stringline between the two newel posts to determine the height and positioning of the two railings.

3) Mark out the appropriate joinery for either a socket or lapped fit.

4) Remove the waste wood of the joint.

Note: If you are fastening the railings with a socket fit, the mortise waste wood can be removed with a router or drill.

Drive a hardwood wedge part way into the end grain of the tenon end of the railing. Then, when the railing is driven into the mortise, the wedge will spread the end and prevent loosening of the joint.

5) Apply glue to the surfaces of the joint before final assembly.

Figure 15-19
Socket and
lapped fit railing
attachments to
newel posts.

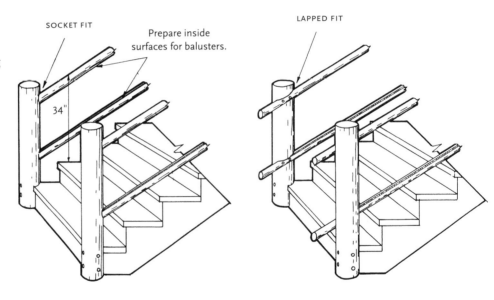

13. Fastening the balusters to the railings.

Balusters provide vertical support to the railings, while at the same time providing a partition to keep children from falling off the stairs. For this reason also, there must be no more than 4" spacing between the balusters. The design of the balusters is important, as it can enhance or detract from the house's design as a whole. Below are four methods for fastening balusters to the railings.

Tools: Eye and ear protection, chainsaw, tape measure, chalkline, cross-cut handsaw, hammer and nail set.

For the groove method: Rout with a ³/₄" (19 mm) straight bit.

For the socket method: Use a 1¹/₂" (38 mm) hand auger.

Materials: Baluster material, wood glue, finishing nails.

Procedure:

1) Prepare the balusters by sanding and staining them (see section 14, below).
2) Fasten balusters between the railings, with one of the methods shown in Figure 15-20.

Figure 15-20
Fastening
balusters to
railings.

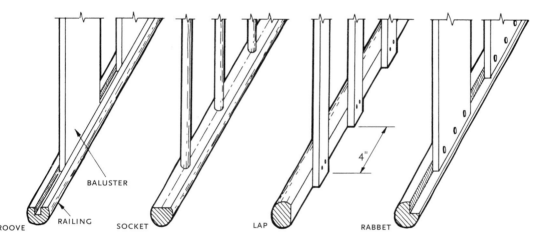

GROOVE   BALUSTER   RAILING   SOCKET   LAP   4"   RABBET

14. Baluster design and construction.

The balusters are the parts of the staircase that make the most immediate visual impression. Spindle balusters can be as rustically simple as peeled pole saplings, or as ornate as lathe-turned columns. The final choice will depend largely upon the design and decor of the entire house (Figure 15-21).

The board baluster with cut-out patterns is simple to construct, yet offers a great deal of design flexibility. This type of baluster provides more design opportunities for utilizing the negative space (where the wood is cut away) than does the spindle baluster.

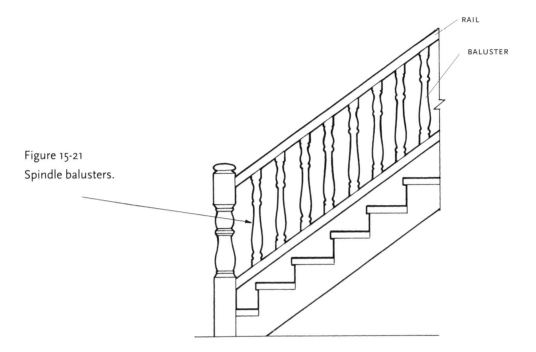

RAIL

BALUSTER

Figure 15-21
Spindle balusters.

Tools: Board baluster: Eye protection, router with 3/8" (9 mm) straight bit and template guide; Spindle baluster: Eye protection, table saw with combination blade.

Materials: Baluster material, 1/8" (3 mm) hardboard template material.

Procedure:
1) Make up the hardboard templates to your design.
2) Tack-nail the template to the baluster board as shown in Figure 15-22. Ensure there is extra material for the bevel cut for attachment to the top railing.
3) Secure the baluster board and rout the design as shown.
4) Attach balusters between the railings.

15. Constructing a timber spiral staircase.

A circular stairway affords the opportunity to transform the common stairway into the interior's most dramatic feature.

Constructing a circular stairway with curved, laminated stringers is both complex and costly. A fan-type, circular stairway in which treads are spread out around an axis pivot simplifies construction and reduces

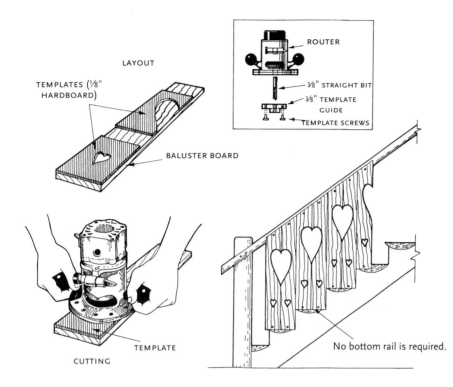

LAYOUT

TEMPLATES (⅛" HARDBOARD)

ROUTER

⅜" STRAIGHT BIT

⅜" TEMPLATE GUIDE

TEMPLATE SCREWS

BALUSTER BOARD

TEMPLATE

CUTTING

No bottom rail is required.

Figure 15-22
Making board balusters.

costs. Common fan-type spiral staircases are fabricated out of steel. The timber spiral staircase shown here (Figure 15-23) uses the same basic approach of fanning the treads around an axis. This is done with a quick and simple method which allows the builder to construct an impressive circular staircase with a minimum of experience, tools, and materials.

In an average house with an approximate 8' (2400 mm) total rise between floors, the timber circular staircase will need approximately 180° or half of a circle (semi-circle) to complete its total run. It is recommended that the radius of this semi-circle be between 42"–54" (1066–1370 mm), so that two people may pass each other comfortably on the stairs. For a still greater passage space, increase the radius. Timber tread materials must be dry, since green wood will shrink, causing a reduction of the stair's height.

A. Determining the total rise, total run, and tread size.

1) Determine the total rise by measuring the distance between the finished floors of the two storeys. For example: 96" or 2400 mm (Figure 15-24).

Figure 15-23 & 24
A timber spiral
staircase—
measuring
between floors
for total rise.

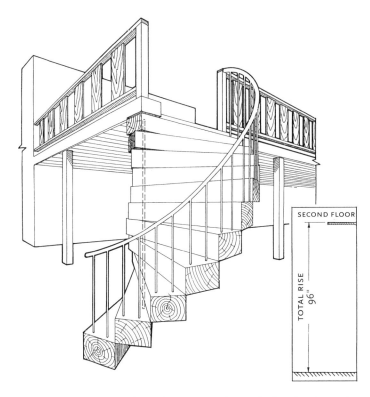

SECOND FLOOR

TOTAL RISE
96"

2) Determine the number of risers and treads by dividing the total rise by the optimum riser height. For example, 8", or 200 mm.

96" (2400 mm) ÷ 8" (200 mm) = 12 risers and treads.

There will actually be 11 risers and treads, since the second floor landing forms the 12th tread riser.

3) Determine the total run by multiplying the number of treads by the optimum tread width. For example, 12", or 300 mm. These timber treads are designed to be wider than usual to allow for more usable exposed tread.

11 treads × 12" (300 mm) = 132" (3300 mm) total run.

4) When this has been done, proceed with the subfloor layout, the directions for which follow.

B. Layout on the subfloor.

1) Begin the layout on the main floor by establishing the location of the second storey landing. Lines can be chalked on the floor to represent the landing, as shown in Figure 15-25.

2) Next, chalk a parallel line $6^{1}/_{2}$" (165 mm) from the landing representation as shown. The $6^{1}/_{2}$" allows for the last stair tread to run parallel with the landing with $^{1}/_{2}$" (12 mm) clearance. This parallel line then forms the base of the semi-circle. Locate the axis point as indicated, so that the tread will be flush with the edge of the landing.

3) Draw the semi-circle arc. This can be done by embedding a nail at the axis and then using a length of wire and pencil to scribe an arc equal to the radius (in this case, 50"/1270 mm) (Figure 15-25). The total run of the staircase is along the arc of this semi-circle. To determine if more than a semi-circle is required for the total run of 132" (3300 mm), it is necessary to calculate the circumference of the semi-circle. The formula for a semi-circle is:

(Pi) times radius. Pi is a constant equal to 22/7 or 3.1416.

3.1416 × 50" (1270 mm) = 157" (3990 mm)

Since the total run is only 132" (3300 mm), the staircase will fit within the semi-circle.

(The formula for a circle is Pi times diameter.)

4) Lay out the tread centers along the arc line, remembering that the landing constitutes the last tread. Begin from the base line (the center of the eleventh tread), and step off eleven 12" (300 mm) units around the arc, as shown in Figure 15-25.

5) Proceed with an actual stair construction, as described below.

Note: To achieve a wider tread closer to the axis (i.e. for an 18" line of travel) simply fan out the treads.

C. Stair construction.

Tools: Electric drill with 1" (25 mm) and $^{5}/_{8}$" (16 mm) auger bits, level, tape measure, crescent wrench, pencil.

Materials: Iron rod $^{3}/_{4}$" × 100" (19 × 2540 mm) long threaded 16" (400 mm) at one end; two pieces of plate iron, 3/16" × 4" × 4" (4 × 100 × 100 mm); $^{3}/_{4}$" (19 mm) nut and washer; 10" (250 mm) lag screws (2); tread material (dry).

Procedure:

1) Mill eleven treads to the dimensions 8" × 12" × 56" (200 × 300 ×

Figure 15-25
Spiral stair layout
on the subfloor.

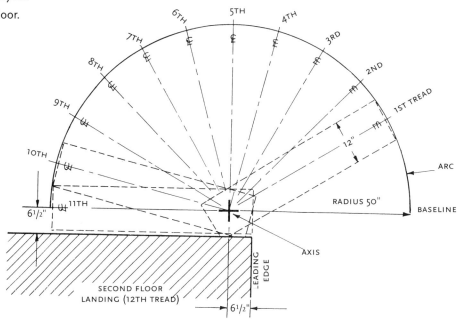

1422 mm) (Figure 15-26a). The tread width can be a variance of 12"–24".

2) Using the template as shown in the diagram, locate, and then drill a 1" (25 mm) hole in one end of each tread. Plane and sand the tread surfaces.

3) Fabricate an axis rod by welding one plate iron piece to the end of the rod as shown in Figure 15-26b. The second plate must have a 3/4" (19 mm) hole drilled through its center.

4) Position the rod and first tread on the axis mark located on the subfloor, as in Figure 15-26c. With the first tread placed in its correct location, secure it to the floor with countersunk lag screws.

   Note: Ensure there is adequate support under the subfloor for the weight of the stairs.

5) Stack the remaining treads on the rod as shown, then cinch down the nut with plate and washer to firmly hold the stacked treads.

Figure 15-26
Constructing
the staircase.

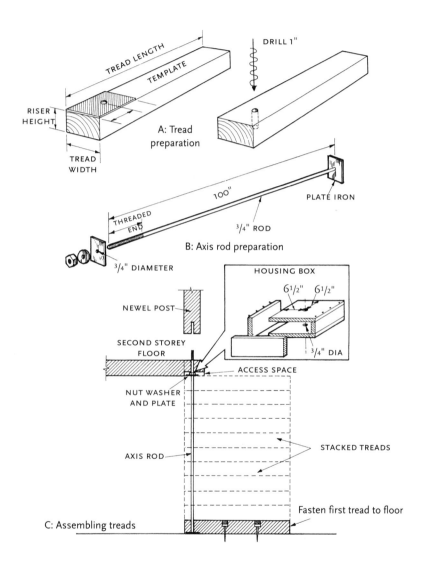

DRILL 1"

TREAD LENGTH

TEMPLATE

RISER
HEIGHT

A: Tread
preparation

TREAD
WIDTH

100"

THREADED
END

PLATE IRON

3/4" ROD

B: Axis rod preparation

3/4" DIAMETER

HOUSING BOX

6 1/2"   6 1/2"

NEWEL POST

SECOND STOREY
FLOOR

3/4" DIA

ACCESS SPACE

NUT WASHER
AND PLATE

STACKED TREADS

AXIS ROD

Fasten first tread to floor

C: Assembling treads

6) Anchor the rod to the second floor landing. One way of doing this is to install a housing box like the one shown in the inset of C. An access space must be left under the housing box to permit tightening of the nut if the treads loosen as a result of shrinkage.

7) Fan out the treads to their respective center marks then firmly tighten the nut. Use a plumb bob or straightedge and level to match the treads to the layout marks. The completed spiral staircase should look like the one in Figure 15-23.

8) The railing and baluster will help to secure the ends of the treads. A curved storage closet can be made by framing in the space under the stairs, using the arc line for reference. This closet framing can be extended to form the balustrade and handrail, thus providing maximum support for the stair treads as well as utility.

Wood Finishes

"Weathering" is the very slow breakdown and wearing away of the wood's surface fibers, a change in color, and roughening of the wood's surface. As long as wood has ventilation and is protected from rot and insect damage due to ongoing damp conditions, it is only for aesthetic reasons that weathering may be considered undesirable. Over time unfinished wood will age to a natural patina finish. Certain wood species (i.e. cedar) have increased resistance to decay and would be better suited as sill beams where exposure to moist conditions is greater. Refer to Appendix II. Traditionally, where wood comes in contact with the ground it is preserved using either a method of charring by fire or by application of natural creosotes and resins. Wood that has been soaked in sea water for a time is somewhat "pickled" by the salt brine. Anything beyond letting the wood age naturally requires an ongoing maintenance of exterior finishes as described below.

EXTERIOR FINISHES

The design of the building should include wide roof overhangs to protect the exterior walls. Once the walls and roof of the building are complete, an exterior finish may be applied. Exterior finishes fall into two categories: the penetrating type, such as stains, oils, and preservatives, or the surface type, such as paints, varathanes, and varnishes. Surface finishes should be avoided on wood with a high moisture content, as blistering will result from trapping of moisture between the wood and the coated surface unless it is breathable. Even those good quality exterior varnishes which contain ultra-violet absorbers are limited in their effectiveness and suffer from early cracking and peeling.

Penetrating Finishes

Preservatives

Wood is visibly affected by mold and mildew. Mold and mildew fungi can begin to grow and discolor a newly peeled log within 48 hours if conditions are warm and humid. If mildew growth has already begun it can be removed by cleaning the log with a solution of water, detergent, and bleach. The strength of the solution depends on the extent of discoloration.

Exterior preservative finishes are often used in coastal and other damp regions where mildew and decay are likely. Water-repellent preservative finishes contain waxes, oils, resins, preservatives, and, optionally, pigments. The waxes, oils, and resins cause the wood surface to repel water, while the preservatives impart mildew and decay resistance. Pigments add color and protect the wood surfaces from deterioration caused by ultra-violet light. The finish's life is related to its pigment, ranging from two to four years. One application of a preservative finish is usually sufficient. Maintenance is also simple. The surface is cleaned and washed with soap and water before another coat of finish is applied.

Note: Repellents could cause additional finishing problems unless another repellent finish type is applied over top. The water repellent carriers will prevent rain leaching out the initial fungicidal treatment on freshly peeled logs. *WARNING: Since fungicides and mildewcides are extremely toxic they must be handled with great caution, using appropriate protective gear identified on the product container.*

Pigmented stains

Pigmented stains are a popular finish because they are easy to apply, attractive, and easy to maintain. Stains are classified by the solvent carrier in which they are dispersed. The most common solvents are water, alcohol, and oil. Water stains perform satisfactorily. Spirit (alcohol) stains dry very rapidly, making them more difficult to apply. Oil stains are slower to dry and easier to apply evenly. Most pigmented stains are oil-based. This type of finish is recommended for drier regions, but also works well in wet areas if a fungicide is added.

Semi-transparent stains are most often used on wood surfaces as they do not hide the natural grain and texture of the wood. Opaque stains hide the grain and should be avoided unless desired. Depending on climatic conditions, an established stain finish can be expected to last up to five years. Because the surface film is thin and flexible, stain will not peel, crack, or blister.

Stain finishes are easy to maintain. The surface is washed down with soap and water and a new coat applied about every two years.

Note: Exposed wood such as railings require more frequent coats.

Oils

Most contractors tend to blanket the house, both inside and out, with an oil finish. Oils are easy to apply and don't peel or crack, but they tend to darken the wood. Most oil finishes perform best in dry areas. Boiled linseed oil and tung oil are the favorites of many builders, though too heavy an application can cause the oil finish to remain soft and tacky so that insects and dirt particles may stick to it. This is even more true of raw linseed oil, and mildew may form as well.

All three of the above penetrating finishes are best applied by brush to a clean and dry wood surface. A maintenance coat of finish should be applied before the old finish has deteriorated badly. It is best to apply oil to wood on a hot day as the oil flows more freely into the pores of the wood.

INTERIOR FINISHES

The purpose of interior wood finishes is to add depth, warmth, and character with a clear finish or a slightly pigmented stain. In addition, interior finishes give protection against scuffs and scratches. Toxic preservatives are not required since with an inside air moisture content of less than 20 percent no mildew will grow.

Clear finishes

Waxes used to be popular as flat, interior wood finishes, but have been largely replaced by synthetic varnishes which have high water and abrasion resistance. Furthermore, a wax finish is virtually impossible to remove, as well as being difficult to refinish with other products, should one decide to do so.

Polyurethane varnishes are available in a full range of glosses. They produce a hard, tough finish that is resistant to oil, water, alcohol, and heat. The long drying time that was a problem with the traditional varnishes has been eliminated in the polyurethanes. To allow greater penetration into the wood and reduce the possibility of a poor finish due to a wood's excessive moisture content, the first coat of varnish should be thinned with 15%–20% of solvent. The second coat can then be applied in full concentration.

Exterior finish formula

There are a myriad of commercial products available, some of which are very good. Depending on the amount of exterior wood surface you are covering, however, these products can become quite expensive. As an alternative I include a do-it-yourself formula.

The Madison formula

The Madison formula is a modified, semi-transparent, oil-based stain developed by the Forest Products Laboratories of the Canadian Department of the Environment and the U.S. Department of Agriculture. The mixture is intended to produce the color of western red cedar. A formula for other woods can be mixed by altering the type of pigment. (See Appendix I for a pigment chart.)

Basically, the Madison formula is an all-around exterior finish which incorporates all the qualities of a preservative, a stain, and an oil. It contains paraffin wax to increase the linseed oil's water-repellency, and pentachlorophenol to inhibit mildew. Because the formula includes wax, no finish can be successfully applied over it which does not also contain wax.

Madison formula for natural cedar color

Boiled linseed oil	3.1 gal (U.S.)	12 L
Mineral spirits	1 gal	4 L

Burnt sienna color-in-oil	1 pt	0.5 L*
Raw umber color-in-oil	1 pt	0.5 L*
Paraffin wax	14 oz	0.4 kg
*Pentachlorophenol concentrate 10:1	2 qts	2 L
Zinc stearate (keeps wax in suspension)	1³/₄ oz	50 g

Pour the mineral spirits into an open-top 7 gal (25 L) can. Heat paraffin and zinc stearate in the top of a double boiler and stir until the mixture is uniform. Pour this into mineral spirits, stirring vigorously. This should be done outside to avoid the risk of fire.

Add fungicide and linseed oil to the cooled solution. Stir in the colors until the mixture is uniform.

One quart (liter) covers 350–450 sq. ft. (8–10 sq. meters) on a smooth surface and 175–225 sq. ft. (4–5 sq. meters) on a sawn-textured surface, depending on how porous the wood is.

*As pentachlorophenol is a highly toxic ingredient the builder may wish to substitute it with the less toxic zinc napthenate.

Alchemy

Years ago it was discovered that oak wood stored in a horse barn eventually turned a smoky grey color, caused by the ammonia content of urine reacting with the natural tannens of the wood.

Ferrous sulfate dissolved in warm water provides a safe, inexpensive wood patina the color of walnut when combined with a finish coat of oil. The movie industry has discovered this as a method of quickly aging wood (roof shingles, etc.). Pine wood is a particularly difficult species to stain due to the blotching which occurs around the knots. My experiments with a dilution of sulfuric acid applied to pine on a warm, sunny day resulted in a beautiful redwood patina when combined with a finish coat of oil. The process seems to be photo- and/or heat-reactive as without those climatic conditions present no patina resulted. Also the drawback with acid is the corrosive factor, damaging cloths and rusting metal tools.

There are many old-time concoctions long forgotten or tucked away in dusty books only waiting to be rediscovered. As the cost of commercial preparations keeps rising more individuals will be seeking the alternatives.

Appendix I

This chart may be used in coordination with any of the finishes listed in Chapter 16.

Color Desired	Pigment required	Quantity for 5 gallons (19 liters)	
Cedar	burnt sienna	1 pint	(0.5 L)
	raw umber	1 pint	(0.5 L)
Light Redwood	burnt sienna	1 quart	(1 L)
Chocolate Brown	burnt umber	1 quart	(1 L)
Fruitwood Brown	raw sienna	1 pint	(0.5 L)
	raw umber	1 pint	(0.5 L)
	burnt sienna	1/2 pint	(0.25 L)
Tan	raw sienna	1 quart	(1 L)
	burnt umber	3 fluid oz.	(85 cl)
Green Gold	chrome oxide	1 pint	(0.5 L)
	raw sienna	1 pint	(0.5 L)
Forest Green	medium chrome green	1 quart	(1 L)
Smokey Gray	white house paint	1 quart	(1 L)
	raw umber	6 fluid oz.	(170 cl)
	lamp black	2 fluid oz.	(57 cl)

Appendix II

Tree Species and Wood Properties: The softwood and hardwood tree species identified in this chart list the geographical sources, physical properties of the wood, and the parts of a post and beam building for which each species is best suited.

A letter grade (see key) is given for the wood's properties and suitabil-

			PROPERTIES					SUITABILITY					
TREE SPECIES	Strength	Decay resistance	Movement resistance (lack of spiral grain)	Checking resistance	Workability		Ground sills	Posts	Top plates	Walls	Floor members	Roof members
Ash, Silvertop (*Eucalyptus fastigata*); Australian states of N.S.W., Victoria, and Tasmania.	G	N/A	G	G	G		M	G	G	G	G	G
Ash, White Mountain (*Eucalyptus regnans*); Australian states of N.S.W. Victoria, and Tasmania.	E	M	G	G	G		G	G	E	G	E	E
Blackbutt (N/A); Australian states of N.S.W. and Queensland.	G	M	G	G	G		M	G	G	G	G	G
Cedar, Atlantic White (*Chamaecyparis thyoides*); eastern U.S.	P	E	G	G	G		E	G	P	E	P	P
Cedar, Eastern Red (*Juniperus virginiana*); eastern U.S. and Canada.	P	E	G	G	G		E	G	P	E	P	P
Cedar, Western Red (*Thuja plicata*); western U.S. and Canada.	P	E	G	G	G		E	G	P	E	P	P
Cottonwood, Black (*Populas trichocarpa*); western Canada, northwestern U.S.	P	M/P	M	G	G		P	G	M	G	M/P	M/P
Cottonwood, Eastern (*Populus deltoides*); middle and eastern U.S. and Canada.	P	M/P	M	G	G		P	G	M	G	M/P	M/P
Elm, White (*Ulmus americana*); middle and eastern U.S. and Canada.	E	M	M	M	G		M	G	G	G	G	G
Fir, Amabilis (*Abies amabilis*); Pacific coast of Canada and northern U.S.	M/P	M	M	G	G		M	G	M	G	M/P	M/P
Fir, Balsam (*Abies balsamea*); middle and eastern Canada.	M/P	M/P	M	G	G		M	M	M/P	G	M/P	M/P
Fir, Douglas (*Pseudotsuga menziesii*); western U.S. and Canada.	E	M	G	G	G		E	E	E	G	E	E
Fir, Grand (*Abies grandis*); Pacific coast of U.S. and southern Canada.	M	M	G	G	G		M	G	M	G	M	M
Gum, Blue (*Eucalyptus globulus*); Australian states of Tasmania and Victoria.	G	N/A	M	M	G		M	G	G	G	G	G
Gum, Spotted (*Eucalyptus maculata*); Australia coast of New South Wales and Queensland.	E	G	G	M	G		M	G	G	G	G	G
Hemlock, Eastern (*Tsuga canadensis*); southeastern Canada to middle eastern U.S.	M/P	M/P	M	M	M		M/P	M	M	M/G	M/P	M/P
Hemlock, Western (*Tsuga heterophylla*); western U.S. and Canada.	G	M/P	G	G	G		M/P	G	G	G	G	G
Jarrah, Curly (*Eucalyptus marginata*); western Australia.	E	G	M	M	M		G	M	G	G	G	G

Letter Grade Key

E = Excellent
G = Good
M = Moderate
P = Poor
N/A = Not available

ity. For example, the three species of cedar shown have excellent decay resistance but are poor in strength. Hence cedar would be well-suited for a building's ground sills which are exposed to repeated wet conditions, but would not be suitable for top plates and floor or roof structural members, unless the member is made sufficiently large to support the load.

TREE SPECIES	PROPERTIES					SUITABILITY					
Letter Grade Key E = Excellent M = Moderate G = Good P = Poor N/A = Not available	Strength	Decay resistance	Movement resistance (lack of spiral grain)	Checking resistance	Workability	Ground sills	Posts	Top plates	Walls	Floor members	Roof members
Karri (N/A); western Australia.	E	M/P	M	M	M	M	M	G	G	G	G
Kauri, New Zealand (*Agathis australis*); New Zealand.	G	G	G	G	G	G	G	G	G	G	G
Larch, European (*Larix decidua*); Alps, western Poland into Russia and Carpathian mountains.	E	E	G	G	G	E	E	E	G	E	E
Larch, Japanese (*Larix leptolepis*); Shinano province in Japan.	E	E	G	G	G	E	E	E	G	E	E
Larch, Tamarack (*Larix laricina*). Throughout northeastern U.S. and Canada to eastern British Columbia.	G/E	E	G	M	G	E	E	E	G	G/E	G/E
Larch, Western (*Larix occidentalis*); northwestern U.S. and eastern British Columbia.	E	E	G	M	G	E	E	E	G	E	E
Oak, White (*Quercus alba*); eastern U.S. and Canada.	E	M/G	G	G	G	M/G	E	E	G	E	E
Pine, Eastern White (*Pinus strobus*); eastern Canada and northeastern U.S.	M	M	M/P	G	G	M	M	M/P	G	M/P	M/P
Pine, Lodgepole (*Pinus contorta*); western Canada and northwestern U.S.	M/G	M	M/P	G	G	M	G	M/P	G	M	M
Pine, Ponderosa (*Pinus ponderosa*). Scattered throughout western Canada and U.S.	M/G	M	G	G	G	M	G	G'	G	G	G
Pine, Red (*Pinus resinosa*); northeastern U.S. and eastern Canada.	M/G	M/G	G	G	G	M/G	G	G	G	G	G
Pine, Scots (*Pinus sylvestris*). Throughout Europe and England.	G	M	G	G	G	M	G	G/E	G	G/E	G/E
Pine, Western White (*Pinus monticola*); southwestern Canada and western U.S.	M	M	G	G	G	M	G	G	M	M	M
Poplar, Balsam (*Populus balsamifera*). Throughout Canada and northern U.S.	P	M/P	M/P	M	M	M/P	M	M/P	G	P	P
Spruce, Black (*Picea mariana*). Northeastern U.S. and throughout Canada, except the Southwest.	G	M	M/P	M	G	M	M	G	G	G	G
Spruce, Engelmann (*Picea engelmannii*). Along North American Rocky mountain range from western Canada to New Mexico, U.S.A.	G	M	G	G	G	M	G	G	G/E	G	G
Spruce, Norway (*Picea abies*). Extending eastward from England to the Alps, Carpathians, and Russia.	G	M	G	G	G	M	G	G	G/E	G	G
Spruce, Sitka (*Picea sitchensis*); Pacific coast of U.S. and Canada.	G	M	M	G	G	M	G	G	G/E	G	G
Spruce, White (*Picea glauca*). Throughout Canada and northeastern U.S.	G	M	M/G	G	G	M	G	G	G/E	G	G
Tallowwood (N/A); western Australia.	E	G	G	G	G	G	G	G	G	G	G

Note: As species wood properties vary in accordance with different locales, this chart is intended as a general guide. Builders should consult local information sources for more detailed information on species properties and suitability.

Appendix III

STRUCTURAL BEAM LOADING AND SIZING

Before one can determine the size of the support beam needed to carry a load, it is first necessary to determine the proportion of load the beam carries. Figure III-1 shows floor support girders. In A, the single girder provides a center support and carries half the weight of each floor joist resting on it. Thus, the girder carries half the weight of the floor, while the two foundation walls carry the other half.

In B, a single girder is placed slightly off-center to support a bearing partition. Again, the girder carries half the floor weight, and only the pro-

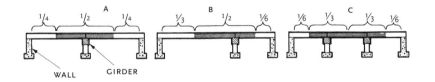

WALL   GIRDER

Figure III-1
Proportions of
floor weight
carried by
girders.

portion of weight carried by the foundation walls changes.

In C, there are two support girders, and each beam carries a third of the floor weight, while the foundation walls carry a sixth each, or a total of a third of the floor weight.

The girder serves to bisect the floor joist into two or three sections, depending on the number of girder supports. The support beams of a roof operate in the same manner.

A roof is like a floor with its middle pitched up to form a peak and with its sides sloped. The rafters function in the same manner as the floor joists, and the ridge pole and purlins function like floor girders. The proportion of roof weight these beams carry is determined in the same way

Figure III-2
Two ways of
distributing
roof weight
on rafters.

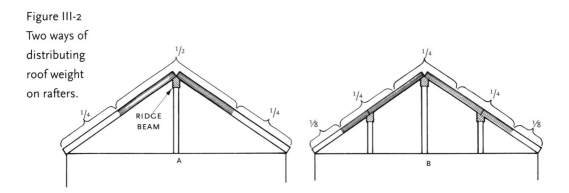

as for floor girders. In Figure III-2a the ridge pole beam carries half the weight on the roof, while the walls carry the other half.

In B, a purlin beam is included on each slope. Here the ridge beam carries an eighth of the weight of each roof slope, or a quarter of the weight of the roof, while the purlins each carry a quarter of the weight of the roof. The side walls carry the other quarter of the roof weight, or an eighth of the weight each.

Figure III-3
Calculating
beam size of
example
house.

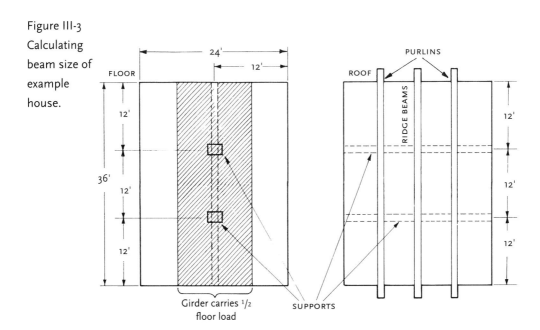

Defining loads

The loads carried by floors and roofs are broken down in the following manner.

DEAD LOAD: The weight of the building alone.

Floors: 10 lbs per sq. ft. or .48 kilonewtons per sq. meter (kN/m²).

Roofs: 20 lbs per sq. ft. or .95 kilonewtons per sq. meter (kN/m²).

LIVE LOAD (on the floor only): Occupants and furnishings.

Main floor: 40 p.s.f. or 1.9 kN/m².

Second floor: 30 p.s.f. or 1.43 kN/m².

SNOW LOAD (on the roof only): This varies with geographic area; check with building authorities.

Note: Sloped roofs hold only a percentage of the total ground snow load. Apply the weight reduction as follows:

Metric roof slope	Standard roof slope	% of Ground snow load
0/250	0/12 (Flat roof)	100 (no weight reduction)
80/250	4/12	80 (20% weight reduction)
165/250	8/12	70 (30% weight reduction)
210/250	10/12	60 (40% weight reduction)
250/250	12/12	50 (50% weight reduction)
295/250	14/12	40 (60% weight reduction)
375/250	18/12	30 (70% weight reduction)

Calculating beam size

Once the proportion of the floor and roof load that the beam will carry has been determined, it is easy to calculate the size of the beam needed. Below is a sample house with steps shown on how to calculate the size of floor girder and roof ridge and purlin beams.

Sample house data: Single storey 24' × 36' (7.315 × 11 m)

Single floor girder supported at two equal spacings.

8/12 pitch roof (165/250 cut of the roof)

Ridge pole and purlins supported at two equal spacings.

Local snow load 30 p.s.f. (146 kg/m²) (variable upon geographic location)

A. Determining floor girder size

		Standard measures	Metric measures
1)	Determine the total floor load per sq. ft. (sq. meter). (Refer to page above.)	Dead load = 10 p.s.f. Live load = 40 p.s.f.* Total load = 50 p.s.f.	Dead load = .48 kN/m² Live load = 1.9 kN/m²* Total load = 2.38 kN/m²
2)	Determine proportion of joist floor load carried by the girder. (Refer to page 339.)	Span = 24 x ½ = 12'	Span = 7.315 x ½ = 3.658 m
3)	Find the distance between the girder supports (given).	(given) = 12'	(given) = 3.658 m
4)	Find the linear foot (meter) load on the girder by multiplying the proportion of girder load carried by the total floor load.	12' x 50 p.s.f. = 600 p.l.f.	3.658 m x 2.38 kN/m² = 8.70 kN/m
5)	To find the total load of the girder, *multiply the linear foot (meter)* load on the girder by the span between the girder supports, as in the example.	600 p.l.f. x 12' = 7,200 lbs	8.70 kN/m x 3.658 = 31.8 kN

6) Find the beam size needed from the beam size table, below. In the column *Span in Feet/ meters* locate 12' (3.6 m) and follow the figures down until the number approximating 7,200 lbs (31.8 kN) or the next largest number appears (e.g. 8,537 lbs, or 38.0 kN). Now move horizontally to the left until you are under the heading *Solid Beam Size*, where the dimensions are given. In this case an 8" x 10" (200 x 250 mm) girder or 9" (230 mm) diameter log is needed. (Note beam dimension in relation to strength explained below.)
Girder size needed = 8" x 10" (200 x 250 mm) timber 9" (230 mm) log

*main floor

B. Determining roof ridge and purlin beam sizes

		Standard measures	Metric measures
1)	Total roof load	Dead load = 20 p.s.f.	Dead load = .95 kN/m²
		Snow load (8/12 pitch =	Snow load = 165/250 =
		70% of 30 p.s.f.) = 21 p.s.f.	70% of 1.43 kN/m2 = 1.0 kN/m²
		Total load = 41 p.s.f.	Total load = 1.95 kN/m²
2)	Proportion of roof load carried by the ridge beam (See Figure III-1)	Span = 24 x ¼ = 6'	Span = 7.315 m x ¼ = 1.828 m
3)	Distance between supports (given) =	12'	3.658 m
4)	Linear foot (meter) load on the ridge beam or purlin.	6' x 41 p.s.f. = 246 p.l.f.	1.828 m x 1.95 kN/m² = 3.56 kN/m
5)	Total load carried by the ridge beam or purlin	246 p.l.f. x 12' = 2,952 lbs.	3.56 kN/m x 3.658 = 13.0 kN
6)	Ridge beam and purlin size needed (see beam size, below, under Span in Feet/meters) (e.g. 12', or 3.6 m) then left locate beam size	4" x 8" timber or 6" log	100 x 200 mm timber or 150 mm log

BEAM SIZE IN RELATION TO SPAN AND TOTAL LOAD*
Assumed no material defects: Allowable Fiber Stress 1400 p.s.i.
(9.6 Megapascal, MPa)

Solid Beam Size in Inches/millimeters	Span in Feet/meters						
	6 (1.8 m)	7 (2.0 m)	8 (2.4 m)	10 (3.0 m)	12 (3.6 m)	14 (4.2 m)	16 (4.8 m)
2 × 6 (50 × 150 mm)	1318/5.9	1124/5.0	979/4.4	774/3.4	636/2.8	536/2.4	459/2.0
3 × 6 (75 × 150 mm)	2127/9.5	1816/8.1	1581/7.0	1249/5.6	1025/4.6	863/3.8	740/3.3
4 × 6 (100 × 150 mm)	2938/13.1	2507/11.2	2184/9.7	1726/7.7	1418/6.3	1194/5.3	1023/4.5
6 × 6 (150 × 150 mm)	4263/19.0	3638/16.2	3168/14.1	2504/11.1	2055/9.1	1731/7.7	1483/6.6
2 × 8 (50 × 200 mm)	1865/8.3	1865/8.3	1760/7.8	1395/6.2	1150/5.1	973/4.3	839/3.7
3 × 8 (75 × 200 mm)	3020/13.4	3020/13.4	2824/12.6	2238/10.0	1845/8.2	1560/6.9	1343/6.0
4 × 8 (100 × 200 mm)	4165/18.5	4165/18.5	3904/17.4	3906/17.4	2552/11.4	2160/9.6	1802/8.0
6 × 8 (150 × 200 mm)	6330/28.2	6330/28.2	5924/26.4	4698/21.0	3873/17.2	3277/14.6	2825/12.6
8 × 8 (200 × 200 mm)	8630/38.4	8630/38.4	8078/35.9	6406/28.5	5281/23.5	4469/19.9	3851/17.2
2 × 10 (50 × 250 mm)	2360/10.5	2360/10.5	2360/10.5	2237/10.0	1848/8.2	1569/7.0	1356/6.0
3 × 10 (75 × 250 mm)	3810/17.0	3810/17.0	3810/17.0	3612/16.1	2984/13.3	2531/11.2	2267/10.1
4 × 10 (100 × 250 mm)	5265/23.4	5265/23.4	5265/23.4	4992/22.2	4125/18.4	3500/15.6	3026/13.5
6 × 10 (150 × 250 mm)	7990/35.5	7990/35.5	7990/35.5	6860/30.5	6261/27.9	5312/23.6	4593/20.4
8 × 10 (200 × 250 mm)	10920/48.6	10920/48.6	10920/48.6	9351/42.0	8537/38.0	7244/32.2	6264/27.9
2 × 12 (50 × 300 mm)	2845/12.7	2845/12.7	2845/12.7	2845/12.7	2724/12.1	2315/10.3	2006/8.9
3 × 12 (75 × 300 mm)	4590/20.4	4590/20.4	4590/20.4	4590/20.4	4394/19.6	3734/16.6	3234/14.4
4 × 12 (100 × 300 mm)	6350/28.3	6350/28.3	6350/28.3	6350/28.3	6075/27.0	5165/23.0	4474/19.9
6 × 12 (150 × 300 mm)	9640/42.9	9640/42.9	9640/42.9	9640/42.9	9220/41.0	7837/34.9	6791/30.2
8 × 12 (200 × 300 mm)	13160/58.6	13160/58.6	13160/58.6	13160/58.6	12570/55.9	10685/47.5	9260/41.2
2 × 14 (50 × 355 mm)	3595/16.0	3595/16.0	3595/16.0	3595/16.0	3595/16.0	3199/14.2	2776/12.3

*Total load in body of table is expressed in pounds and kilonewtons. This table is calculated for Douglas fir, southern pine or an equivalent. Sound round logs approximating square beam sizes are assumed to be 20 percent stronger than square timbers.

BEAM DIMENSIONS AND RELATIVE STRENGTH

 = x load.

 = 2x Doubling the *width* of a beam doubles its load carrying capacity.

 = 4x Doubling the *depth* of a beam increases its load carrying capacity *four* times.

Appendix IV

Common Rafter Lengths

Degree of Roof Slope	Metric Roof Slope	Standard Roof Slope	Constant	×	Building Run	= Rafter Line Length
15°	60/250	3/12	1.03	×		= Rafter Line Length
20°	81/250	4/12	1.05	×		=
23°	103/250	5/12	1.08	×		=
26.5°	123/250	6/12	1.12	×		=
30°	144/250	7/12	1.16	×		=
33.5°	166/250	8/12	1.20	×		=
37°	188/250	9/12	1.25	×		=
40.5°	210/250	10/12	1.30	×		=
45°	250/250	12/12	1.41	×		=
49.5°	295/250	14/12	1.54	×		=
53°	335/250	16/12	1.67	×		=
56.5°	375/250	18/12	1.80	×		=
59°	415/250	20/12	1.95	×		=
61.5°	460/250	22/12	2.09	×		=
63.5°	500/250	24/12	2.24	×		=

The line length of a rafter can be determined from this table by locating the roof slope (in degrees/ metric/ or standard) in one of the three left hand columns. Then, on the same line to the right, the constant number is obtained. Multiply this constant with the building run measurement to find the rafter length. To this figure add wastage and overhang allowance.

Example: Find the rafter line length for a 45° (250/250, 12/12) slope, whose building run is 15' (4572 mm).

Standard (12/12) 1.41 × 15' = 21'2" rafter line length

Metric (250/250) 1.41 × 4572 mm = 6446 mm rafter line length

Appendix V

Truss Specifications

Figure V-1
A nailed "W"
truss.

When fabricating dimensional frame trusses, the gusset placement is important. The information given below is intended to supplement the conventional trussed roof system described in Chapter 12, section 2.

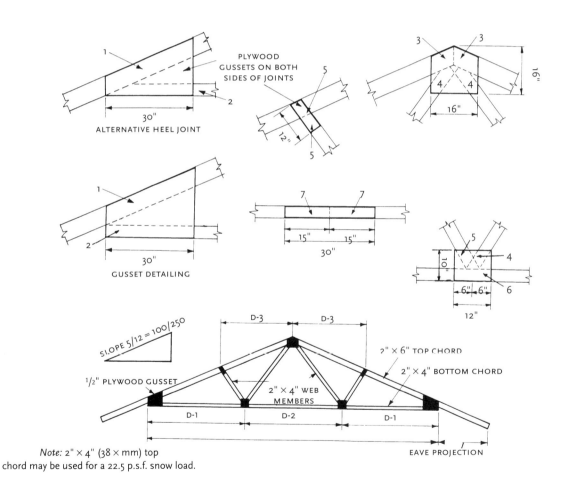

Note: 2" × 4" (38 × mm) top chord may be used for a 22.5 p.s.f. snow load.

Nailed 'W' Truss

Slope: 5/12 (100/250) only
Spans: 28'4" to 34'4" (8.64 to 10.46 m)
Gusset materials: 1/2" (12 mm) plywood

Nailing procedures

Roof Snow Load	Slope	Span "L" ft in		Joint Location 1	2	3	4	5	6	7
22.5 lbs/ft²	5/12	30	4 (9.24 m)	12	12	4	4	3	4	8
1.07 kN/m²	100/250	32	4 (9.85 m)	13	12	4	4	3	4	8
		34	4 (10.46 m)	14	13	5	5	4	5	9
30 lbs/ft²	5/12	30	4 (9.24 m)	15	14	5	5	4	5	10
1.43 kN/m²	100/250	32	4 (9.85 m)	16	15	5	5	4	5	11
		34	4 (10.46 m)	17	16	6	6	5	6	12
37.5 lbs/ft²	5/12	28	4 (8.64 m)	17	16	5	5	4	5	12
1.79 kN/m²	100/250	30	4 (9.24 m)	18	17	5	5	4	5	12
		32	4 (9.85 m)	19	18	6	6	5	6	13
		34	4 (10.46 m)	20	19	7	7	6	7	13

Dimensions

Span		L = 28'4" = 8.64 m	L = 30'4" = 9.24 m	L = 32'4" = 9.85 m	L = 34'4" = 10.46 m
Dimensions	D–1	10'1" 3073 mm	10'10" 3302 mm	11'7" 3530 mm	12'4" 3759 mm
	D–2	8'2" 2489 mm	8'8" 2641 mm	9'2" 2794 mm	9'8" 2946 mm
	D–3	6'4" 1930 mm	6'9" 2057 mm	7'2" 2184 mm	7'7" 2311 mm

Materials

Lumber

No. 1 Grade Spruce or equivalent for top and bottom chords.
No. 2 Grade Spruce or equivalent for web members.

Nails

Use 3" (75 mm) common steel wire nails.

Nails should be in staggered rows and clinched perpendicular to the direction of the plywood face grain.

Solid blocking should be used under gusset plates during nailing.

Plywood

$^{1}/_{2}$" sheathing grade Douglas fir or equivalent throughout.

The plywood's grain direction should face parallel to the bottom chord except for plates joining web to top chord at quarter points.

Directions

a) To ensure maximum stiffness, the upper chords must be in good bearing contact at the peak.

b) Trusses with spans whose sizes fall between those listed must be nailed in a way that is not less than that shown for the larger span.

Note: Roof snow load = 80% of ground snow load (for example, 5/12, 100/250 roof slope).

Trusses are spaced 24" (600 mm) on center.

Appendix VI

Log and Frame Dimensions

Table 1: Log–Frame Conversion

3¹/₄" (82 mm) diameter log = 2" × 4" (38 × 89 mm) or 2" × 5" (38 × 114 mm).

4¹/₄" (108 mm) diameter log = 2" × 6" (38 × 140 mm).

5¹/₄" (133 mm) diameter log = 2" × 8" (38 × 184 mm).

6" (152 mm) diameter log = 2" × 10" (38 × 235 mm).

7" (178 mm) diameter log = 2" × 12" (38 × 286 mm).

Table 1 gives log to frame conversion equivalents. A given diameter log equal in strength to the corresponding dimensional material given. This conversion table can be used for quick reference in sizing floor joist equivalents. Increasing the width of the frame material corresponds with an increase in log diameter size.

Table 2 gives the minimum log diameter size needed for a given span and spacing. This table can also be used as a quick reference to determine the size of log floor joist members.

Table 2: Log Floor Joist Sizes (40 p.s.f., or 1.90 kN/m2, main floor)**

Joist Diameter	Spacing	Span
4¹/₄" (108 mm)	24" (610 mm)	8' (2.4 m)
5¹/₄" (133 mm)	24" (610 mm)	11' (3.3 m)
6" (152 mm)	24" (610 mm)	14' (4.3 m)
7" (178 mm)	24" (610 mm)	17' (5.2 m)

*Assumed no major log defects

**Assumed 2" × 6" (38 × 130 mm) tongue & groove flooring

Bibliography

Design Books

Brand, Stewart. *How Buildings Learn*

Chang, Amos Ih Tiao. *The Tao of Architecture*. Princeton, NJ: Princeton University Press, 1981.

Elgin, Duane. *Voluntary Simplicity*. New York: William Morrow and Co., 1981.

Engel, Heinrich. *The Japanese House*

Greene, Charles/Henry. *The Ultimate Bungalow*

Itoh, Teiji, and Yukio Futagawa. *The Classic Tradition in Japanese Architecture*. New York, Tokyo: Weatherhill/Tankosha, 1971.

———. *The Elegant Japanese House*. New York, Tokyo: Weatherhill/ Tankosha, 1967.

Itoh, Teiji, and Kiyoshi Takai. *Kura: Design and Tradition of the Japanese Storehouse*. Seattle: Madrona Publishers, 1981.

Kern, Ken. *The Owner Build Home*. New York: Charles Scribner's Sons, 1972.

McHarg, Ian. *Design with Nature*. New York: Doubleday/Natural History Press, 1969.

Stickley, Gustav. *More Craftsman Homes*. New York: Dover Publications, 1982.

Olgyay, Victor. *Design with Climate*. Princeton, NJ: University Press, 1963.

Walker, Les, and Jeff Milstein. *Designing Houses*. New York: Overlook Press, 1976.

History Books

Barbeau, Marius. "The House That Mac Built." *The Beaver Magazine Quarterly* (December 1945): 10–13.

Bugge, Gunnar, and Christian Schultz-Norberg. *Stav Og Laft*. Oslo: Byggekunst, 1969.

Callen, Mary K. *History of Fort Langley 1827–96*. Ottawa: National Historic Parks and Sites Branch, 1979.

Cook, Kathleen, trans. *North Russian Architecture*. Moscow: Progress Publ., 1972.

Hansen, Hans Jurgen. *Architecture in Wood*. New York: Viking Press, 1971.

Kavli, Guthorm. *Norwegian Architecture Past and Present*. Oslo: Dreyers Forlag, 1958.

Lindholm, Dan, and Walther Roggenkamp. *Stave Churches in Norway*. London: Rudolf Steiner Press, 1969.

Moogk, Peter N. *Building a House in New France*. Toronto: McClelland and Stewart Ltd., 1977.

Peeps, Calder. "Fort Langley in ReCreation." *The Beaver Magazine Quarterly* (Autumn 1958): 30–39.

Shurtleff, Harold R. *The Log Cabin Myth*. Gloucester, MA: Harvard University Press, 1939.

West, Trudey. *The Timber-frame House in England*. New York: Architectural Book Publishing Co., 1971.

Log Building Books

Janzen, Vic. *Your Log House*. Gardenvale, PQ: Muir Publishing Co., 1981.

Langsner, Drew. *A Logbuilder's Handbook*. Emmaus, PA: Rodale Press, 1982.

Mackie, Allan B. *Building with Logs*. Prince George, BC: Log House Publ. Co., 1972.

———. *Log House Plans*. Prince George, BC: Log House Publ. Co., 1979.

Mann, Dale, and Richard Skinulis. *The Complete Log House Book*. Toronto: McGraw-Hill Ryerson Ltd., 1979.

Phleps, Hermann. *The Craft of Log Building*. Ottawa: Lee Valley Tools Ltd., 1982.

Stonework Books

Kern, Ken; Magers, Steve; and Penfield, Lou. *Stone Masonry*. Oakhurst, CA: Owner/Builder Publications, 1976.

Schwenke, Karl, and Sue Schwenke. *Build Your Own Stone House*. Charlotte, VT: Garden Way Publishing Co., 1975.

Timber Frame Books

Benson, Tedd, and James Gruber. *Building the Timber Frame House*. New York: Charles Scribner's Sons, 1980.

Elliott, Stewart, and Eugene Wallas. *The Timber Framing Book*. Kittery Point, ME: Housesmiths Press, 1977.

Nakahara, Yasuo. *Japanese Joinery*. Vancouver: Hartley & Marks Publishers, 1983.

Tool Books

Arcand, R.D. *Log Building Tools & How to Make Them*. Sorrento, BC: R.D. Arcand, 1976.

McDonnell, Leo P. *Hand Woodworking Tools*. New York: Delmar Publishers, 1962.

Newberry, Bill. *Handbook for Riggers*. Calgary: Commercial Printers, 1967.

Tree and Wood Books

Constantine, Albert, Jr. *Know Your Woods*. New York: Charles Scribner's Sons, 1959.

Findlay, W.P.K. *Timber Properties and Uses*. London: Crosby Lockwood Staples Publ., 1975.

Hoadley, Bruce R. *Understanding Wood*. Newton, CT: The Taunton Press, 1980.

Hosie, R.C. *Native Trees of Canada*. Ottawa: Ministry of Environment, 1973.

Lloyd, C. *Australian Carpenter*. Melbourne: The MacMillan Company of Australia PTY Ltd., 1965.

Pinces Risborough Laboratory. *A Handbook of Softwoods*. London: Dept. of Environment, Millbank Tower, 1957.

Glossary

Anchor fastener: A bolt, bar, or spike protruding from the foundation, used to anchor the sill.

Backcut: The final felling cut in felling a tree.

Backfilling: Replacing the excavated soil around a foundation wall.

Baluster (also banister): An upright support of a handrail on a staircase.

Bar (or blade): The part of the chainsaw on which the cutting chain travels.

Bay: A uniform division of a building, such as the spaces between a series of four posts.

Beam: A principal horizontal support member in the building's floor or roof frame.

Bearing partition: A wall which carries second storey or roof loads.

Beetle: A large mallet (15–20 lbs) used to gently "persuade" tight joints to fit.

Bent (framework): A framework of vertical posts and horizontal beams.

Birdsmouth: A V-shaped joint resembling a bird's open beak, used to join a rafter to the top plate.

Blade: See Bar.

Blockwork: A method of horizontal notched corner log and timber construction.

Brace: A diagonal support member used to stiffen unstable walls or frames.

Buckling: To saw a felled tree into log lengths.

Bulhuse: A 16th century Danish term, referring to post and beam construction methods.

Butt: The large end of a log or tree sawn from the stump.

Butt joint: Any joint made by fastening two members together without overlapping.

Camber: An upward arch given to a beam or girder to prevent its becoming concave due to its own weight or the weight of the load it must carry.

Cantilever (beam): A projecting beam that supports a structure such as a balcony or overhang.

Carrier: Water, oil, or a solvent used to disperse a preservative or finish on a wood surface.

Caulk: To make tight against wind and water using a sealing material.

Chamfer: A sloping or beveled edge for decoration of a timber. Also used for tenon joints for easier insertion into a mortise.

Check: A longitudinal crack in a log or timber caused by too-rapid seasoning.

Chinking: The process or materials used to fill gaps between horizontal wall logs or half-timbers.

Chipper chain: The cutting teeth of a chainsaw chain whose round backs allow for planing and curved cuts.

Chisel chain: The cutting teeth of a chainsaw chain whose straight-edged backs prevent planing or curved cuts, and allow only straight cuts.

Collar-tie: A horizontal member connected at the midpoint between two rafters to reduce spreading or sagging of the rafters.

Common rafter: One of a series of support members extending from the top of an exterior wall to the ridge of a roof.

Compression: A pressing or crushing type of force.

Conduction: Movement of heat through a material.

Cord: The principal top or bottom member of a truss.

Countersink: Burying the head of a pin, screw, or bolt into an enlarged hole, which is then usually plugged.

Course: The tiered layers of logs or half-timbers used in solid wood construction.

Crawl space: A shallow space between the lowest floor of a house and the ground beneath.

Cross grain: Grains that run perpendicular to the straight grain of wood. In wood joinery it is more difficult to work in the cross grain.

Crosscut saw: A saw designed to cut across the wood grain.

Crown: Convex side of lumber or timber.

C.R.M.S.: Cold rolled mild steel, harder than H.R.M.S. (hot).

Cull: A tree or log considered unmarketable because of defects.

Cut (of a roof): The metrically measured angle of incline of a roof.

Dado: A rectangular groove in wood which runs perpendicular to the grain, usually cut with a dado plane or router.

Dado groove: See Dado.

Darby: A plasterer's float made of a narrow piece of wood or metal with two handles, used to smooth a stucco surface.

Dead load: Total weight of the building's structure (floor, walls, roof, etc.).

Defect: A fault or irregularity in wood materials which reduces strength, durability, or appearance.

Depth: The vertical thickness of a beam.

Diagonals: Used in the squaring procedure for establishing right-angle accuracy when laying out a foundation, or testing frame accuracy.

Dogs, chainsaw: Pointed metal teeth located between the blade and motor of the chainsaw. Used when felling, bucking, or flat-surfacing wood and pivoting the saw to maintain position while sawing.

Dovetail: A tenon and mortise shaped like a dove's fantail; a locking joint.

Dowel: A wooden peg used to aid in fastening two pieces of wood together.

Drift pin: A metal punch of slightly smaller diameter than the pin or spike, used to embed the pin or spike into a countersunk hole.

Drip cap: Flashing or molding placed to prevent rain water from entering the building. A groove in the underside of a sill or header serves the same purpose.

Drywall: Interior wall and ceiling finishing material similar in appearance to plaster.

Eave: The part of a roof which projects beyond the face of a wall.

Excavate: To dig a cavity, such as for the foundation.

Expanded Polystyrene (E.P.S.): Rigid insulation used in building construction. *Uses no C.F.C.s in manufacture.

Expansion joint: A joint in concrete or plumbing designed to permit expansion without damage to the structure.

Extruded Polystyrene: Rigid insulation used in building construction. *Uses C.F.C.s in manufacture.

Facia: A finishing board around the face of eaves and roof projections.

Felling: The process of tree cutting.

Fiber failure: Structural failure of wood resulting from excess loading.

Firmer chisel: A heavy-duty chisel strong enough to be hit with a mallet.

Fish wire: A wire or string used to pull electrical wire through a service hole.

Flashing: Sheet metal or other material used to shed water away from the building.

Flush (cut): An even cut which is level with an adjacent surface.

Fork and tongue joint: A modified mortise and tenon joint used for joinery of timber rafters at the peak of the roof.

Frame: A structure comprised of vertical and horizontal members.

Framework: The braced frame timber construction method.

Framing square: A steel L-shaped metal layout tool used for laying out joinery and roof members; also doubles as a rafter square.

Furring: Wood nailing strips laid on a roof for the application of wood shakes, and on walls to support finishing material.

Gable: The triangular portion of the end wall of a building formed by the roof.

Gable roof: An A-shaped roof with two equal slopes meeting at the ridge.

Girder: A principal beam used to support loads.

Golden Section: Mathematical proportion applied to sizing of cabinetry.

Green (wood): Freshly cut wood which has not been seasoned.

Groove: A rectangular slot running parallel to the wood grain.

Gusset: A wood or metal plate attached to one or both sides of a joint to increase its holding power.

Half lap: A joint in which half of the opposing wood of each member is removed and the connection lapped.

Half-timber: A log whose sides have been flat-surfaced while the top and bottom are left round. Used as a wall infill material in post and beam construction, where the rounded width portions may be scribed and fitted together.

Hardwood: Referring to broad-leaved deciduous trees, rather than to the hardness of the wood.

Header: The horizontal wood member above a window or door.

Hew: To square a timber or half-timber by hand using a scoring axe and broad-axe.

Holding wood: A portion of wood left uncut between the undercut and backcut of a tree, which acts as a hinge for controlled felling.

Housing: A mortise or cavity cut to receive the end of a beam, for example, a floor joist.

H.R.M.S.: Hot-rolled mild steel, which is softer than C.R.M.S. (cold).

Hudson's Bay frame: An English term referring to the short log post and beam construction methods of early Canada.

Hypotenuse: The sloping side of a right-angle triangle.

Infill (panels): The material, such as log, half-timber, or stackwall, which is placed between the bays of a post and beam frame.

Jamb: The side member of a doorway or window lining.

Jig: A device used to hold work during the manufacture of an assembly, such as a panel.

Joinery: The craft of joining wood to form a structure with the use of various joints.

Joint: A connection between two wood members.

Joists: The horizontal wood members used to support a floor or ceiling.

Kerf: A saw cut.

Kickback: An uncontrolled jerk of the chainsaw bar which is a common cause of cuts. Kickbacks most often occur when working near the nose of the chainsaw bar.

King-post: The vertical member in the center of a truss.

Knee brace: A timber member placed diagonally between a post and beam, used to stiffen a frame.

Laft work: A Norwegian term for the blockwork method of construction.

Lag screw: A heavy wood screw with a square head and coarse thread.

Layout: The process of drawing a joint's dimensions in preparation for cutting.

Linear dimension: Measurement along a line.

Live load: The occupancy weight added to a building (people, appliances, furnishings, etc.).

Lofting: A layout process in which graphic representation, as of the roof truss, is drawn full scale.

Main stack: The main vent pipe of a house's plumbing system.

Mallet: A $2^{1}/_{2}$ lb (1 kg) hardwood hammer used to drive a chisel.

Member: A building component, such as a log, timber, or half-timber.

Moisture barrier: A material used to prevent the passage of moisture.

Mortise: A female socket designed to receive a male tenon to form a joint.

Nominal size: The dimensions of undressed lumber.

Notch: The groove in a log or timber to receive another log or timber.

Oakum: Tar-impregnated hemp used for caulking joints.

On center: Identified by the center line symbol, it represents the center of a member, and is used to take measurements from when laying out spacings for joists, rafters, etc.

Overall length: The total length of a member, including tenons, overhang allowance, etc.

Overhang: Projection of the roof beyond the wall.

Partition: A wall which separates rooms.

Perimeter: The outer boundary of a structure.

Pièce-sur-pièce: A French term for the all-wood post and beam building methods of early Canada; also called *pièce-en-pièce.*

Pin: A steel peg or spike used in fastening two pieces of wood together.

Pitch: A roof's angle of incline expressed in standard measurement.

Plumb: Vertical; or to test for the vertical plane.

Pocket: Similar to a mortise or housing.

Pony wall: A short partition often used instead of a girder beam to support a floor.

Post: The vertical log or timber posts of a post and beam frame.

Post and beam: A term referring to a log or timber frame of posts and beams historically built with log or half-timber wall infill.

Purlin: A horizontal, structural roof member spanning the gable ends, which may be supported midway depending on the span distance.

Pythagoras' theorem: In a right-angle triangle, the sum of the squares of the sides is equal to the square of the hypotenuse: $a^2 + b^2 = c^2$. Used in calculating foundation, roof, and kneebrace lengths.

Rabbet: A long, step-shaped groove cut along the edge of a board or timber, which may be cut to receive a window or door.

Rafter: A sloping support member of the roof frame which extends from the top plate to the ridge.

Red River frame: The English term for the all-wood and post and beam building methods of early Canada.

Reisverk: A Norwegian term referring to the vertical posts of early post and beam construction.

Ridge beam: The topmost horizontal roof member spanning between the gable ends; also ridge board and ridge pole.

Rip saw: A saw designed to cut parallel to the wood grain.

Rise: The vertical height measured from the top plate to the ridge of a building.

Roof slope: The roof's angle of incline; termed "pitch" when expressed in standard measurement and "cut of the roof" in metric measurement.

Rough-in: Enclosing the electrical and plumbing lines in the floors, walls, and ceilings.

Rough opening: An opening framed or cut to receive a window or door.

Round: See Course.

Run: The horizontal distance from the building's outside wall to the ridge line; half the span distance.

Sash: The framework which holds the glass in a window.

Scarf joint: A joint for splicing two wood members end to end.

Scribe: The process of duplicating the contours and dimensions of one surface onto another for the purpose of joinery.

Scriber: A common tool used in log building for scribing two irregular surfaces for the purpose of joinery.

Seasoning: The drying of wood to reduce its dimensional shrinkage.

Settling factor: A calculated amount of shrinkage based on 1/2" (12 mm) per vertical 12" (300 mm) or horizontally laid green wood.

Settling space: The space, based on the calculated settling factor, which is left above a window or a door that has been installed within a solid wood infill wall.

Shakes: A defect in wood showing a partial or complete separation between the wood's growth rings.

Shear: A force causing slippage between layers of wood fibers.

Sheathing: A covering of plywood, boards, or waterproof material on the exterior of a building.

Shim: A thin tapered material, such as a cedar shingle, used in leveling a window or door frame.

Sill: The horizontal member that rests on the foundation; also the lowest horizontal member of a window's rough opening.

Skids: Poles which elevate wood materials above the ground. Also used to provide a stable work surface.

Skirting board: A board used to conceal a settling space.

Slip joint: An attachment to a log wall designed to permit the natural, unimpeded settling of the wall.

Sod roof: A roof whose covering includes two layers of grass turf, originating in northern Europe.

Soffit: The materials attached to the underside of a roof overhang.

Softwood: Refers to needle-leaved coniferous or evergreen trees, rather than to the softness of the wood.

Solid wood construction: A term referring to the methods of all-wood post and beam or blockwork construction.

Span: The horizontal distance between a building's side walls. Also the distance between supporting members, such as beams, rafters, and joists.

Spiral grain: A corkscrew-shaped grain pattern most often found in woods such as Tamarack and Black Spruce. Excessive spiral grain can cause posts or beams to twist out of position.

Spline: A rectangular strip of wood which, when fitted into grooves in two adjoining members, locks them together.

Squaring-off: To cut wood at a right angle. Also refers to the process of taking the diagonals of a rectangle to establish right-angle corners.

Stackwall: A wall infill using stacked cordwood embedded in mortar. (Usually a double wall system with an insulated middle cavity.)

Stave construction: See *Reisverk.*

Stav og laft: A Norwegian term for combined *reisverk* and *laft* construction.

Stress: The internal force of a material which resists or promotes change in shape or size. External forces (rain, sun, and heat) cause stress in wood which can lead to cracking during the seasoning process.

Structural trim board: The load-supporting boards which also serve to conceal a settling space.

Strut: A structural member whose placement in a structure such as a truss serves to resist loading forces by acting in compression.

Stub wall: See Pony wall.

Stucco: A cement-like material used as an exterior wall covering, similar to plaster in its properties and appearance.

Stud frame: A framework of dimensional studs (2", or 50 mm, nominal thickness) using external sheathing to provide rigidity.

Sway brace: To temporarily strengthen a wall which might otherwise be unsafe.

Template: A full-size pattern made of a hard material used in layout and checking joints.

Tenon: The male projection of a wood member formed to join with the female mortise.

Tension: The stress that resists two forces pulling away from each other.

Thermal mass: A body of material which acts to store heat. The amount of thermal storage potential is relative to the quantitative mass.

Thermal resistivity: The ability of a material to resist heat conduction. The higher the thermal resistivity (R factor), the better the insulation material.

Tie-beam: A beam spanning between the two side walls of a building and locking them in place to prevent spreading caused by forces exerted by the roof rafters.

Timber: A large four-sided wood member.

Timber frame: A braced frame infrastructure using timbers joined and doweled together.

Tongue and slot: A traditional method of joining solid woodwall infill to the posts, where the infill pieces are fashioned with tongues which fit into a slot or groove in the post.

Top plate: The top horizontal member in the building's wall system which serves to tie the walls together and forms a level, flat surface to support the roof.

Truss: A structural framework designed to withstand external loading, such as a roof truss.

Undercut: A wedge section cut from the base of a tree to cause it to fall.

Vapor barrier: See Moisture barrier.

Wall channel: A vertical groove removed from a log wall to allow connection with a slip joint and a partition.

Wane: The rounded edge of a square sawn timber.

Waste wood: The portion of wood cut away to reveal the joint.

Width: The horizontal thickness of a beam or post.

Wood lath: A thin, narrow piece of wood used as a base for applying plaster or stucco.

Index

James Mitchell is the founder of the
Island School of Building Arts
3199 Coast Road
RR#2, Site 29, C-7
Gabriola Island, BC
Canada VOR 1XO

PHONE: 250-247-8922
FAX: 250-247-8978

WEBSITE: http://www.island.net/~bldart
E-MAIL: bldart@island.net